Innovation

Innovation
The communication of change in ideas, practices and products

W. R. Spence

Emeritus Professor of Communication
The University of Ulster
UK

CHAPMAN & HALL
University and Professional Division
London · Glasgow · Weinheim · New York · Tokyo · Melbourne · Madras

Published by Chapman & Hall, 2–6 Boundary Row, London SE1 8HN, UK

Chapman & Hall, 2–6 Boundary Row, London SE1 8HN, UK

Blackie Academic & Professional, Wester Cleddens Road, Bishopbriggs, Glasgow G64 2NZ, UK

Chapman & Hall GmbH, Pappelallee 3, 69469 Weinheim, Germany

Chapman & Hall Inc., One Penn Plaza, 41st Floor, New York NY 10119, USA

Chapman & Hall Japan, Thomson Publishing Japan, Hirakawacho Nemoto Building, 6F, 1-7-11 Hirakawa-cho, Chiyoda-ku, Tokyo 102, Japan

Chapman & Hall Australia, Thomas Nelson Australia, 102 Dodds Street, South Melbourne, Victoria 3205, Australia

Chapman & Hall India, R. Seshadri, 32 Second Main Road, CIT East, Madras 600 035, India

First edition 1994

© 1994 W R Spence

Typeset in $10\frac{1}{2}/12$ pt Times by Best-set Typesetter Ltd., Hong Kong
Printed in Great Britain at The Alden Press, Oxford

ISBN 0 412 54220 X

A catalogue record for this book is available from the British Library

Library of Congress Catalog Card Number: 93-74434

∞ Printed on permanent acid-free text paper, manufactured in accordance with ANSI/NISO Z39.48-1992 and ANSI/NISO Z39.48-1984 (Permanence of Paper).

Contents

viii   Contents

Preface and Acknowledgements

Of making many books there is no end.

Ecclesiastes 12: 12

Even a book of this kind, which is based upon personal experience and presents much new material in both form and content, is necessarily influenced to some extent by the work of others. Where I am aware of any indebtedness I have offered due recognition in the appropriate chapters and/or bibliography. With regard to that pioneer in the field of rural sociology, Prof. Everett R. Rogers, I hope that reference has been kept down to a level which avoids tedious repetition.

In respect of historical material I would thank Messrs Prentice Hall of New York for permission to reproduce a diagram which appeared in Rogers' *Social Change in Rural Society*, originally published by Appleton-Century-Crofts in 1960, as Fig. 7.4. I am also grateful to the Rural Sociological Society for permission to use as Fig. 4.1 a diagram which was published in vol. 23, *Rural Sociology*, in 1958. With regard to Fig. 7.5 it is, I know, based on a drawing which I saw in a publication some years ago but I cannot now recall the source. I regret that, in this case, I am not able to express my appreciation to an author or publisher but I shall gladly do so if an appropriate name can be drawn to my attention.

My thanks are due to Mr Mark Wellings, commissioning editor with Chapman & Hall, who has taken a lively interest in the progress of the manuscript and offered timely advice. My profound indebtedness to the members of my own family unfortunately defies appropriate expression. However I promise them not to write any more books – after I finish the next one! I hope that I have not overlooked anyone who should have had a mention. If so I offer my apologies as well as thanks.

Since the 1960s there have been very many people who have encouraged me to pursue my work on the adoption and diffusion of innovations, and I owe a particular debt of gratitude to my former students of all ages and diverse occupations in many countries. It is for those who follow in their footsteps that this book has been written.

W. R. Spence
1993

Introduction 1

Even God cannot change the past.
Agathon, 447–401 BC

Study the past, if you would divine the future.
Analects of Confucius, c.550–478 BC

The seeds of great discoveries are constantly floating around us, but they only take rest in minds well prepared to receive them.
Walter B. Cannon (1945)

Theory and facts must be closely related to each other.
Kurt Lewin (1936)

In this introductory chapter we consider the importance of trying to find out how and why new ideas spread. We look at the origins of research into what causes changes in attitudes, practices and products, and outline how various aspects of both theory and practice will be dealt with in the text.

INNOVATION AND YOU

Anyone, such as yourself, who is curious enough to be reading this page must surely belong to that present-day category of people who feel that they would derive some benefit from a better understanding of innovation. Included are those readers for whom success in their occupations or interests depends on knowing how new ideas, practices and products actually spread. At the heart of this process of diffusion and adoption lies the fundamental act of personal decision-making. This often results from being put under pressure to change, which might well be a good thing although it is useful to know how best to resist such influence at times! For some really motivated people it precipitates the action to bring about change instead of waiting for it to happen.

In our present age of rapid technological and social change this book provides an introductory insight into those basic personal and social processes which operate when there is an attempt to introduce variation or modification of any kind. Nowadays a study of innovative processes is not confined to practitioners in specialist areas such as education, advertising, marketing, sales promotion and public relations. Many students are involved in even more wide-ranging activities related to sport, the church, medicine, politics and social welfare. The material in this book is relevant to them all because they tend to share a common characteristic – they frequently ask questions such as the following:

Are there any specific factors which can persuade an individual to accept something which is new?

What aspects of that new idea, practice or product are the most important and need to be emphasized?

What kind of characteristics help to identify the probable adopters?

What practical benefits can be derived from an understanding of the innovation processes?

What worthwhile applications can I transfer to my own particular activities or occupation?

How can I make the most effective use of these in the light of current knowledge and techniques?

WHAT THIS BOOK IS ABOUT

If you would like to be able, in the first instance, to answer questions such as those above then this book is meant for you! So far as is possible it is written in everyday language rather than technical jargon. Should you wish to pursue higher level studies it indicates additional works to which you can refer. This book has been produced specifically to assist students rather than to impress academics. It aims to introduce the reader gradually to the essential concepts and basic practices related to the adoption and diffusion of innovations. This requires some insight into the fundamentals of innovation theory as indicated by appropriate observation, contemplation and research. In addition there is critical examination of a range of case studies from around the world. In this way theory and practice are considered together in the context of various geographical and occupational circumstances. You do not require previous knowledge of any of the social sciences in order to understand this because any necessary sociological and psychological material is introduced in the text. Special attention is paid to relevant contributions from the fields of communication and decision-making. In addition, where some terms or expressions might be unfamiliar (or are used in an unusual or very specific way) these are explained when they first appear.

The prime concern of innovation is with things *as they appear to us*. There are well-known optical illusions, such as those shown in Fig. 1.1, which indicate just how misleading our visual perceptions can be. Perhaps it would be more accurate to say that it is not necessarily our perceptions (ie what we see) that are faulty. It is more likely to be our cognitions (ie the sense which our brains try to make of the perceptions). This can cause problems for hard-headed folk whose primary concern is with reality. How real is a rainbow, for example? We can not only see it,

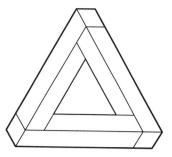

(a) It is impossible to join all three corners as shown

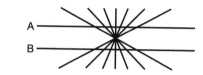

(b) Lines A and B are both straight and parallel

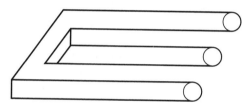

(c) It is possible to see things which do not exist

Fig. 1.1   Optical illusions (part (c) reproduced by permission of John Wiley and Sons Inc. New York).

we can call our friends to confirm that it is visible to them also; we can take a photograph to show to others who could not be present at the time of its appearance – and yet it has no objective existence. It cannot be located by us in the physical world. We have to remember, therefore, that in respect of all our senses it is how we *see* things, not so much with our eyes as in our minds, that is important.

We can all find some difficulty in coping with whatever is new to us. Although experience of such matters differs a great deal from person to person there is real practical advantage in exploring the general personal and social implications of the inevitable adjustments which we all have to make from time to time as an inescapable part of our changing human condition.

   To do so will give us basic understanding of the processes which are universally involved in the acceptance and spread of innovations, whatever their nature. This, in turn, should enable us not just to respond sensibly to situations where change takes place but actually to initiate desired change in those areas which are of personal, professional, social or commercial concern to us.

What is new to some individuals may encompass a very wide range of factors indeed. These may include issues and actions as diverse as switching from one brand of soap powder to another, undertaking a change of job, moving house, considering the probable unhealthy effects of cigarette smoking, or anticipating the prospect of a low pay rise (or none at all).

THE BASIS OF INNOVATION

'When I use a word,' Humpty Dumpty said in a rather scornful tone, 'it means just what I choose it to mean, neither more nor less.' This can be true of others outside of Lewis Carroll's *Alice Through the Looking Glass*. For instance the word **innovation** is often used loosely to indicate something newly created or produced. It is still, in particular, frequently confused with **invention**. Inventions are certainly innovations since, by definition, they are something new but innovations need not be inventions. They may be long-established ideas, products or practices which are found to have a fresh application. They are then regarded as new by some people.

Many thinkers over the last century or more have wondered why some ideas spread better, or faster, than others. An understanding of this would obviously be of particular importance to those who, for example, sell goods or services as well as to those who advertise them. In addition people who wish to influence personal or public opinion in other ways, such as through teaching, journalism or public relations, could also benefit. At the present time the demand to extend such insight to include sectors of human welfare, particularly in social work, counselling and nursing indicates that the scope for practical application is in no way restricted to mainly commercial enterprises.

Perhaps the earliest writer to consider the matter logically was Gabriel Tarde who in 1903 wrote a book called *The Laws of Imitation*. He said 'Our problem is to learn why, given one hundred innovations conceived of at the same time – innovations in the form of words, in mythological ideas, in industrial processes etc – ten will spread abroad while ninety will be forgotten.' Despite his useful but primitive analysis of what he regarded primarily as a form of imitation, it was many years before anyone else attempted to pursue more refined investigation into this aspect of human choice and decision-making. When this was done it was in the context of the diffusion and adoption of innovations.

THE START OF ADOPTION/DIFFUSION RESEARCH

As with so many other aspects of human existence it is difficult to say precisely just when methodical investigation into the spread of new ideas and practices began. But it would not be misleading to suggest that basic scientific investigation really developed in earnest in the land-grant colleges of the United States towards the end of the Second World War. At first it was not initiated as an academic study; on the contrary, it was a very practical attempt to produce a solution to the problem of food shortages facing many countries at the end of a thoroughly devastating international conflict. Those land-grant State colleges which had originally been established many years earlier to further, amongst other things, the scientific study of agriculture found a new impetus to the development of an academic discipline now widely recognized as Rural Sociology. Agriculture was, and remains, the world's most basic and important industry. Despite a continuing decline in the labour force it is still responsible for the employment of vast numbers of people whose whole way of life is geared to the production of the essential foodstuffs without which we could not survive.

Towards the end of the war many ordinary foods were both scarce and becoming scarcer even in those parts of the USA where shortages had previously been virtually unknown. Consequently the federal government wished to increase home production quickly and economically. In order to do this government officials tried to speed up the flow of information to farmers from government agricultural research stations which had been established to investigate ways of increasing food production in general.

The two ways of attempting this were by:

1. developing new techniques to improve traditional farming practices; and
2. encouraging the growing of different varieties of crops, previously largely untried in the United States.

At the beginning the efforts of researchers were directed almost entirely towards gaining ready acceptance of government advice, proposals and instructions by farmers. It soon became clear, however, that the agricultural environment was ideal for assessing the effectiveness of different approaches intended to persuade the potential adopter. This was because the acceptance of innovative ideas could be observed easily in farming practice and the quality and quantity of subsequent yields could be readily assessed. As a result, the predicted outcome of different types of influence could be tested for efficacy and accuracy.

In the course of time there evolved, from the accumulated factual information, some of the basic theoretical principles which still provide a reasonable insight into the adoption and diffusion of innovations today. This was an important element in the early development of rural sociology as a formal study, later recognized as a genuine discipline which comprised conceptual as well as empirical elements. This in turn contributed something to the growth and academic credibility of other interdisciplinary areas such as those related to human communication. While the study of communication itself covers a very wide remit indeed, many aspects of it still remain interrelated with those of innovation since all communication may be considered as having the basic intention of exerting an influence for change on the recipient.

THE NATURE OF INNOVATION

What is important about an innovation is that it is something which is *perceived* as novel whether it is new or not! It is the newness to the individual which determines the response to it. As will be seen later in the book this can influence something as basic, but as commercially important, as changing the packaging of an existing brand to improve its customer appeal, or amending a political party manifesto and redesigning its logo to attract more support from the 'floating' or uncommitted voters.

Things which are seen to be new bring about a change of some sort in the personal circumstances of the individual concerned. Any change implies a possibility of risk, and not all people are risk-oriented to the same degree. Some will welcome every novelty; more cautious individuals will accept something which is different only after persuasion and much deliberation; and a few will stubbornly resist anything that might be characterized as an innovation, however reasonable it might appear to be and however beneficial to their circumstances.

Reaching an individual decision will be influenced by a number of different factors, the most important of which are:

- the nature of the innovation itself;
- the personal characteristics of the individual;
- the cultural climate of the society; and
- social pressures exerted by the working environment as well as those of the residential neighbourhood.

All of these merit the fullest consideration because of the range of factors involved and their impact, combined as well as separate, on the actions of the individual in society.

It is possible to regard many contemporary issues as having major dimensions of innovativeness. Examples could include the implications of political independence for the constituent states of the former Soviet Union; the economic consequences of having a Channel tunnel between France and England; the implications for the international money market of introducing a common European currency; development of the techniques of diplomacy to allow for hostage negotiation; the creation of a unified command structure for a United Nations military force . . . the list is almost endless and the topics do not have to be on such a grand scale as these. It needs only the introduction of a new activity into a school curriculum, or a different sandwich filling to the menu of a fast food bar to be equally significant in their own context, ie they are matters of real importance to those people most likely to be affected by them. No matter how different the issues may be in nature or in scale the same principles and practices apply to all and the full range is examined in detail in this text.

ASSUMPTIONS ABOUT HUMAN NATURE

We all make assumptions about other people. Often these are based on past experience, prejudice, instinct or intuition. While some assumptions require explanation and may need some defending there are others which seem reasonable enough and have the support of distinguished academics. One well-known sociologist was Talcott Parsons whose works contributed much to an understanding of the sheer complexity of the human being. In general, his views of the broad characteristics of human behaviour are that:

- all human actions are directed towards goals of some sort;
- individuals possess some degree of freedom to choose between alternative courses of action;
- in human behaviour there is both a cognitive element as well as one which seeks gratification of personal needs; and
- there is some sort of order brought to our lives by the acceptance of commonly shared values.

While my simplistic summary of his sociological criteria may be lacking in academic precision it does provide an indication of the broad assumptions which underpin some of the expressions employed in this book. One of the assumptions which I am making at this stage, for example, is that you accept my view that perceptions are the impressions which we all receive via our senses and cognitions are the interpretations which we place on them. Few people would, at the outset, want a more technical explanation.

HOW THIS BOOK IS ORGANIZED

In reading this book it is not necessary for you to follow the King of Hearts' directive to Alice to 'Begin at the beginning, and go on till you come to the end: then stop.' However there is certainly an advantage in reading the chapters consecutively, at least initially, because in that way you will become familiar with the principal terms and concepts as they are first presented. Each chapter has basic objectives specified at the outset. These indicate broadly what the key issues are. If you wish, you could use this as a kind of checklist to gauge your progress.

Four brief sections are appended to each chapter. They are:
1. a summary of the chapter itself;
2. some material to stimulate personal reflection;
3. an opportunity to apply theory to practice; and
4. some suggested further readings.

These should help you to integrate the different elements of the subject matter dealt with in each chapter and to learn how to consider theory and practice together in a wide range of situations. In addition there are actual case studies in Chapters 10, 11 and 12. These, by their nature, often involve the bringing together of various elements of knowledge from different sources. In addition to any evidence presented to you it will be necessary for you to use critically your own personal insight, beliefs, value judgements and experience.

In ideal circumstances theory is always illuminated by actual experience, and practical techniques are constantly underpinned by theory. Your acquired knowledge and present endeavours are therefore invaluable for identifying, in conjunction with the text, how to achieve the desired improvement in whatever situation is important to you.

This book will provide some practical illustrations and examples of theory which has been put into practice. However it is quite definitely *not* a cookbook with a set of recipes for dealing with every difficulty involving change. It does not pretend to supply ready-made solutions which you can apply to all the problems which you may encounter. Nonetheless you should be able to find direct answers to many of your questions in the chapters which follow. You will also discover what factors are likely to be most relevant to a wide range of decision-making situations and how best to deal with them. This can contribute in no small measure to identifying the approach which is ideally suited to your own personal circumstances.

I trust that you will find this book really worth reading – and reading again.

Characteristics of social change 2

There is nothing permanent except change.
Heraclitus, 520 BC

Observe always that everything is the result of a change.
Marcus Aurelius, 200 BC

The one certainty about change is that it takes everyone by surprise.
Chesterman and Lipman (1988)

There was never any thing by the wit of man so well devised, or so sure established, which in continuance of time hath not been corrupted.
Book of Common Prayer, original preface, 1549

In this chapter we will reflect on the nature of change, particularly social change, in relation to a few relevant theoretical concepts. We will consider briefly the relationship between alteration and progress and examine how desired change might be brought about by the achievement of both general aims and specific objectives.

Objectives
When you have completed this introductory chapter you should be able to:

- indicate at least one way in which western society today appears to differ from that of, say, the Middle Ages;
- outline one of the theories which exerted some influence on early thoughts about social change;
- distinguish between aims and objectives;
- state the major difference between an invention and an innovation;
- specify what elements might be of importance in bringing about change.

WHY IS CHANGE IMPORTANT?

There is nothing new about the concept of change. Indeed change itself is both commonplace and universal. However what has become strikingly different in recent times is the accelerating *pace* with which it now takes place. This is especially evident in the case of technological developments. In manufacturing industry today, for example, there are products being manufactured for sale, particularly those incorporating micro-technology, which will be obsolete very soon after they reach the purchaser. Changes of design, methods of construction, probable cost and predicted application have often been decided for an updated product long before the current production has been completed.

Social change is not always as evident as technical change but it is of the greatest importance in ensuring an orderly development of our civilization. It is easy to understand how, in circumstances where alteration of any sort is taking place, people can sometimes feel insecure and reluctant to make a decision about accepting something different unless and until necessity forces them to do so. A modern-day example is the dilemma of a potential house purchaser in England where there is a situation in which house prices and property values often tend to change at very short notice in a volatile market. In addition there are variable interest rates and uncertain taxation laws. While change in technology is important for all of us we can usually come to terms with it since its effects are often so visible that there is both the opportunity and the necessity to consider the possible implications. However, change in the fabric of our society, which is absolutely vital to our very existence, is usually so insidious in its effect that it can go virtually unremarked until its consequences – often unfortunate – make themselves known. At the present time in Europe, for instance, many people in former 'Eastern Bloc' countries are struggling to come to terms with what is meant by a market economy. Few people from the Western world, however experienced in business, would be capable of explaining it satisfactorily since most of us have only a vague notion of the interacting demand-supply forces.

That is why in this book, while not pursuing any definitions for their own sake, we must make some attempt at the outset to understand what the term **social change** actually means. Remember that it can be said, with some certainty, that everything that we are and do is determined largely by the sort of social environment in which we live. We must therefore take account of the fact, for it is a fact, that the dominant feature of contemporary society is one of continuing alteration. Most of us are engaged in trying to bring about change, even if it is only in respect of achieving an improvement in our own lives. Many of us, in addition, function as agents of change in our roles as teachers, managers, or whatever job descriptions we would apply to ourselves. But we, in turn, are on the receiving end of the process and it is this which necessitates our own continuous adaptation to change brought about by others.

In the world today, wherever we are, change is regarded as a typical condition and stability (other than temporary) is the more abnormal. This differs markedly from, say, the Middle Ages when philosophic thought, both sacred and secular, tended to provide a rationalization of the *status quo*. There was recognition of the established 'order of things' which persisted until well into Victorian times when, as one hymn-writer was still able to express it, God had put 'the rich man in his castle, the poor man at his gate'.

Because the majority of human individuals do not live in isolation but in the company of (or at least in close proximity to) others, change takes place not only in a social setting but, indeed, acquires whatever real meaning it may have only in this particular context. This is because what we recognize as an alteration is a comparison with some previously existing pattern or standard. Because of this we have to look first of all at the broad concept of social change itself since this provides the background for our subsequent analyses of more specific movements. This concerns the careful examination of individual decisions which we all have to make in relation to modification, the factors which influence our own decision-making, and particular consequences or implications of the subsequent outcomes.

IS CHANGE DESIRABLE? – OR INEVITABLE?

Change has always appeared to many of the elders in society as something to be endured rather than encouraged, mainly because of its potential for creating dramatic, as well as continuing, instability. Change came to be tolerated largely as a necessary intermediate stage in the process of moving towards something more desirable which would thereafter persist unchanged, ie a **steady state** when perfection had been attained. Even the philosophers of change, from Plato to Marx, tended to regard the process largely as a means of attaining an eventual stable condition which would be infinitely better than the one which it would displace. Socially and theologically, therefore, it was believed that when the ideal desired condition had been reached no more change would occur simply because it would no longer be needed. Any movement towards change in these circumstances would be viewed with a degree of reserve as to its nature, and a measure of suspicion concerning its outcome, because of the element of risk involved in confronting the unknown.

Note that not all change was necessarily directed towards achieving some future Utopia. On occasion it was instituted in order to try to regain that which, it was felt, had been lost from times past. The religious Reformation of the sixteenth century, for example, can be viewed not so much as an attempt to overthrow the Church of Rome and lead to new theological orthodoxies, but as something which emerged, almost incidentally, from the efforts of people like Martin Luther to try to restore their religion to its former perceived purity.

Four hundred years on the major kingdoms, empires and societies of the world have undergone striking changes. Many of them, in fact, have long since disappeared! Some have survived but have changed gradually and almost imperceptibly over many generations. Others have altered more swiftly and strikingly. Nevertheless for much of that intervening period right up until comparatively recent times stability was not only accepted as the social ideal; it was also the normal social condition.

Today perpetual change seems to be the norm for much of the world's population, and any stability is largely accepted as abnormal. The changeover period for this reversal of social conditions is indeterminate; the balance did not tilt at any particular point in time but shifted gradually over many generations. It was not, in fact, until near the end of the eighteenth century that thoughts which had gradually been forming for decades finally took shape in the idea that change in itself could actually be desirable. Furthermore (it was tentatively proposed) it might, after all, even be defensible to try to bring it about.

Around a century later those thoughts had advanced still further to the stage where change which was considered worthwhile began to be considered also as ultimately inevitable. The implication was, in effect, that it was not only essential that it should happen but also that it was desirable that it should be encouraged! The very concept of social progress therefore introduced the innovative notion that people themselves might, by their own efforts, try to produce improvements in the quality of their individual lives. This was a completely new perspective which emphasized that bringing about change could, at least on some occasions, not only cause things to be different but might also make them better. Such a major ideological breakthrough even made impact on some of the ecclesiastical thinking of the time. The proposition that perhaps God helped best those who tried to help themselves began to gain some credence. This offset the somewhat fatalistic attitudes inherited from earlier generations who had been prone to accept certain aspects of their lives as predetermined and therefore beyond their control. In 1859 Samuel Smiles published his famous book, *Self Help*, to encourage people to exert themselves in their own interests. However, it has always been obvious, to even the most casual observer, that the outcomes of any human endeavour tend to be largely unknown in advance and the benefits, if any, are therefore inevitably uncertain.

An attempt at improvement, however conceived or defined, can often result in unpredictable consequences in the short term even if it continues to sustain momentum towards an originally specified long-term goal. To some extent this may account for the persistence of the belief that any advance, of whatever form, often depends upon an evolutionary, rather than a revolutionary, style of development. With such a point of view it is possible to consider as genuine progress any movement towards eventual change which does not necessarily achieve a satisfactory outcome at each individual stage in the process.

CHANGE AND ALTERATION

It is axiomatic that we tend to think of change as proceeding from bad to good, from good to better and from better to best. The level of attainment is evaluated on an **evolutionary** scale; for example we often say that something is 'a step in the right direction'. One plausible reason for adopting this approach is because it is virtually impossible in some situations to point to improvement, even although there is every reason to believe that it has come about. A prime example is in preventative medicine. How can it be shown conclusively that people who might otherwise have become ill or died have *not* done so because some prophylactic approach has been effectively adopted? This is also difficult in other areas; for instance the development of a good police force which achieves genuine progress in respect of its first principles, ie crime prevention, might actually be thought to have become less effective when judged against the former success criteria of secondary objectives, ie arrests, prosecutions and convictions. One British Chief Constable is on record as saying that his officers are successful, in the course of the year, in preventing four out of every five serious crimes from being committed. Since this cannot be demonstrated the ordinary citizen tends to view such claims with scepticism. The matter is of some importance to British police forces at the moment since the publication of the Sheehy Report in June 1993 proposed, amongst other changes, the introduction of performance-related pay for police officers. What criteria could be used to prescribe appropriate performance indicators?

You must remember that change is basically only alteration. It need not mean that things have become better, only that they have been made different. Change itself is relatively easy to bring about. Not only can we all do it but, in some respects at least, we all have undoubtedly done so. It may be, indeed, that some of us are employed largely in order to cause change to take place. As indicated above any particular alteration does not necessarily bring about any real or lasting improvement since this is difficult to attain or even, on occasion, to identify. There are two principal reasons for this:

1. It is not enough to know what we want to achieve; we must also possess the necessary skills and sufficient determination to employ them.
2. No matter what is achieved or what benefit results, there will be some individuals who will remain unconvinced that it was worthwhile. There are always those who prefer to believe that things were better as they used to be.

Progress is a highly subjective judgement! For many people *any* change, however slight, creates a temporary state of uncertainty. They are temporarily put off balance and this can produce unease, insecurity and some actual loss of former competence. There may even be feelings of not being able to cope at all. Such a phase passes – more quickly for some than for others – being succeeded by renewed confidence and extra poise gained as a result of some personal accomplishment in the new situation, such as the acquisition of additional skills or fresh knowledge. This is an experience familiar to those who complete any course of study or engage in any training exercise or educational learning process.

WHAT KINDS OF CHANGE ARE THERE?

While many kinds of change can take place it is often convenient to group them broadly into two categories, social or technological, although in practice this is actually a difficult distinction to make. If the changes concern primarily people then they may reasonably be considered as being **social** in nature. On the other hand if they appear to be fundamentally about material products and related processes then they can be more easily viewed as **technological**.

However, you should remember that all technology inevitably has a strong social dimension because it arises first in the individual mind, is brought into existence by human beings, is operated by them, and its consequences are likely therefore to influence many other people. Feedback from them modifies the technology so that people and, indeed, society itself are involved at every technological stage of any invention, development or application.

Just as two categories of change may be postulated so also there can be two ways of regarding *how* change may occur:

1. Change which happens whether it is wanted or not (like growing old). All that we can do in such cases is to try to adjust to the alteration which results.
2. Change which is intended to be brought about by human endeavour (such as the overthrow of a dictatorship). In these situations we have to anticipate what actions are likely to be most appropriate to achieve the objectives which we had in mind.

In both instances it would be wise to try to predict what the possible consequences might be in the case of either success or failure.

The words 'change' and 'innovation' have both been used so far and in everyday usage these terms are frequently interchanged, although their meanings differ. An innovation is not necessarily something which is new (such as an invention) but it is something which is seen by many people to be new to them. Examples of innovations could include the invention of a new mechanical device, the creation of a different consumer product, the development of a novel form of personal relationship, an addition to our existing knowledge in a particular specialism, or the emergence of a fresh theory marking some advance in human thought. The terms innovation and change differ in meaning, yet they are closely related because change has often come about as a result of innovation.

In this respect change, even significant change, is really a modification of what already exists, so that even with fairly dramatic alteration there is still **continuity**. This provides a basis for stability in society but without stagnation. Consequently we are able to accept moderate revisions and amendments to worthy, long-established ideas to pass on, virtually unaltered, to future generations. This approach is the foundation of every school and college curriculum, every educational system, throughout the world.

PRODUCING CHANGE

The involvement of young people in promoting social change has always aroused doubts in the minds of older folk as to their maturity of judgement, yet it is often the young who introduce the most significant advances. It is also commonplace to find that, irrespective of the skills of the inventors or the technical merits of their products, there are reservations, by long-established practitioners, as to what is really worthwhile in the field of new technology. Because of this even modest changes for the better, both social and technological, may well be resisted, perhaps vigorously.

Current examples include several proposals for changes in legislation in Britain. Suggested alterations in the law which would allow the police to conduct random breath tests to identify drunken car drivers have met with considerable opposition in England and Wales. Despite the continuing high level of annual road accidents caused by drunkenness on the part of drivers, civil rights campaigners and others persist in holding the view that such police action would infringe the citizen's personal liberties. In these present circumstances there is no likelihood of any early change in the law, because most democratic governments, which depend on periodic votes of the populace in order to hold power, are reluctant to undertake actions which might cause them to become unpopular. The British government is no exception. On the other hand, the South African government has made great strides in changing both its legislation and its longstanding practices in respect of apartheid. This has brought it favourable recognition from some other countries but only continuing, and even escalating, trouble at home where every change appears to be opposed by blacks and whites alike despite the alterations being claimed to be in the best long-term interests of both.

Sometimes resistance can be in the form of support for an entrenched position of power and privilege. The two basic categories of practising lawyers in England provide an apt illustration. Barristers vigorously repudiate the possibility of their profession merging with, or having any closer professional relationship with, their legal colleagues, solicitors. Dismissing what appears to be unthinkable, ie that a solicitor might be enabled eventually to become a judge, they are reported as objecting to solicitors (who normally appear only in the 'lower' magistrates courts in respect of relatively minor offences) even being allowed to speak in any type of higher court. Power, of course, does not belong exclusively to any professional group – as was demonstrated by the Synod of the Church of England in 1992 when approving a recommendation for the future ordination of women priests. It was in the two Houses of Bishops and Clergy that the required two-thirds majority vote was first obtained. Only the House of Laity provided strong opposition to the proposal, which they ultimately supported by only two votes.

THE PROCESS OF CHANGE

To understand social change we must attempt to discover some kind of pattern in it. Social change is, on the whole, an orderly process by which an alteration occurs in the structure or function of a society composed of individuals and groups. It can take many forms but consists basically of the three distinct stages which characterize all change processes:

1. The creation or production of something which is new or different.
2. The spread or communication of the innovation to the other members of the social system.
3. A stage consequential on the other two, and involving both personal and social outcomes. These occur when the effects of adoption or rejection by members of that society become evident.

The word 'change' does not indicate a 'process', social or otherwise, since it does not imply any law, direction or continuity. Only when there is a continuous movement, often in a step-by-step manner, is it really possible for us talk about a process. A **process** implies going from one state or stage to another. When, in addition to continuity, there is also a change of direction or emphasis then other terms such as 'evolution' can be used. Evolution implies some sort of gradual growth in form or nature as well as in size. It is usual to think of this as on a forward or upward scale. When we add value judgements or ethical values, progress tends to imply movement towards some final desired goal. Because change involves risk many people are unhappy during the transition period. For instance, some statesmen in the US and elsewhere are currently expressing grave misgivings about the dissolution of the centrally-controlled Soviet state and its replacement by a consortium or loose confederation of a dozen different states. Formerly the Soviet Union, or USSR, was viewed as the principal enemy of the US but an acceptably stable form of confrontation had been developed which, for a long time, suited both countries and, indeed, the rest of the Western World. Now there is social, political and economic instability which will continue to cause great unease until some kind of mutual interface has again been determined, this time with the more decentralized Commonwealth of Independent States, some of which seem determined to obtain complete autonomy.

On a smaller scale, perhaps, but an issue which may still become vital to global peace is the confrontation which continues to rage so bitterly between the ethnic groups in the former Yugoslavian state. Even nearer to home, the recent democratic change of government in Sweden, after many years of socialist rule, has made life difficult for the administrators of that welfare state. They can not, like the previous politicians, put forward plans for changes in taxation and welfare benefits based on the superficial plausibility of previously accepted egalitarian dogma. The French government also has succumbed to a change of heart by the electorate, in an already confused and unstable political system.

BASIC THEORIES OF SOCIAL CHANGE

In an effort to try to understand and explain change two fundamental theories have dominated our thinking in the past:

1. The **cyclical** approach;
2. The **evolutionary** approach.

Cyclical interpretation of change

The oldest theory of change is founded on the cyclical approach. Many people have sought reassurance in homely analogies as an indication of how change can be incorporated naturally into everyday life. Based on the human life cycle of birth, growth, ageing and death, a theoretical frame of reference for understanding social change suggests that it could be cyclical in nature and that there are forces for development or decay which tend to operate continuously in all spheres of human activity.

This certainly applies with respect to the annual climatic seasons and, in a statistical sense, to certain phenomena such as the Trade Cycle, atomic processes, astronomical observations and fashion trends. Cyclical change can also be illustrated, it has been argued, by examples of the great civilizations which have arisen, flourished, decayed and disappeared over the centuries. Some features of a cyclical process obviously help to shed light on particular social problems such as unemployment, although even here there are obvious discrepancies. A recent example was a proposal in 1992 to make 30 000 British miners compulsorily redundant by closing down virtually all the remaining coalmines in the country. Issues of this magnitude do not fit easily or smoothly into any neatly recurring theme.

However, speculative theorizing as a means of producing any generalizable frame of reference for viewing change fails to stand up to critical analysis of objective data. Observations show that while there are, indeed, rhythmic fluctuations in most forms of change, not all occur at the same rate or in the same direction, nor even on any common time scale. Thus an all-embracing cyclical theory has no scientific foundation.

Evolutionary interpretation of change

The second type of theory is also based largely on observation of so-called natural processes. It views change as evolution, or literally an unveiling, of some latent or hidden dimensions of the situation. For instance, one of the evolutionary aspects of society is held to be the increasing identification of particular work patterns as a result of division of labour within particular distributions of population. Such task allocation, it is held, leads to specialization of functions, the rise of occupational guilds, the concept of apprenticeship, the emergence of trade unions, the development of professions, the institutionalization of hierarchical structures in employer-employee and manager-worker relationships and, inevitably, the class structure of civilized society. Occupational classification enables some societies to be categorized as more developed than others, ie some are perceived as 'higher' than others. We often continue to make such value judgements from comparisons of this sort and, although highly subjective, they inevitably provide much of the foundation for the interpersonal relationships which make our lives not only possible but meaningful.

Some other attempts at identifying the meaning of change were more marginal in that they did not tackle the issue of social change itself head-on. Instead they tended to be based more on accounting for observed differences than on any attempts to try to understand the more fundamental underlying operation of forces or types of influence. For example, one historically based perspective queried whether social change proceeds in the direction of achieving eventual perfection of the society or, alternatively, whether it ultimately brings about the extinction of that society in which it occurs. This was a philosophical approach which attempted to provide a universal overview. Naturally, it is both difficult and misleading to portray generalizations on the basis of individual cases.

Since civilizations have been located in a wide range of different global settings it was inevitable that some more local interpretations of the meaning of change would therefore periodically be devised. **Geographic determinism** was one such example. The suggestion in this case was that, in the northern hemisphere, the more northerly the location the more likely it was that the inhabitants would be dour, hardworking, industrious and thrifty. Those resident in the more southerly parts (it was said) tended to be more carefree, lazy, indolent and spendthrift. In the southern hemisphere the mirror image was said to be the case. In response to this interpretation climatologists were at pains to point out that it was more likely climate, rather than location, that caused the variation, the colder regions producing and supporting the human characteristics that made for individual industry, progress, economic enterprise and social advancement. What was being sought here and in other propositions of similar kind, regrettably, was the setting up of a cause-effect relationship, where in reality none existed. Also there was a total preoccupation with changes of direction; consequently the fact was overlooked that many really important changes which have occurred are not of direction but of *intensity*. When people are persuaded to change their attitudes, for example, they may not develop different ones to replace those previously held. Instead they may cling to their former beliefs with even greater conviction, a point which is of some consequence in contemporary political and social studies.

More recent insight into the nature of change incorporates modern understanding of both the psychology of individuals and the sociology of different types of society. This will be referred to in greater depth in Chapters 10, 11 and 12 (ideas, practices and products). These chapters in turn will be underpinned by the immediately preceding ones on change agents and opinion leaders.

Whether the perspective on change is ancient or modern it is still a characteristic of the social sciences that, unlike the physical sciences, there are no genuine laws which can specify categorically that a particular cause will produce a predictable effect. Indeed a 'cause' is often extremely difficult to identify. There are, of course, logical steps which can be taken to ensure that the uncertainty is considerably diminished. This requires what is nowadays encompassed in such processes as forward planning.

PLANNED CHANGE

Essentially, change can only come about if there exists a gap between what *is* and what *could be* (some people would be more specific and prescribe 'what ought to be'). This provides a basis for identifying **need** which, in its broadest meaning, can be thought of as what is required to fill any identified gap. However, need is often more closely targeted on some obvious lack of provision endangering human progress or even basic existence. Purposeful change could be seen as an attempt to satisfy or reduce that need. Need might also be identified as something which is merely *wanted* by an individual or group. However not all wants are needs since the underlying basis of need is necessity, not desire, although many changes in modern society are responses to just such expressions of longing.

In any case it is as true today as it has been throughout history that change takes place in a wide range of different forms. Some of these will not only be unwished for but may have consequences that could be unacceptable and sometimes even disastrous for both people and nations. Most changes still come about by deliberate design in order to alter existing conditions for some economic, social or ideological reason. Such alteration focuses on desired objectives or is motivated by stated aims. Some kind of overall planning is necessary, taking into account the adequacy of total available resources to obtain the desired outcomes. If this were not the case, decisions would be on an *ad hoc* basis. While planning cannot guarantee success, the risks are at least minimized.

Essentially, planning is concerned with two main functions:

1. Striving to eliminate, or at least reduce, uncertainty and replace it by calculable risk.

2. Providing the means of discriminating between the many choices which might exist in respect of that risk.

AIMS AND OBJECTIVES

In order to bring about consciously any desired change it is necessary to have some goals in mind. These may be identified as either **aims** or **objectives**. As with other terms in everyday use the two are often used interchangeably but there is an important difference. In basic terms:

- Aim implies strategy;
- Objective employs tactics.

It is useful to consider an aim as being concerned more with general policy than with day to day achievement. In other words it employs strategy rather than tactics. This is usually long range, rather imprecise in its description and often almost impossible to achieve – or at least to know when it has been accomplished. Examples include such aims as 'producing good citizens' or 'education for all'. Objectives, on the other hand, are quite specific and more recognizably attainable. Examples are 'the basic rate of income tax will be reduced to 20% by next April', or 'a community centre will be built within two years'. All objectives, without exception, are defined as achievable and assessable. Indeed they are often the milestones which indicate how much progress has been made *en route* to the larger goal. Sometimes the term **goal** is used by writers to indicate something less vague than an aim but not as well-defined as an objective. I think that this is an unnecessary *complication* of a fairly straightforward distinction between those things which can definitely be seen to be attainable and those where it would be difficult to know.

It is assumed that you are reading this chapter because you genuinely would like to understand the nature of change and innovation. A desire to know more about the phenomena may have been your aim in starting to read this book. As one of your primary objectives (whether or not you actually thought of it in this way) you will consequently have set yourself the task of reading this chapter. You should certainly know when you have achieved this objective. But when, if ever, will you be able to say that you have fully achieved your original aim?

In setting objectives there are certain procedures which provide appropriate guidelines. These may be summarized as follows:

- Know that a definite goal actually exists.
- Be able to specify clearly what it is.
- Identify what steps will be necessary to achieve it.
- Verify that it is possible for these steps to be taken by yourself and/or others who are to be involved.
- Perhaps most importantly, establish that making the effort is accepted by all participants as being truly worthwhile!

Guidelines such as these lessen the risk of failure to achieve perceived goals. Such lack of success, when it occurs, tends to come about because of one or other of two fairly common human shortcomings:

1. A failure of understanding – this is an inability to see how something can actually be achieved.
2. A failure of confidence leading to a lack of real commitment. In this case there is undue hesitancy because while the target may be accepted as possible there may be a feeling that it may not succeed.

Aims do not necessarily have to be on a grand scale. An aim and an objective may differ qualitatively while appearing to be almost identical. For example it has already been stated that one of your objectives may have been to read this first chapter and this is capable of verification. You know when you have finished reading the number of pages allocated to the chapter. You could not, however, have had as an objective 'to understand' this chapter. It is possible to read without gaining understanding and, in any case, how is understanding to be measured effectively? Even long-standing recognized public examinations often test the accuracy of recall more than the ability to comprehend and apply. Hopefully your own understanding of this chapter should be assisted by the summary, notes for reflection, opportunities for practical application and examples throughout the book. Your original aim could be achieved in its highest form at the very end. By that stage your insight into innovation theory and practice should have become much more than just the sum of the various adoption, diffusion and communication elements contained in these fourteen different chapters.

SUMMARY

Change is inevitable but it may not always be of the kind which is wanted. Every alteration is unsettling because not all of the consequences are predictable. Many people are more content when things are not undergoing such movement because then they have fewer adjustments to make. Change which is wanted can be planned to happen. This requires the identification of aims or goals and the setting of objectives. While the desired change may actually take place it may not be considered by everyone to be any improvement on what had previously existed.

REFLECTION

At this stage there is not too much in the way of new material to reflect on. However, regarding all new information, the instruction to 'think on these things' (Philippians 4: 8) is both timely and appropriate. You will therefore find items for reflection towards the end of each chapter since it is useful to check, before going on to apply any theory to practice, that you have achieved the objectives specified at the beginning of each chapter.

APPLICATION

There is an old saying (origin unknown) that 'Change is what you should prepare for in prosperity and pray for in adversity.'

What message do you think this is intended to send? To whom? Why? What, if anything, does it mean to you?

Try to write down brief notes on which you would base an answer. Do *not* write an essay. When you have given the matter some thought turn to the Appendix and consider the points indicated there. Compare your own notes with the suggestions and examine any differences to see whether or not these should be further explored by you.

This chapter does not follow the pattern of the rest of the book. Where it has been general in its content the other chapters are more specific and focus on the subject matter indicated in their titles. They are concerned in increasing detail with the nature and impact of change as it affects individuals in everyday life, especially those who find themselves acting as change agents or would wish to do so. These types of people influence individuals and often sell products, make purchases, communicate with others or assist them to make decisions. There is wide-ranging examination of the complexities of various kinds of change and how change may be brought about and/or appropriately responded to. Questions and issues for contemplation may be direct or indirect but are always relevant. If, at the end of this chapter, you are interested enough to want to read more about the general topic of change, and particularly its social characteristics, you might find some of the following books helpful (subject to availability).

RECOMMENDED FURTHER READING

Hills, Philip (ed.) (1980) *The Future of the Printed Word*, The Open University Press, Milton Keynes.
A fascinating and thought-provoking book on the social implications of advances in information technology.

Johnson, Elizabeth S. and Williamson, John B. (1980) *Growing Old*, Holt Rinehart and Winston, New York.
A study of attitudes towards one change which is generally conceded to be inevitable.

LaPiere, Richard T. (1965) *Social Change*, McGraw-Hill, New York.
This should be available in public libraries and will certainly be found in the sociology departments of colleges and universities. It is definitely not bedtime reading! Read the first chapter only for an interesting (but rather lengthy) review of a wide range of theories of social change.

The other chapters are more specifically concerned with sociological theory.

Laver, Murray (1980) *Computers and Social Change*, Cambridge University Press, Cambridge.

Very pleasant easy reading concerning the effects which developing computer systems can have on our lives.

What is an innovation? 3

Everything has been thought of before, but the problem
is to think of it again.

J.W. von Goethe (1799)

The (White) Knight said . . . 'It's my own invention.'
Lewis Carroll, Alice Through the Looking Glass

There is no new thing under the sun.

Ecclesiastes 1: 9

This chapter considers the meaning of innovation, how it may
occur, and how it may be perceived by the individual. We also look
at a number of factors which usually influence the extent of its
acceptance.

Objectives
When you have read and reflected on this chapter you should be
able to:

- give an example of an innovation and describe what constitutes
  its 'newness';
- select two features of an innovation known to you, identifying
  one which could aid its acceptance while indicating another which
  could retard acceptance;
- specify two possible sources of innovation and give an example
  from each.

THE NATURE OF INNOVATION

An innovation might be something which has never previously existed.
Conversely it could be something quite new to our own personal situation or capable of having a fresh use at the time that we become aware
of it. Because of this we may be willing to consider using it ourselves –
provided of course that we believe it to be not just different but also
better than its comparison. To think of things being better or worse
involves us in making value judgements with which other individuals
may not agree.

It will be obvious to many people from past experience that not everything new (however 'new' is defined) is necessarily good. And of those things which might be good not all become well known. Even then only a few of the 'survivors' prove to be of really widespread interest, and of those which are, not all will be taken up at the same time. It is as though each new idea has to pass through a series of filters before being able eventually to be put into practice.

What influences help to determine the actual patterns of this kind of situation? That is what much research into the adoption and diffusion of innovations is largely concerned with.

An understanding of what makes an innovation attractive (and when) can obviously be of immense value to manufacturers, politicians, teachers and others, all of whom sell either products, ideas or services. In some respects the process of innovation might be regarded as being concerned with overcoming a kind of 'sales resistance'. This would be far too restricted a view for us to take although it certainly is related to the bringing about of change to which there is often a widespread reluctance. Some resistance, or at best indifference, to change applies even at the level of general interpersonal communication as will be evident when we look more closely at adoption and diffusion processes later in the book.

In practice, much of our decision-making can be seen to be subject to two major influences:

1. The features of the innovation.
2. The characteristics of the decision-makers.

The first influence arises from the attributes of an innovation itself and the way in which these present the possibility of improvement or advantage. The second is a reflection of personal characteristics such as attitudes, beliefs and human values. At this point, therefore, we will focus attention on the implications of the first group of factors since they are capable of being more readily identified and defined. The more complex personal and social features of the second group of factors are of such vital importance that they will be dealt with at length in the immediately succeeding chapters.

ASPECTS OF INNOVATION

As indicated in the previous section, an innovation can be an invention; something produced or developed which is strikingly different from anything already in existence. In this case the question of newness is not in doubt. However an innovation might not be a material product but a fundamental change of practice which is new because it puts an entirely different emphasis on well-established procedures. An example might be that of a former communist country now endeavouring, with 'inherited' staff and methods of operation, to achieving capitalist style objectives.

The matters which need examination must include the following factors because they are all vital to any form of decision-making:

- Cost
- Complexity
- Visibility
- Divisibility
- Compatibility
- Utility
- Collective action.

Some of these factors may be defined differently, and additional ones may be considered for inclusion, but none of the essential characteristics of those listed above can be omitted without lessening the rationality of reaching a sensible conclusion. While they are described as factors there is no implication that theoretically each one has a unique and intrinsic content and structure. It is simply a term of convenience (as most categories are) and there are many dimensions at even the simplest level of description. We will now examine each factor in more detail.

FACTORS RELATED TO INNOVATION

Cost

Any new product or practice which is high in financial cost is likely to be adopted more slowly than one which involves lower expenditure, even if the eventual return for outlay is likely to be proportionately higher. This is a phenomenon well-known to the commercial retail sector. In general people will accept what appears to be a bargain knowing that it represents somewhat lesser quality in return for an appropriately lower price. Many would prefer to do this rather than pay 'extra' to ensure such features as additional safety, economy, durability or aesthetic appeal. Particularly in respect of consumer products many of these features are precisely those aspects which are emphasized in advertisements in the 'quality' press, designed to attract the more affluent or discerning consumer. One imported European beer, for example, sells under the slogan 'Refreshingly Expensive'.

While the risk associated with adopting an innovation invariably has some cost factor in it this need not necessarily be always, or only, a financial one. For instance a new approach to medical treatment of, say, human infertility may require some experienced general practitioners to forsake traditional approaches in favour of new clinical practices, resulting in a temporary lowering of competence levels. In such circumstances they might find themselves unwilling or unable to come to terms with this. The inevitable feelings of insecurity which arise might also not be thought worth the risk. The high price which might have to be paid in human terms is a real personal-factor cost to the individual concerned.

When considering the implications of cost, it is also worth noting that **opportunity cost** is a valid concept for many people, especially administrators or managers who have limited resources available for a wide choice of projects. This term highlights the missed opportunity to do one thing, rather than another, when both are desirable but only one can be supported. The decision to incur actual financial outlay on any one project in a series should therefore take into account the opportunity cost as well as the actual expenditure. In many institutions of higher education there are new courses being provided regularly in response to the emergence of fresh requests. Yet few, if any, of the existing courses are discontinued until enrolments fall to a level of non-viability. In such circumstances, a concern about adequate resources often focuses as much upon opportunity cost as on the basic financial burden. The implications in a case of this sort often relate to what might have been done to promote even more new courses instead of continuing to respond to demands for repetition of those programmes already in existence.

Complexity

Ideas and practices which are relatively simple to understand and operate by the end-users tend to be adopted more readily and quickly than those of greater complexity. Television as an enjoyable pastime, for example, has an almost universal entertainment appeal. There is probably no other leisure provision which offers so much in return for so little knowledge, skill or effort. On the other hand, television used for business conferencing, although technically feasible, cost-effective and only marginally more difficult to operate than the domestic product, has not yet progressed much beyond the pilot-scheme stage. In a different but related context the manufacturers of card games and board games know just how difficult it is to extend the market for such products. Despite some increase in demand for chess, backgammon, bridge, Monopoly and Trivial Pursuit these pastimes are of relatively minor commercial consequence in comparison with the vast numbers of purchasers who apparently prefer to play less intellectually demanding games. Especially for the young the button-pushing wizardry of pocket-sized electronic games obviates the need for learning traditional elementary skills such as shuffling, dealing or remembering rules and moves. The complexity instead lies in the design and construction of the machine itself while the controls are simple to understand, being no more complicated than those of a TV set. At the same time computer games demand new types of personal skills, which young people can often master more readily, centring on manual agility and quickness of response in a situation where the opponent is a space-age machine.

Visibility

An innovation is likely to be adopted more readily and more widely if it is open to inspection and, above all, if it can be seen to work. This transparency is what communication is fundamentally very much concerned with. Knowledge must not only be transmitted but also received if it is to have any chance of being acted upon. However it is essential that, in addition to being received, it must also be understood. This, as we shall see later, cannot be taken for granted. Relatively few gardeners, for instance, apply pre-emergent weedkiller in their gardens because there is no visible evidence that it actually works to prevent undesirable growth. Instead there is a proliferation of *weedkillers* of every kind (all with very satisfactory summer sales figures for the manufacturers) which people apply quite happily to their weeds once they have allowed them to grow. The unwanted vegetation, being destroyed in a highly visible way, provides proof of the weedkillers' effectiveness. On a different scale it could be noted that, at least until comparatively recently, the National Health Service in the United Kingdom was actually operating largely as a remedial service. No proactive assistance was available to those who were reasonably healthy and wished to remain so, but appropriate hospital and other provision was made for those who actually fell ill. This was because, universally, government expenditure of public funds on preventative medicine can be politically hard to justify in the absence of any obvious results of effectiveness, whereas statistics concerning bed occupancy or number of operations performed is proof to the electorate of money going precisely where it really does some good.

Divisibility

Something which can be tried in part before any commitment has to be made to the whole enterprise will generally tend to be adopted more readily than something which cannot be approached in this way. Examples can be seen in a wide range of situations but one from my own experience will serve to demonstrate the principles involved.

Some years ago my proposed introduction of a departmental library within a college did not meet with the approval of the college librarian who wished to exercise centralized control. A shelf of my own books was accordingly made 'temporarily' available for student borrowing from my own office. This proved to be so popular that soon a whole bookcase had to be provided to give access to a larger selection of such volumes. To ensure accurate record-keeping of books on loan my secretary initially looked after the issues and returns but soon had to seek assistance in order to cope. Eventually a spare room had to be set aside with a part-time clerical assistant in charge, at length replaced by a full-time assistant to cope with increased demand. Finally the room was equipped as a departmental library (subject to certain restrictions in respect of staffing and funding). This very satisfactory outcome would have been unlikely had more direct confrontational methods been used. In fact this library was highly specialized and contained no reading material of the slightest interest to students other than those following my own courses.

Compatibility

The attitudes and values which most people hold in relation to an innovation tend to be affected by their past experience with related ideas. The new idea must not conflict with the values and beliefs which they have developed otherwise it has little chance of success. One instance of this would be the absence of artificial aids to family planning in a country such as Spain where church teaching has made powerful impact on personal morals. In such a situation there can be no form of public approval for artificial methods of contraception and no approved spread of information about such matters. There will therefore be no change unless, which is unlikely, a new value system is first adopted. Such adoption, should it happen, would be an example of a non-material innovation, the newness consisting in the transference of both idea and practice from outside to within an environment where it had previously been viewed as alien.

Utility

If something new can be seen to be a major improvement on what currently exists then it could well be adopted fairly quickly. There are plenty of physical examples to be seen, such as instant coffee, pocket calculators, laptop computers, mobile telephones and automated cash dispensers. On the other hand, many new things which have previously seemed to offer only novelty value or at best, only slight improvement were somewhat delayed in their adoption. Examples include contact lenses instead of spectacles, electronic organizers instead of diaries and word processors instead of typewriters. Eventually they all did achieve acceptance. Others failed. For example, we still use the old-fashioned and inefficient mechanically-derived QWERTY keyboards on even the most modern computers, despite the availability of efficiently designed ergonomic input facilities. And then there are the video telephones which hardly anybody seems to want, despite the fact that they have been demonstrated for decades!

Where a rational decision is made on the basis of assessing the probable advantage of making a change, some account has to be taken of what improvement, if any, is likely to arise from it. This may be measured in social, as well as economic, terms. For example a change in an individual point of view may be needed just in order to stimulate a desire to possess the most modern or up-to-date version of something. Some people prefer to use the term **marginal utility**, which is (or was) more common in the field of economics, to indicate a preference for something which gives only a slight social or personal advantage. The commonest example in recent years must be the annual August bulge of new car purchases in England in order to get the distinctive fresh letter on the car's registration plate. This ploy by the government to spread car sales over two peaks each year instead of having just one every January, enables car purchasers in August of any year to obtain what is effectively the succeeding year's registration letter for the vehicle. In spite of the fact that this does not fool anyone it still remains a popular requirement, even though a few months later the registration loses at least some of its cachet when genuine January registrations take place.

Collective action

While most decisions tend to be made at individual level there are some situations which require group decision-making, a point of some importance which arises especially in the context of organizations. These are dealt with in Chapter 13. For the present we can reflect that it would usually be of little immediate consequence if a few fairly isolated residents who were miles from a main electricity supply circuit decided to seek electrification for their homes. In order to have a supply extended to that particular location the applicants would normally need to rally the support of as many other potential consumers as possible. This could make the provision of the service an economic possibility for the suppliers and result in a reduced installation charge for the consumers. Sometimes group action is simply not possible, as is the case with domestic medical practice in the Australian outback. To serve the outback and isolated homesteads the Royal Flying Doctor service is a substitute for the family doctor of the conurbations. Perhaps the most common recurring example of the different approaches by individuals as compared with groups is seen in the continuing popularity of fluoride toothpaste. Purchases by individuals continue to grow in Western countries while, at the same time, there is normally a public outcry whenever any proposal for general fluoridation of domestic water supply is suggested.

FORMS OF INNOVATIVE PROCESS

Bearing in mind the factors mentioned above, and any related matters, it is important to recognize that there are several different ways in which an innovation may arise. Each will have its own unique influence on the acceptance of what is new. In this respect we can regard innovations as having three possible main attributes:

1. planned to occur;
2. improvements; or are
3. fundamental in nature.

Innovations are planned

They are planned at least in the sense of being deliberate, ie they are devised and/or disseminated in order to assist in the achievement of certain goals. The very term innovation comes from the Latin *innovare* (to renew) and therefore implies a purpose and some motivation underlying the impetus to change. These qualities may apply either to the originator or the recipient (or both). The ability to review conditions from time to time and then update them as required is obviously essential in any connection where the situation has not become completely static.

Innovations are improvements

Whether or not any alteration is an 'improvement' is likely to remain a largely subjective judgement since not everyone will apply similar criteria in their assessment of it. However, innovations are created or spread in an attempt to bring about some improvement, technological and/or social. All innovation has a positive approach to change. It does not usually contain anything rebellious or revolutionary in the sense of, say, political overthrow. It seeks acceptance and approval rather than attempting to bring about any alteration by force. As such there is an absence of coercion, although the circumstances of some situations may well exert pressures which influence an individual to become involved in action for which there is little personal enthusiasm. This is a very important point to bear in mind when considering subsequent issues in innovation in this text.

Innovations are fundamental in nature

They are fundamental in the sense, at least, that they inevitably cause widespread repercussions far beyond their original intentions. It is axiomatic that outcomes are unpredictable and that the effects of even minor change often spread like ripples on a pond. All change, however personal and private, inevitably produces more widely related social impact and thus may contribute (albeit only marginally) to modifications in the structure and fabric of society itself.

THE EMERGENCE OF INNOVATIONS

Some of the implications of these considerations will be examined later. In the meantime it is relevant to consider the principal ways in which the emergence of an innovation can come about.

Sources of innovation include:

- research
- invention
- discovery
- development
- problem-solving.

The principal impetus for innovation is to be found in one or other of these categories.

Research

This is probably the first source to come to mind, especially in respect of new products. Research is a significant part of every manufacturing activity today as well as being an inescapable part of the activities of a vast range of agencies and diverse enterprises. These include institutions of higher education, hospitals, libraries, pharmaceutical suppliers, food processors and armaments manufacturers. Research has tended to be associated more with invention than with innovation. However, invention may relate to new *processes* rather than material *products* and involve problem-solving as well as creativity. Not all research is concerned with finding answers to specific problems facing human beings. Its activity often relates more to the pursuit of truth for its own sake, wherever it may be found, whatever form it may take and whatever the consequences may be. By its very nature applied research does look at the practical applications of the possible end results; this depends on the initiative and purpose of the investigators involved. In this context the end user may or may not be the prime motivator for the generation of new knowledge; however, their expressed desires will not be ignored. What needs have actually been identified may have come from some form of investigation such as 'market research' or may simply have been specified on the basis of 'brainstorming' or intuition.

Invention

As I have already made clear this refers to the creation of something completely new, ie something which did not previously exist, at least in any directly comparable form. This is the most obvious and readily understood form of innovation especially in relation to technological artefacts. The atomic bomb, to cite one example, would illustrate clearly something which had not previously existed and which was entirely different in every way to previously known conventional explosives. However, the invention of artificial silk, as rayon was first called, was equally an invention since nothing even remotely like it in terms of chemical structure and physical characteristics had ever existed prior to Chardonnet producing it in 1884. Looking at the numbers of annual applications in many different countries for the registration of patents it is clear that, in the technological field at least, invention proceeds today at an undiminished rate.

Discovery

This term denotes a state of mental recognition of something previously unknown. Whether it was always there but hidden from our understanding or whether it is new in a creative sense is largely a matter for philosophical debate in the appropriate context. It is, for example, often stated that knowledge is created rather than discovered. Discovery and invention do have a fairly direct linkage in that one almost inevitably leads to the other. The existence of X-rays was a discovery which led directly to the construction of the X-ray machine, an indispensable tool in medical diagnosis. For most people the difference is not particularly significant since the general term innovation covers both and, in any case, for most of us nothing exists until it has been discovered. We often talk of inventions and breakthroughs in various scientific and technical fields as discoveries and any such discovery, whether tangible or intangible, may be just as innovative as any invention. While inventions may be pursued as issues requiring resolution, discoveries may be accidental. Indeed many really important discoveries have been made precisely in this way by people who were seeking something else when they almost literally fell over the new discovery in the process. This was the case with penicillin, the vulcanization of rubber and the discovery of America. These three examples, so different in character, time and place, illustrate the lasting importance of the accidental dimension in any situation where chance might just be a factor – and there are very few situations where this is not the case!

Development

This term relates more to the improvement of something which already exists than to original creation. Few innovations are perfected at their inception. It is usual for there to be a period of modification and refinement while a product, process or thought is reshaped or fine-tuned. On occasion the final version may differ greatly from that which was originally put forward and, in that respect, the process may have a particular dimension of problem-solving in it. Those who make an improvement, however significant, on something which already exists do not usually receive the same acclaim as the original inventor who created something which had no precedent. Neither, of course, do they experience the same sort of difficulties, mental or social, as did the inventor. Nevertheless many people consider development to be a distinct form of re-invention as it very often contains a great deal of original work both in creative thinking as well as in actual construction.

Problem-solving

There is an old saying that 'necessity is the mother of invention'. This is usually taken to mean that new approaches are devised to improve aspects of our society because there are certain conditions which require modification or improvement. In other words it is considered that at least some innovative effort is put forward in order to assist problem-solving. It is a truism that, in order to solve a problem, it is necessary first of all to recognize that one exists. The existence of a problem points to something needing to be resolved. Whatever the response to this it should, if it is appropriate, lead to a reduction of the perceived need which originated it. When dealing with other people's problems there is often the anxiety of knowing whether or not to accept the existence of a difficulty which they alone can see. In this situation it has to be recognized, however, that for them *their* perception is the only real one. This is because the world we live in is the world as it impacts on our own senses, irrespective of any objective criteria evident to other people. The acceptance of this viewpoint will be a forceful introduction to the core of innovation for some people who have no doubts about objective reality but have reservations about any other kind. However in terms of *subjective* reality the world in which we live and to which we respond is essentially the world which we perceive. In other words, for those people who genuinely believe that they have a problem their belief will govern their actions. They must, therefore, be regarded as being in real difficulty and consequently in need of appropriate guidance and assistance.

THE CONTEXT OF INNOVATION

In so far as the total environment supporting innovation can be identified it could be said that, in actual fact, little seems to have changed in respect of its essential elements since the time of the Industrial Revolution. The universal conditions providing a supportive environment still appear to be much the same as they were then. Factors supporting innovation might be briefly summarized as follows:

- Entrepreneurship
- Mobility of labour
- Effective communication
- Democratic structure
- Market orientation.

These terms are now explained.

Entrepreneurship

This is an awkward term but an important one. An entrepreneur is often regarded today as someone who starts his own speculative new small business. However the broadest term, and in many ways still the best, was defined around the year 1800 by the French economist J. B. Say who identified an entrepreneur as one who 'shifts economic resources out of an area of lower and into an area of higher productivity and greater yield'. This need not imply that the population of an entrepreneurial society must be such as to turn it into a nation of shopkeepers. It does, however, indicate an underlying motivation to sell, persuade, convert or in some way influence others to the benefit of at least one party to the interaction – and preferably both. The entrepreneur is often an innovator. He has one of the most essential qualities for such a role. He is prepared to take a risk!

Mobility of labour

Mobility does not refer only to the willingness to undertake geographical movement but also to versatility of attitudes and values in respect of issues such as training. This is especially important in processes such as reskilling rather than deskilling, a matter of contemporary importance at a time of increasing redundancies in a range of specialized occupations worldwide. The essence of this approach is to recognize the fact that nowadays, unlike previous generations, very few of us are likely to continue for the rest of our lives in the employment in which we started. Many people will change occupations twice or more in the course of their working lives. Additional training or qualifications will have to be gained for at least some of these changes. An innovative approach to re-training programmes is long overdue in every country in the world.

Effective communication

All information supporting change must be effectively communicated in order to produce action. Communication involves both human and tech-nological aspects and will be considered in detail in Chapter 7.

Democratic structure

Without a reasonably democratic society in which differing ideas may be freely expressed and discussed there cannot be that genuine progress which is often the outcome of unfettered reflection and debate. There is genuine benefit, personal and social, in being able to 'think out loud' on occasion. Indeed in some business and commercial undertakings there are regular 'brainstorming' sessions where no idea is too far-fetched to be considered and no value judgement is attached to any individual contribution. Even today that cannot be done in every country without fear of being censured by bureaucrats or, at least, causing embarrass-ment to colleagues. The fact that some former dictatorships have been replaced by governments avowedly committed to democracy offers hope for an extension of such structures and processes in the future.

A market orientation

While all the previous factors can be seen to have a contribution to make to the support of innovation this is sometimes overlooked because of its commercial label. It is, however, absolutely essential that to be widely accepted an innovation must be capable of being received by as many people as possible. This will only happen when it supplies an answer to some felt need. In other words, it must be able to sell itself. Even the most competent salesman has to sell himself first, and it is what we all do at interviews and the like. Just a very slight stretch of the imagination is needed to confirm that, in that one sense at least, all of us are already involved in a market economy of some importance.

SUMMARY

All inventions are innovations because they create something which did not previously exist. Not all inventions, however, are material artefacts. An innovation is not necessarily an invention but can be a new way of perceiving something which may already be in existence. There are features of all innovations, whatever their form, which tend to make them readily acceptable to at least some people. But there may well be an absence of such features in some instances (or the existence of contradictory ones) which could slow down or even completely halt such acceptance. Innovations can arise from any one of a number of different sources but are all similar in that they require a suitable environment in which to flourish.

REFLECTION

The following points are not questions to be answered but indications of areas of thought to be explored as a preparation for issues which will arise later.

1. Re-read this chapter in order to jot down any key words and terms which you may wish to remember, for example, **invention**, **development**, **compatibility**, **mobility**. Can you explain such terms using your own words?
2. Try to name one innovation which you believe to have failed. This could be a political manoeuvre, a theory, a mechanical device, a medically prescribed drug . . . anything.
   Why do you think that it failed? What, in your opinion might have made it succeed? Are there any lessons to be learned from its appearance and/or disappearance? (You will be returning to points such as this later in the book.)
3. Can you identify any one specific innovation which has really impressed you? Why did it do so? How, if at all, has it made (or is it likely to make) any contribution to your own life?
4. In what sense, do you think, might it still be possible to argue that there is nothing new under the sun?

While it is not necessary to produce written responses to these points there is much to be gained in doing so. It will, for example, enable you to check whether you can confidently and accurately express yourself in writing (a widely different form of communication from that of oral expression).

APPLICATION

After you have read the following extract you may find it worthwhile to try to answer the question at the end. A sample answer (which is not to be taken as the only acceptable or correct one) is given later in the Appendix.

A powerful determinant of consumer choice is habit or inertia. It suits the consumer to treat much of her activity as a matter of routine. To indulge in a process of conscious deliberation at every purchase would take an enormous amount of time and mental effort which, not unnaturally, there is a strong drive to avoid. Any satisfactory model of consumer choice is bound to give a large weight to the brand previously purchased.

Timothy Joyce (1967) What Do We Know About How Advertising Works?

J. Walter Thompson Co. Ltd, London.

In the light of these comments try to suggest an innovative approach which might be taken in order to overcome customer inertia towards:

1. a particular type of product; and
2. a particular brand of that type of product.

Indicate what degree of success might be expected in each case and give reasons for your answer.

RECOMMENDED FURTHER READING

It is not necessary for you to do any further reading until you have covered a bit more ground in respect of basic theory.

However, if you would like to do so at this stage there are several books which might be available in your library. Each of the following could provide something worthwhile although they are recommended more to be skimmed through than read thoroughly.

Drucker, Peter F. (1986) *Innovation and Entrepreneurship*, Heinemann, London.
A very technical book aimed at Graduate Business School students, written by an American professor. Have a look at a library copy if one is available. If it happens that you are a management student and/or a business executive then maybe this is one you should get – some day. At the moment, however, it would be very hard going!

Dyer, Gillian (1982) *Advertising as Communication*, Methuen, London.
Deals with the wider issues of advertising such as the cultural implications of the alternative world portrayed in commercial advertising, for example on television.

Ehrenberg, A.S.C. and Pyatt, F.G. (1972) *Consumer Behaviour*, Penguin Books, Harmondsworth.
This consists of a number of separate papers by different authors on various aspects of buying and selling. It is a little bit dated now but still deals with some of the fundamentals which never really change. Worth looking at – briefly.

Packard, Vance (1965) *The Hidden Persuaders*, Penguin Books, Harmondsworth.
This is the classic text which is well worth reading – and it is easy to

read – for sheer enjoyment as well as insight into what makes people behave as a result of manipulative pressures. If you can still find a copy for sale, buy it! There will almost certainly be one in your local lending library.

Who are the innovators? 4

'Why, that I cannot tell,' said he.
   Robert Southey, The Battle of Blenheim (1774–1843)

A traitorous innovator, a foe to the public mind.
   Coriolanus, Act 3, Sc 1

If a man does not keep pace with his companions,
perhaps it is because he hears a different drummer.
   H D Thoreau (1906)

This chapter considers the personal characteristics of people in respect of their response to innovations. It examines personal and social factors which may influence individuals to accept or reject things which appear to them to be new.

Objectives

When you have studied the contents of this chapter you should be able to:

- recognize the five traditional adopter categories;
- identify some personal and social qualities which might influence the response of an individual to a new idea, product or practice;
- appreciate the kind of influence which can be exerted on individuals by their physical and social environment.

THE RANGE OF INNOVATIVENESS

In the previous chapter we looked at some possible characteristics of innovations. These can be very important in helping to determine whether something which is seen as new can also be seen as acceptable. However past experience indicates that only one thing is certain: whatever the nature of the innovation not all people will accept it and, of those who do, not all will adopt it at the same time.

There is a gradation or continuum of innovativeness which stretches over a very wide range of acceptance behaviour. The first people to adopt are those generally known as the **innovators**. They are not the inventors or the initiators of whatever has emerged as novel. They are simply the first people to be persuaded that there is advantage to them in incorporating a particular innovation into their personal way of life. It is usual to divide the entire range of adopters into several categories for ease of examination and the diagram in Fig. 4.1 indicates how these categories have been traditionally determined.

The graph demonstrates the bell-shaped curve which characterizes the statistically 'normal' distribution. This has been obtained by plotting the percentage of adopters at regular time intervals over an adequate period of adoption (it is actually rare to have a complete time scale since total adoption is both difficult to define and even more difficult to determine). The mean, or arithmetic average, is then taken as the starting point for moving first one, then two, standard deviations to left and right. This partitions the area under the curve into six sections, only five of which are usually given attention.*

These categories are not watertight compartments in real life and in conceptual terms are closer to what some theorists might consider to be 'ideal types'. A parallel can be drawn in the classification of social groups, where no sharp dividing line can be drawn even on measurable dimensions such as income. It is, however, even more complicated in respect of innovations since people may at any one time be in a high class with regard to one particular innovation and in a lower class for another.

The most clear-cut category, to which only one person in every forty belongs, appears to be that of the innovator. It also happens to be one of the most important since it identifies a person who invariably is the first to try, *and then adopt*, a new product or process. Note that simply trying something does not in itself make you an innovator; it is the continued use of whatever you may try that is the yardstick. As already indicated, however, it is possible to identify even innovators who may be progressive in relation to technological equipment but demonstrate a noticeable reluctance to change in respect of, say, political outlook. It is therefore necessary to consider all categories in order to put our understanding of the innovators into proper context.

ADOPTER CLASSIFICATION

While there are no discrete categories it is useful to accept that some can be created by the labelling of certain groups of people who share some defined characteristics. There are five convenient classifications of adopter behaviour characteristics:

1. Innovators
2. Early adopters

---

*There is no need for you to worry about any statistics or calculations. I mention this here only to show the basis for allocating the categories (which are, after all, only for convenience in promoting examination and discussion). However, if you would like to check on any statistical terms such as means and standard deviations you will find an appropriate text listed in the recommended reading at the end of the chapter.

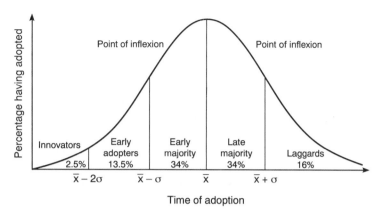

Fig. 4.1   Adopter categories.

3. Early majority
4. Late majority
5. Laggards.

The latter could actually include a very small sixth category, that of the **resistors** or **rejectors**, since (as already stated) complete adoption is unusual. Especially in the world of the marketplace such individuals still merit attention. It should be remembered, of course, that these are wide generalizations founded on data collected from various sources in different countries over a great many years and individual exceptions have to be expected. It is important to emphasize that, as in all attempts at human prediction, the descriptions are guidelines to tendencies or probabilities and are not specific criteria. For the purposes of such categorization on the basis of adoption it is assumed that the innovations on which judgements are based have definite relevance to the needs of the potential adopters.

Category 1 – innovators

These are the first people to adopt what they perceive to be a new idea, buy a new product regularly or put into practice a fresh or revised technique. They constitute about 2.5% of the total population who eventually accept the innovation in question. They are more venturesome than most people; indeed this is their most typical characteristic, and they are usually younger than many of their neighbours or colleagues. Their contacts are fairly wide-ranging so that they are not restricted to a local social network of family, relatives and friends. Instead they have a wider cosmopolitan type of social relationship which includes people with similar interests and occupations, often in other countries. They are inclined to travel further and more frequently than many of their contemporaries and sometimes appear to do so deliberately in order to extend their range of experiences and contacts.

For the most part they are better educated than their contemporaries and often hold academic and/or professional qualifications. They tend, in any case, to have jobs requiring specialized knowledge or training, and most of them enjoy relatively high incomes. They are usually passive members of a number of formal organizations, both social and occupational. These are often outside as well as inside their local community. Although seldom participating in such organizations (and rarely holding any office) they can be widely regarded as of fairly high status both personally and occupationally. They invariably read more than the average person and their newspapers are more often national than local. They also regularly read such publications as educational and research journals which make them aware of new ideas, discoveries and developments long before many of their acquaintances or friends. Not only do they become aware of innovations earlier than most people, they also require less time to consider them and decide whether or not to adopt.

While they have a reasonably high intellect, it is ultimately their ability to think confidently in the abstract which most clearly identifies them. Unlike so many others they do not have to have the actual experience of seeing or handling something in order to be able to assess its probable usefulness or attraction. They are also able to understand and process complex material readily. Having made a decision they tend to abide by it instead of constantly trying to gain reassurance that it was a correct one to make. The financial security which they possess, not only in income but more especially with respect to capital assets, supports them in this approach. Furthermore it also enables them to absorb the occasional loss which may arise from their high-risk ventures, which are often single-minded in the extreme.

Category 2 – early adopters

Within this category are those early adopters who are just a little more cautious than the innovators although well ahead of the average person in their readiness to accept and adjust to change. In comparison with innovators they are likely to be slightly younger and better educated. They usually take an active part in formal organizations and are often to be found holding office in those centred on the local community. They are universally somewhat parochial compared with their more innovative peers. Many of them, indeed, manage to be securely integrated with the local social system in a way that the innovator never has been and is never likely to be. They can have, however, just as much social status and quite definitely do have the greatest degree of opinion leadership in most Western social systems. Opinion leadership is a measure of the amount of influence which they can exert on others and is considered at length in a separate chapter.

The early adopters are often respected by their acquaintances as embodying the selective and successful use of new ideas. They have the advantage of being seen to be those who only accept something comparatively new when the evidence that it is worthwhile has really started to accumulate. Because in this way they act as legitimators for so many people in the community they receive a great deal of attention from change agents (the people such as teachers, salesmen, politicians, and others whose job it is to influence the attitudes and values of others). They are the established type of people to use as a reference point in respect of anything relatively untried. Because they are not too far ahead of the field there is no real communication gap between them and their compatriots such as can arise with the innovators. Also their credibility and respect are not liable to be dented when they indulge in some change as they are known to be not too easily swayed by novelty alone.

Category 3 – early majority

These people are exceedingly deliberative when making any decisions. However, they eventually follow their more innovative companions while not being known, in general, to act as leaders themselves. In practice they adopt new ideas just a little before the average member of their social system and they are indistinguishable from such people on most of the observable dimensions such as age, education, income and so on. However, by occupying a position which lies between the progressive and the traditional, they serve a very useful and necessary, though incidental, function. This is to accord approval, by their own procedures of delayed verification, of the eventual more widespread acceptance of certain new products and practices. Many of them belong to local organizations where they can be quite active but do not often hold any official position. They are well known as providers of information to many people who would look to them for guidance when personal decisions might have to be made. They therefore supply an essential counselling service for those who need it. Their actions alone supply whatever is necessary for legitimization without any more sophisticated involvement on their part. Change agents with some message to be spread abroad invariably believe that these are useful people to involve in such an activity since, in practice, they can actually do a substantial part of the change agent's job (sometimes without knowing that they are doing so!).

Category 4 – late majority

Overwhelming pressure from their peers is needed for these people to arrive at any decision to adopt anything which is different from what they have known in the past. Weight of public opinion has to be considerable before they will move, and even then it will tend to be in a ponderous manner. The tend to regard with scepticism the probable value of any change, and therefore lag a long way behind the average person in implementing any new ideas or processes. To some degree they can be influenced by those people who are somewhat more change-oriented than themselves, but they are also stubbornly supportive of one another and will use every possible delaying tactic to extend the limit required for decision-making. Generally they are middle-aged and share many of the attributes of Category 3. They are not particularly receptive to mass media and tend to ignore or discredit anything transmitted via the television, the radio or the press. Nearly all of them appear to be virtually immune to influence which does not emanate from sources already known to and respected by them. They do not actually have many lines of communication open to them outside their immediate neighbourhood.

More than in any of the other categories, their acceptance of any new practice is determined by basic financial considerations. However, the possible economic advantage of something new wins only sluggish acceptance – even when endorsed by many of their friends or close neighbours. Because these people normally have small, and often un-certain, incomes it is understandable that they may have genuine reasons to fear taking a risk, but ironically, while they are among the last to accept an applicable innovation they are almost certainly at the forefront of those who would have benefited most from early adoption of it.

Category 5 – laggards

These are the slowest, and also the last, people to adopt anything. They are very traditional in their outlook and not only are they resistant to change but can frequently be openly hostile to those who would wish to bring it about. They are nearly always older people, poorly educated and with little, and maybe intermittent income. They do not read much and, in any case, have a long history of disbelieving much of what is written. Their social contacts are so few that some of them are virtually isolated, particularly those in rural areas. They do not usually belong to any formal organizations. There is a high level of belief in superstition of different sorts, especially that relating to good and bad luck. Indeed success or failure is commonly attributed to luck rather than being seen to bear any relationship to individual effort or ability. There is an almost fatalistic submission to their economic and social condition and their only willing acceptance appears to be in the form of hearsay and gossip.

Only the most intense interpersonal influence ever brings about any modification of their circumstances. Even when this does happen it occurs with so much reluctance that it might be thought that there was a desire to see it fail. Personal outlook is rarely changed to any great extent. By the time some attitudes have been altered, what was 'new' has already been replaced by something which is yet more advanced and accepted by the progressive types. Laggards are alienated from what must seem to them to be a world which is moving far too fast. Most of them indicate that they just want to be left alone. It is hardly surprising that, even in the most backward communities, they fail to display any great cohesiveness or active involvement in their environment. They are the kind of people often described as drop-outs.

That people tend to be spread over some sort of continuum, whether categorized as above or not, might reasonably be anticipated. Clearly, simultaneous adoption by all potential users must always be an unrealistic expectation. What might be astonishing, however, is that the range can be so wide. The one small category which falls outside the range of adopters considered above is that of the **rejectors**. For the time being they are located at the bottom end of category 5 since there are very few in this totally intractable state. At this stage, then, it would be appropriate for us to consider whether we can outline what personal and social factors are likely to influence the adopter category into which each of these different individuals could be considered to fall.

FACTORS INFLUENCING INNOVATIVENESS

The following clusters of factors summarize the results of my research from different countries of the world over the last couple of decades. It is neither necessary nor appropriate in this introductory book to go into fine detail with any of them but even in their briefest outline they are capable of contributing something to an understanding of the innovativeness of individuals, a trait which may be characterized as human progressiveness. The term 'progressiveness' is, of course, a value judgement

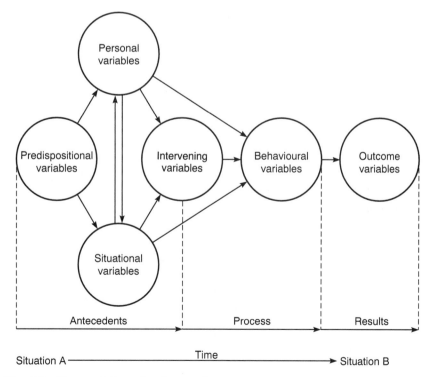

Fig. 4.2 Factors influencing innovativeness.

since it implies satisfactory progress towards an approved goal. For the possible route, I have postulated a relationship between the factors demonstrated in Fig. 4.2 which indicates the probable direction of the different influences towards such a goal without in any way attempting to portray their relative strengths.

The factors related to progressiveness are:

1. predispositional;
2. personal;
3. situational;
4. behavioural;
5. intervening;
6. outcome.

The following brief comments on each may provide some useful information for assessing their relative importance.

1. *Predispositional factors*

   These comprise the internal forces and hereditary tendencies within individuals which predispose them to react or behave in a particular way in a given situation. Individuals do not, of course, have to succumb to such influences – there is still a high degree of free will whatever the genetic inheritance. There is no suggestion that behaviour can be predicted, only that some kinds of actions are more likely than others. Included in this category would be personality factors: attitudes, beliefs, values and goals. These may be modified by individuals but represent something of a racial or familial legacy from which they are never completely freed and every decision retains some trace of their inheritance.

2. *Personal factors*

   For the most part these serve to identify individuals, both to themselves and to others, in terms of age, sex, ethnic origins and other factors about which they can do nothing and which are incapable of genuine alteration. Included also are those which might be less clear cut such as duration and type of schooling, standard of education, employment experience and the like which cannot be changed retrospectively. These factors are the ones most likely to lead to interpersonal tensions and communication problems.

3. *Situational factors*

   These are external to the individuals concerned but are within the environment in which such people exist and act out their lives. Examples would include size of family, nature and number of dependents, kind of employment, extent of income and standard of living. The nature of the community, society and nation also exert, in varying degrees, an influence on each individual because of the services which they provide or the conformity which they require. As with the intervening factors, outlined below, there are constraints on the extent to which individuality can develop into eccentricity before it becomes regarded as undesirable or unacceptable deviance.

4. *Behavioural factors*

Basically these concern the personal decision-making process which will be considered at some length in the next chapter. They are related to the actions which may be taken by the individual and arise from personal responses to perceptions of various stimuli.

5. *Intervening factors*

Many of these are not within the control of the individual at all but must be taken properly into account as they often exercise an important influence affecting the human environment. They have the capacity, in particular, to either stimulate or impede personal action. They include aspects of the rationality, strategy and tactics of change-agents, national and/or regional implementation of government policy, variations in climatic conditions, geographical location, community values and especially any particular society's attitude, tolerant or otherwise, towards deviation from accepted or prescribed norms.

6. *Outcome factors*

In a very real sense these can be examined only with the twenty-twenty vision that comes with hindsight. They are not, by definition, factors which precede or influence a decision. They are, however, vital in examining any system of decision-making because not all possible outcomes of a particular process can be anticipated by, or would necessarily be acceptable to, the individual concerned. In such instances there is usually a form of feedback related to the wisdom and success of the original decision which may well occasion a knock-on effect on any subsequent actions. This category, being produced by the interaction of the other five, may cause unexpected changes in future attitudes towards trials, levels of adoption, consequent standard of income and resulting quality of life of the individuals involved.

There are additional complexities introduced when group behaviour and individual behaviour interact, a point which will be examined later. In the meantime, however, one instance of the peculiarities of outcome and, indeed, the absurdity which can characterize innovative situations may be typified by the following example. A normally well-attended rural parish church, renowned both for its beauty and for the standard of its choral work, was chosen for a 'live' televised broadcast of one of its services. The congregation did not wish to miss this special occasion so, on the day of the broadcast, most stayed at home to appreciate it on television! In this instance the behavioural factors of a novel situation had determined these absurd consequences, namely, that people proceeded to act as individuals rather than as members of a group, in this case a congregation.

Such factors as those outlined above should be borne in mind when considering the adoption process which will be examined in the next chapter. In the meantime remember that, in the words of John Donne, 'no man is an island' and that individual actions are often conditioned by both the physical and the social environment. Men and women do not normally choose to live in isolation, cut off from interacting with fellow human beings. The phrase 'individual in society' has a very real meaning for human existence. It is in the social context that basic personal identities are formed, attitudes towards all aspects of human existence established, and maturity of individual judgement fostered. A brief look at the interaction between individuals and their social environment can shed some more light on the most fundamental aspects of innovativeness.

PROGRESSIVENESS IN CONTEXT

The relationship between the individual and the social environment is of prime importance in trying to understand what forces assist or retard the acceptance of innovations. While personal factors undoubtedly underlie the emergence of innovators and other adopters there are, as we know, additional forces at work. Those relating to particular situations or locations must not be underestimated since they contribute significant elements of those attributes such as *esprit de corps* and *patriotisme locale*, the descriptions of which, when translated into English, often appear to be inadequate.

It is usually accepted without too much reservation that communities tend to exhibit characteristics indicative of the dominant individuals, whether in a majority or not, who reside there. In other words we can recognize progressive communities as well as progressive individuals within them. It is not that a community is just an aggregate or sum total of the features of the individuals who comprise it. Many communities exhibit well-known attributes which do not characterize most of the residents. In common parlance we often speak of a 'wealthy community', or 'the stockbroker belt' to convey an image which is not misleading yet, as we know, is not entirely accurate. It does, however, provide a valuable label to help us identify a community which shares a collective philosophy representing achievement for some and ambition for others. Direct mail suppliers, who aim to sell goods direct via the postal service to consumers, have their own territorial maps of neighbourhoods and postal districts which identify locations by such indicators as, for instance, 'Boats and Rotary'. The interrelationship between individual and context is such that it might be said that the one could not really exist without the other.

INNOVATOR CONTINUUMS

It seems defensible, therefore, to say that just as there is a continuum of innovative individuals so it is possible to contemplate a similar meaningful progression of innovative communities. Indeed in rural societies the existence of 'traditional' and 'progressive' communities is more or less taken for granted. If each is regarded as being capable of representation on a continuum then the simple diagram (Fig. 4.3) could serve to illustrate both.

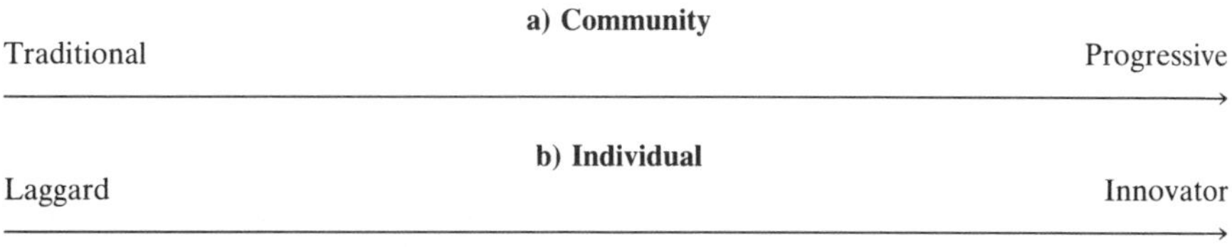

a) Community

Traditional   Progressive

———————————————————————————————→

b) Individual

Laggard   Innovator

———————————————————————————————→

Fig. 4.3   Innovator continuums.

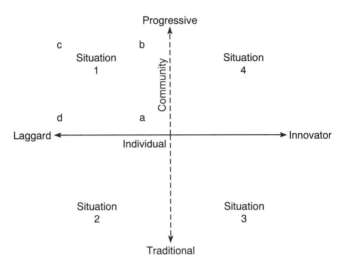

Fig. 4.4   Contextual decision-making.

These basic representations contain the absolute minimum of information – indeed they are incapable of being further simplified. Yet if
these two continuums (or, for some readers, continua) are now cross-
matched the following interesting layout results. This provides a useful
frame of reference for considering the influences which might affect the
judgement of an individual in a decision-making context within his social
environment.

Briefly there are four contextual situations arising from the interplay
of forces indicated in Fig. 4.4:

1. A less innovative person in a progressive community.
2. A less innovative person in a traditional community.
3. A more innovative person in a traditional community.
4. A more innovative person in a progressive community.

THE PROGRESSIVENESS OF INDIVIDUALS IN CONTEXT

The terms laggard and innovator, it should be remembered, really
characterize only those who are towards the extremes of the range. Most
people fall somewhere in between. An examination of situation 1 (Fig.

4.4) should make this clear, remembering that a similar type of simple analysis could be carried out on any of the other three sectors. Four additional positions within this first quadrant have been indicated by points and the letters a,b,c, and d. In reality the number of possible locations is infinite. However, looking at these as exemplars of all the others we can see that in respect of these four persons, all are to some degree below average in personal progressiveness qualities while being located in a somewhat progressive environment.

a. represents an individual who is just below the norm on personal innovativeness and is in a community which is just slightly above the norm on progressiveness.
b. indicates a different individual who is equally just below average but is in a community which is extremely progressive.
c. shows a third person of laggard characteristics located in an extremely progressive community, and
d. identifies a person of laggard disposition situated in a community which, like the first one above, is relatively low in progressiveness.

Many other possibilities exist and the actual placement of an individual on the grid should serve to demonstrate the interplay which might be anticipated between the personal and the social determinants.

Any categorization of an individual should be used in respect of only one specific innovation at any one particular time. Obviously an individual could very well exhibit a genuinely progressive attitude towards, say, a new electronic mail system while continuing to subscribe to extreme fundamentalist beliefs in religious observance and ritual. The labels cannot be used to give any blanket categorizations of people although the looseness of definition in respect of communities has long been sanctioned by common usage. Such communities help to give everyone within them an identity, a sense of belonging and a value reference point. But most people also have other reference groups to which they turn for approval of their beliefs and actions, especially at times of change. This is not necessarily a conscious action on their part and there are many individuals who would deny the existence of such a reference since they are genuinely unaware that it exists.

Nonetheless many people have been indoctrinated to accept just such a frame of reference even if it refers not so much to a group as to an individual – or even to an 'ideal type'. This is usually an image, a hypothetical stereotype. A physical presence is not necessary in order to be effective. For example the concept of the 'good teacher' has, for generations, been held up as a model for aspiring teachers to emulate.

The people who fall into different categories within areas 2 and 4 in Fig. 4.4 are, in respect of any particular innovation, largely conformist to the norms of their community in respect of that particular item. In this respect, at least, their reference groups coincide with their membership groups. Those falling into categories 1 and 3 will employ additional (or, in some cases, alternative) reference groups outside that to which they belong. This, along with a number of other important factors, is relevant to the process of adoption considered in the next chapter.

SUMMARY

Not all people are innovators and even those who are do not necessarily adopt at the same rate or at the same time. It is possible, and customary, to specify five different categories of adopter on a continuum based upon adoption rates over a period of time. Individuals in these categories become progressively slower as the scale moves from Innovator to Laggard. The last people to adopt a particular innovation do so when it is no longer applicable because something better has replaced it. The individuals in each of the specified categories may be identified by certain personal characteristics. In addition they are influenced by other factors relating as much to their physical and social environment as to their own personal traits.

REFLECTION

Look again at some of the terms which you met for the first time in this chapter. Can you, for example, explain the following in your own words?

localite, **laggard**, **point of inflexion**, **traditional**, **progressiveness.**

APPLICATIONS

There are two different, but related, exercises in respect of this chapter. Please consider them carefully before starting to respond.

It would be useful for you to write your responses to these questions in brief essay form, providing an introduction, development of the theme, and conclusion for each.

Part A

In 1711 Alexander Pope, in his *Essay of Criticism (Part II)* said:

'Be not the first by whom the new are tried,
Nor the last to lay the old aside.'

Is this a middle-of-the-road philosophy? What kind of individual in the community do you think might adopt it? Why? What is your own attitude here? Please give your reasons.

Part B

In each of the following two situations what is likely to determine whether the individual specified will be able to make any real impact on the community? To what extent will community influence over the person be the dominant one?

i) a moderately innovative person who moves to live and work in a very traditional or conservative environment.

ii) a very innovative individual who transfers to work in a highly progressive environment.

Again give reasons for your views. Try to base your brief written responses on what you have read and do not turn to the end of the book too quickly to find the outline answers suggested. When you do, please take time to reflect on the implications of the information given there.

RECOMMENDED FURTHER READING

The classic publication by Everett Rogers deals with adopter categories (and very many other issues) very fully indeed, and over the years there have been three different publications of the text. All three are listed here in the expectation that one of the editions will be readily available to you, wherever you may be. No other reading is necessary at this stage although some of you may wish, as suggested in the chapter, to glance at an introductory statistical text which shows, amongst other things, how to produce categories from data and present them graphically.

Rogers, Everett M. (1962) *Diffusion of Innovations*, The Free Press of Glencoe, New York.

Rogers, Everett M. with Shoemaker, F. Floyd (1971) *Communication of Innovations*, The Free Press, New York.

Rogers, Everett M. (1983) *Diffusion of Innovations*, The Free Press, New York.

Spence, W.R. (1976) *Basic Descriptive Statistics* (a programmed text), Dundee College of Education, Dundee.

The process of adoption 5

Let us not go over the old ground, let us rather prepare for what is to come.

Marcus Tullius Cicero, 106–43 BC

Adoption processes are special kinds of decision-making processes.

Van den Ban and Hawkins (1988)

A new scientific truth does not triumph by convincing its opponents and making them see the light, but rather because its opponents eventually die . . .

Max Planck (1950)

In this chapter we consider the essential theoretical underpinnings of the process known as **adoption of innovations**, ie the action of accepting and using on a regular basis something which appears new to the person choosing to adopt. We also examine the possibilities of presenting the process visually by means of suitable models.

Objectives
When you have completed this chapter you should be able to:

- list the five stages in the classic model of the adoption process;
- recognize the main activity in each of these stages;
- see how feedback can affect the adoption process;
- show how an individual's information sources change as progress is made towards making a decision.

THE MEANING OF ADOPTION

When we talk about adoption in the context of innovation we are normally referring to the outcome of a system of personal decision-making which leads, eventually, to the acceptance or rejection of something which is seen as new. To qualify as acceptance the adoption behaviour must be that of intended continued use. Despite this there may be rejection or discontinuance later just as, in the case of initial rejection, there may be subsequent later acceptance. Individuals must go through this sort of mental process in order to reach a decision. In doing so they will employ whatever rational procedures they believe to be appropriate in order to adopt any new idea, product or practice.

The process starts when individuals become aware of whatever appears to be new and concludes when the innovation is put into full operation. At various points along the route to a decision there will be a number of different factors at work. Many of these will be associated with forms of communication. Initially mass media will be seen to be important in creating awareness of the innovation but as the decision-making process nears conclusion it is the personal involvement of friends, neighbours and colleagues which becomes increasingly influential.

The classic model of adoption, which was originally published in the US in the mid-1950s, identified five sequential stages or segments of a process:

1. Awareness
2. Interest
3. Evaluation
4. Trial
5. Adoption.

The idea of stages has tended to persist since then although it was always recognized, even at the very beginning, that no sub-division of the process, however defined, can actually be as self-contained as a discrete stage.

The process was envisaged as following the sequence:

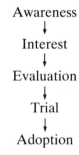

Awareness
↓
Interest
↓
Evaluation
↓
Trial
↓
Adoption

THE RATIONALITY OF ADOPTION

The rationale for assuming a logical and rational process has been based on the premise that, for the most part, human reasoning at even the most primitive level tends to follow an orderly, systematic, fairly methodical and (it could therefore be argued) basically logical and sensible path, although at times the actual bases on which the reasoning is founded may be of doubtful validity. A logical process, of course, may not in itself necessarily produce a valid conclusion. The example in Fig. 5.1 demonstrates that there can be a vast difference between calculating, reasoning and thinking intelligently. For the latter there has to an element of interpretation of information, some cross-indexing to past

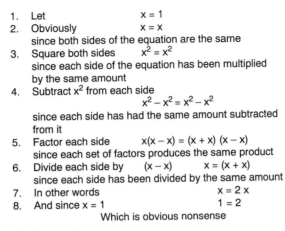

1. Let   x = 1
2. Obviously   x = x
   since both sides of the equation are the same
3. Square both sides $x^2 = x^2$
   since each side of the equation has been multiplied
   by the same amount
4. Subtract x^2 from each side
                         $x^2 - x^2 = x^2 - x^2$
   since each side has had the same amount subtracted
   from it
5. Factor each side $x(x - x) = (x + x)(x - x)$
   since each set of factors produces the same product
6. Divide each side by $(x - x)$ $x = (x + x)$
   since each side has been divided by the same amount
7. In other words $x = 2x$
8. And since x = 1 $1 = 2$
                   Which is obvious nonsense

Fig. 5.1   A logical absurdity.

experiences and their outcomes and, above all, an understanding of the terms of reference employed.

While the manipulation of the *symbols* in this example is logical the conclusion is absurd. This is a paradox produced by having, at one point, a divisor which is actually zero. Having either zero or infinity in a calculation can lead to really weird results! This can, however, happen with purely mechanical processing where, for example, a computer (which cannot, in human terms, **think**) has been inexpertly programmed.

STAGES OF ADOPTION

It is still customary for many people to talk about stages in the individual mental process as though they were real entities although it has long been recognized that there is no boundary point of separation for any of them, other than the first. What happens is that the emphasis on different aspects of adoption shifts as we move from the beginning to the end of an innovative process. Some very sophisticated models have been devised to try to take account of all the possible variables which might be involved. The difficulty with such models is that, as they become more refined, one tends to forget that, rather than portraying the real truth, what they actually do is to encapsulate a few fundamental principles or hypotheses in a way which tends to focus attention on important interrelationships.

At this point in the book it is convenient to continue thinking in terms of stages since this helps to break up a rather complicated process into smaller units which may be more easily understood at introductory level. Bearing that point in mind we can now examine such 'stages' to try to get a clearer picture of the dynamics involved in the related sequence of events. There are five principal stages of adoption:

1. Awareness
2. Interest
3. Evaluation
4. Trial
5. Adoption.

Stage 1 – awareness

This is the only genuine stage, and it is truly unique because you can only become aware of something once. No matter what subsequent views or actions you may develop, the first feeling of awareness can never be repeated. At the start individuals are exposed to an idea previously unknown to them in that form, therefore they are not in possession of any detailed information about it. They may, for example, have had items brought to their attention about membership of a new book or music club, the possibility of acquiring time-share holiday apartments, the availability of massive discounts from a mail order supplier or a startling advance in the design of personal computers. Virtually all of this limited initial information will have come from sources in the mass media, written, spoken or seen. More detailed information from other sources may follow.

Any kind of mass communication channel enables ready transmission of messages from one or more persons to a wide audience. Perhaps in a situation such as this the individual will not feel motivated to make any response because their personal interest has not been captured as a result of any information received. On the other hand he or she may desire to know more. Until it becomes possible for individuals to make some calculated appraisal of any additional information there can, inevitably, be no personal cost-benefit analysis of the situation at its face value, and certainly none in respect of any possible related issues. If, of course, there is even a flicker of curiosity on the part of the individual about such matters then that person may well proceed to the next stage to enable them to relate whatever further details are available to his/her own personal circumstances.

Stage 2 – interest

Here individuals are motivated, for some personally acceptable reason, to engage in purposeful search activity. They will try at this point to find out whatever additional details may be obtainable about the item which has attracted their attention. What they will be looking for is the sort of factual data which will enable them to examine the idea more closely in a personal relationship to their present circumstances, past experiences and prevailing beliefs. Their actions will therefore be aimed towards providing an adequate basis for the making of an evaluative judgement. In other words, they are moving towards the situation of seeing themselves in somewhat changed circumstances resulting from the innovation having been accepted by them and put into practice.

Stage 3 – evaluation

By the time that this third level has been reached individuals are assumed to be trying very hard to apply the new idea mentally to their present situations in order to judge its potential benefit for the future. They may also be not only anticipating but also trying to assess a changed situation where possible attainable advantages might just outweigh any perceived disadvantages, such as extra cost. Other disadvantages to be considered could include uncertainty of operation, eventual obsolescence, probable return on outlay, and ease of making adjustment to the necessary change. Subject to a generally favourable conclusion being reached here the next logical step would be to engage in some initial trial, if this is both possible and practicable, to confirm a decision to say 'yes' or 'no'.

Stage 4 – trial

It might be thought – reasonably – that this stage should come before Stage 3 rather than after it. However the definition of the terms 'evaluation' and 'trial' in the traditional model located it logically in the order already indicated. There *are* alternative approaches and, in any case, we have noted that the concept of stages must not be taken too literally even at this level of study. It is, however, quite a useful basis to start from. Recent refinements arising from psychological and sociological insight can supply a more realistic foundation for revised models, some of which can take better account of everyday factors in a reasonably practical and realistic way.

At this point in the process there is, wherever and whenever possible, the actual implementation of the idea on a reduced scale – the **'micro' approach**. For instance, a farmer might sow a fresh type of hybrid seed on a small plot before deciding whether or not to turn over a large acreage of his arable farmland to growing the new crop. Where the micro approach cannot be used – for example in considering whether to move home to another neighbourhood – the trial may be conducted 'over the fence'. This is an old technique which is very familiar to inner-city dwellers and rural folk alike. By keeping their eyes and ears open they are often able to make a critical assessment of something which they might consider doing by just discovering what happens to other people who try it. It applies in the present-day business world too (but on a somewhat faster timescale) and there are still a few advantages in letting somebody else have a go first – so long as you do not let them get too far ahead!

Stage 5 – adoption

This could just as logically be labelled **rejection**. If individuals are satisfied with the results of the trial they will either proceed to put the practice into operation to the extent that their personal circumstances allow them to do so, *or*, even despite the favourable outcome of a trial, reject the idea for reasons that are valid for them. Whether they decide definitely to adopt, reject or simply postpone making a final decision the adoption process is technically finished for them (at least for the time being) in respect of that particular innovation. Indeed it could be that this stage would lead on to the start of another in parallel, or a repeat in respect of re-evaluating the idea. Most people who intend, or are forced, to abide by the consequences of their actions still commonly seek reassurance that they acted correctly in the light of the information that was available to them at the time. Additionally individuals may wish to actively consider a fresh idea which has just superseded that which they were about to accept. Even immediately after acceptance the innovation may be discarded for what appears to be another one of superior merit. A contemporary example can be seen in the computing world, where those who have initially purchased basic hardware will very quickly upgrade monochrome floppy-disk outfits to full colour hard-disk systems.

THE MEANING OF OVER-ADOPTION

In connection with the topic which we have just been considering it might be worthwhile to reflect on just what constitutes **optimum** (or 'best level') adoption. Earlier in the book it was pointed out that total adoption was a rare occurrence. What, then, is an adequate level of adoption? There is no easy answer to this because conclusions will depend upon expectations and these will vary between suppliers and consumers as well as amongst consumers themselves. Non-adoption, partial adoption and over-adoption are easier to recognize.

- **Non-adoption** in everyday terms is essentially rejection although it is often less definite in form. Theoretically it is characterized by a lack of action whereas rejection implies that a definite (albeit negative) decision has been reached.
- **Partial adoption** is verifiable in the sense that something can be checked to see the extent to which it has 'caught on'. However, in terms of perceived adequacy, when can partial acceptance actually be considered as having gone far enough to be adjudged a success? This is not necessarily maximum adoption because very few products or practices (unless obligatory by law, such as car windscreen wipers or income tax) achieve or require universal acceptance. Also most innovations, particularly those of a technical nature, tend to be overtaken by something even more developed or refined before saturation point can be reached.
- **Over-adoption** occurs when the situation can become 'super-saturated',

to use a term from the physical sciences. This is the peculiar condition arising when some innovation has been utilized far beyond its intended limits and has actually become dysfunctional, ie more of a handicap than the benefit it was originally intended to be. This can give rise to problems illustrated by the impact of two different innovations as described below; one technological, of long standing and universally known, the other (which is non-technological) which has appeared in recent years in the United Kingdom.

TECHNICAL OVER-ADOPTION

Probably the example which might come most readily to the mind of any author or office worker would be that of the QWERTY keyboard. In the early days of mechanical typewriters the letters were impressed upon paper by metal type at the ends of small bars swinging up into position and striking the typewriter's inked ribbon. The key movements were actuated by an operator using a keyboard. Some typists became so fast at the operation that keys constantly got jammed because a fresh one could rise into the printing position before the preceding one had fallen back into place. This happened with quite a range of different layouts in use in the early days. In order, therefore, to slow down the operation and thus give the most commonly used keys an opportunity to return without fouling others, the QWERTY design was produced. The name was derived from the order of the first half dozen letters on the top line. Its prime intention was to impede the operators' movements and to a very great extent it succeeded. It is consequently an anomaly that, at the present time, it is still used universally for computer keyboards in situations where extreme speed is required, not only always of the machine, but often also of the operator.

The situation shows no signs of being changed, in spite of the fact that ergonomically engineered alternatives have been available for years. Many of these require no physical movements of the hands at all: pressure of the appropriate fingers suffice. The fingers may be held poised in their natural position over a much smaller set of keys (sometimes only five for each hand) and can respond much faster and more accurately. The QWERTY keyboard is one innovation which has maintained its position for so many years largely because of the existence of 'secretarial schools' which taught, as some still teach, shorthand and typing. The well-known phenomenon of human inertia meant that it was easier to continue using the traditional instruction manuals since many changes of machine design were cosmetic rather than functional in nature. This attitude was assisted by the manufacturers of all such machines who were happy not to have to re-tool to produce different keyboards as well.

There is, however, no defensible reason for continuing to produce this kind of keyboard for the hundreds of thousands of personal computers now in daily use since most users are, in any case, amateurs employing only one or two fingers anyway. It would be an innovation of quite a different sort if these computer operators (and the technicians who service the machines) decided to learn touch typing as do at least some of their professional counterparts! In the meantime the QWERTY keyboard remains a prime example of over-adoption.

NON-TECHNICAL OVER-ADOPTION

The second instance concerns amateur wine-making in the United Kingdom. There have always been those individuals in various parts of the British Isles who have preferred to brew, ferment or distil their own alcoholic beverages, whatever the views of the law and the excise officers. While it has never been permissible, under British law, for spirits of any sort to be distilled there has long been legislation, peculiarly enough, permitting both brewing of beers and fermenting of wines provided that these are not thereafter offered for sale. Home brewing has, for the most part, involved a stalwart band of enthusiasts supporting products such as 'real ale' because there is little financial saving (although this has recently increased) over the prices charged in licensed premises. The quality of the brew is also less predictable!

The fermentation of wine rested on different support. It was almost entirely confined in years past to rural makers of elderberry, rhubarb and similar homely, and often heady, alcoholic products. Only in recent years has wine-making attracted more widespread interest. That was after package holidays, more than any other factor, had familiarized thousands of people with the favourite grape-derived drinks of other countries. The demand for foreign wine has increased steadily over the years, especially in the south of England, and Great Britain as a whole is now one of the world's great wine-drinking nations.

Naturally any government which sought relatively painless ways of securing increased revenue would find it difficult to resist imposing just a little extra duty on the import of something popular – in this case, foreign wines. But the British government imposed a rate which meant that, for the cheaper wines, the taxation was actually greater than the original cost and this made the modest outlay for home-production appear extremely attractive indeed. A whole new support industry sprang into being virtually overnight. This supplied fermentation equipment, instruction books, yeast, grape extract, bottles, bottling equipment, labels, in fact everything needed to enable the home producer to simulate commercial production. As a result, over time, many people who had acquired their own personalized labels, individually styled bottles etc found (to the surprise of some) that they were not, in the end, actually having the pleasure of drinking an inexpensive but acceptable wine as they had originally intended. Instead they were engaged in laying down a 'vintage', the production displayed in racks, often in the domestic garage doubling as wine cellar. The wine had become a conversation piece rather than something for consumption. The purchase of imported wines, full duty paid, has in consequence continued at an unabated rate with many hosts actually purchasing extra wines for consumption by the guests whom they have invited to see over their 'cellars'. Home production has succeeded for many people in producing only collectors' items where the benefit lies in continuing possession.

In this instance the idea of over-adoption stems from the dysfunctional or pointless nature of the adoption when viewed in relation to the original aims which, for many people, were never achieved at all.

MODELS OF ADOPTION

Simple linear models of adoption, such as the one which we considered earlier, cannot really display possibilities such as those raised by these examples. More sophisticated diagrams are needed – but not just yet. Let us first examine some of the bases on which models of any sort are constructed.

One of the assumptions which we have to make is that all human decision-making behaviour is rational, at least to the individual concerned. This is not too far-fetched because most people do follow what appears to them as a rational path to a decision. What makes some of their conclusions peculiar at times is that they have based their reasoning on partial information, mistaken understanding, inherited beliefs or personal prejudices. The fundamental assumption, then, is that in the majority of cases, certain causes are likely to produce broadly predictable effects. This is because, despite the unknown influence of probability, everything still proceeds in a more or less orderly fashion. In human affairs that fashion is far from being as clear-cut as it is in the physical sciences where 'causes' may be fairly confidently predicted to produce known 'effects', many of these being so well established as to have given rise to 'laws' of cause and effect.

THE IMPORTANCE OF FEEDBACK

Let us look at the original five step sequence, and modify it slightly by incorporating the notion of feedback (Fig. 5.2).

This endeavours to take account of the fact that adoption may not be the end of the matter even in respect of any one particular innovation. Acceptance often leads to reflection and reappraisal. Reassurance is needed that the right decisions were made. Perhaps, instead, discontinuance follows, or a fresh interest arises in something which appears to be even better. It is reasonable to expect a degree of feedback from the acceptance of the new idea that could influence some of the preceding steps for a revision of the decision (even awareness which, although it can not be repeated in its initial sense can, of course, be experienced anew in a modified form). This type of model would accord with the comparable classic communication model which is shown is Fig. 5.3 and about which more is said in Chapter 7 where the nature of feedback

Fig. 5.2   The adoption sequence.

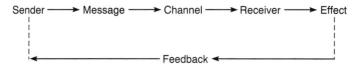

Fig. 5.3   Communication sequence.

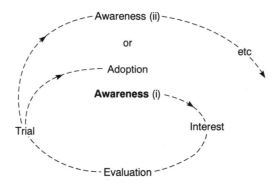

Fig. 5.4   Modified adoption sequence.

is more fully examined. The 'stages' in this communication model are not those through which an individual would pass but merely serve to indicate a sequence of factors which it is useful to analyse consecutively in order to establish a process. This operation originates with the sender of a communication and finishes logically with the receiver, but there is additional information of some sort fed back to the original source.

It would appear from actual observation of everyday human interaction that personal and social processes tend to have a recursive rather than a simple straight linear existence. In other words we seldom come to the end of some simple line of action or thought by experiencing a complete stop. Instead it is much more usual to return to an earlier situation and to find it somewhat changed, ie at a 'higher' level. This suggests that the adoption process might, then, be better represented in circular form than by a straight line. The classic model could accordingly be modified to appear as shown in Fig. 5.4.

Bearing in mind the earlier comments on feedback there is support for the view that, in the final analysis, a spiral might appear to be best of all. The point of return in Fig. 5.4 for the line which might have formed a circle is not closed but is the start of a second loop. This may well repeat the elements of the first loop but at a different level of understanding or operation. The diagram also allows for the finality (for the time being, at any rate) of adoption or rejection.

Models, of course, do not necessarily add anything to our understanding of a situation. They are merely devices to present information in reasonably compact form so as to indicate possible relationships between elements. In respect of any such diagrammatic representation, therefore, you should not ask 'Is this true?' but 'Is this useful?'. At the moment we are considering various graphical layouts because of the need to make the nature of innovation as clear as possible. This is not easy without mathematical formulae and psycho-sociological analysis, but bearing in mind the old adage that 'a picture is worth a thousand words', the few illustrations given here are intended to be of assistance to you when you reflect on the actual process as you, yourself, have experienced it.

COMBINATION OF ADOPTION AND COMMUNICATION

The diagram in Fig. 5.5 suggests a modern representation of theory integrated with practice. I first published it in 1970 and it has remained basically unchanged since then. However it does manage to stay fairly

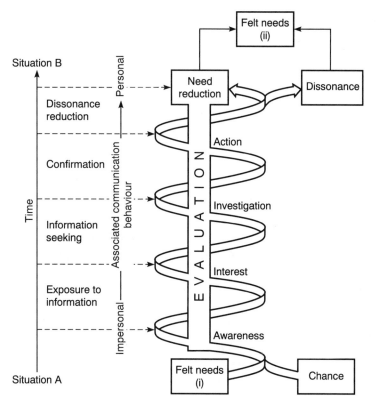

Fig. 5.5 Adoption sequence.

up-to-date in the sense that it is still used today in many universities and colleges as an illustrative device as well as an analytical tool in connection with general decision making. Although it may appear complicated at first glance, it is actually fairly easy to follow and there is no need to go into unnecessary detail about the constituent elements as the rationale for these needs analysis which is beyond the present work. However, by presenting various elements in this way it is possible to include some indication of chronology. This is obviously an important component of all decision-making processes but it is not always capable of being included in presentations because of the difficulty of doing so meaningfully.

The main points to note are as follows. The model initially takes account of the fact that an individual may fall into either of two very different categories which, nonetheless, subsequently have much in common. He may:

- be actively motivated to bring about a change in his particular circumstances; or
- only become aware by chance of the possibility of doing so.

If he is in the first category then he is almost certainly engaging in a problem-solving exercise. This implies that he has become aware that a problem of some sort exists. Accordingly he has to assemble as much relevant information as possible together with valid alternative approaches to a solution. Next a choice has to be made, on the basis of appropriate analysis, of ways and means to achieve the necessary outcome. This is in many ways still comparable to the situation of someone who first of all stumbled upon an innovation and subsequently realized that it could be an answer to an as-yet-unidentified but probable future problem. The portrayal, as with all such models, makes the fundamental assumptions of rationality underlying the process.

The individual decision-making activity as portrayed in Fig. 5.5 culminates eventually in adoption or rejection with all of the consequent probable outcomes. The layout can be likened to a motorway with the main carriageway which has several slip roads at intervals. This design allows for:

- a **direct** route which represents an impulsive response to a stimulus, or a total commitment from first principles, going along the straight road labelled *Evaluation* from *Awareness* to *Action*; and also
- an **indirect** route, which can be exceedingly tortuous if travelled by the more deliberate individuals who decide to turn off the main road to rest, reflect or seek further information as to whether they are going the right way. It is easy to see just how lengthy could be the route travelled by those who reviewed their position at every stage along the way. This is particularly significant when you remember that all of these stages – with the exception of the initial (unchanged) awareness – may be passed through more than once and, furthermore, in any order.

The model itself consists of only four designated elements instead of the original five relatively self-contained defined stages. In this model there are no stages postulated as such because the design allows one area of interest and influence to shade imperceptibly into the next. Thus there are no boundaries to the elements themselves although they clearly occupy sequential positions.

In addition the issue of evaluation has been incorporated centrally and the whole process thus operates around a continuing system of assessment instead of postulating an evaluation stage. This is a more realistic reflection of the characteristics of the real world where we do not just observe but evaluate continuously as we do so. Perception merges effortlessly into cognition. Anyone having any doubt on this issue should pause for a moment to reflect honestly and objectively on the way in which, consciously or unconsciously, they 'weigh up' strangers on first meeting them – a point of which salesmen and school teachers, amongst others, are only too well aware. The initial encounter will invariably involve more – mentally – than the simple fact of just becoming aware that someone unknown has come into view.

Another of the assumptions made has been that we all have needs of various kinds which we would like to have satisfied. To this end we therefore engage in processes leading to **need reduction**, where possible, to minimize risk and maximize achievement of our desired outcomes. Need reduction eventually takes place (in part at least) for any particular individual as a result of his adoption or rejection of something new, or even just a decision to await further developments. It is possible, however, for any of these actions to lead to subsequent doubts and soul-searching. In particular some innovators or very early adopters have been observed purposefully seeking what reassurance might be had in connection with certain new practices which they had adopted and about which, presumably, there was reason for second thoughts.

This tendency can be seen in many different situations. For example an analysis of people asking detailed questions about a particular make of car at a motor show has, in the past, demonstrated that many of them had just recently bought a *different* type of vehicle. They were concerned to prove to themselves that they had made the right decision, or at least a sensible one. Indeed, more effort is often put into collecting evidence to support a decision already taken than was first used to acquire knowledge prior to the decision being made.

This situation is one of **dissonance**, ie a state in which the individual attempts to reconcile conflicting views. Dissonance of some sort often exists after any decision has been made between two possible alternatives, and is certainly there in some form if the range of choices is great. It has been found, nonetheless, that dissonance does not necessarily have to exist in a situation just because there are conflicting, and even apparently irreconcilable, views which may be held by the same individual. A frequently-quoted example used to be the reference to the number of card-carrying communists in Italy and the number of active members of the Roman Catholic Church there. When added together the total exceeded that of the entire population of the country. Assuming the figures to be reasonably accurate one possible interpretation was that there were some people, a fairly large number in fact, who could support communism from Monday to Saturday but became practising catholics on Sunday!

Another feature of the diagram in Fig. 5.5 is the associated communication indicator which accompanies the procedural pathway. It will be noted from the model of adoption and communication that as individuals proceed along the road starting at Awareness their sources of relevant information tend to become more personalized as they near the point of decision. At the beginning they may have obtained information from newspapers or magazines, radio or television. Eventually they want to talk to someone who has appropriate experience or else knows somebody else who has. Often this may be just a matter of listening and reflecting on what others say but sooner or later active support will be sought from someone in a position not only to comment but also to assist with the formation of a judgement.

This is the stage where the influence of the opinion leader is paramount. Chapter 9 is devoted entirely to this topic and investigates the role of the opinion leader in depth.

SUMMARY

More than one model may be constructed to indicate how an individual may reach a decision regarding the adoption of an innovation. Two fundamental approaches underlie all the others. These are usually presented as an adoption process model or a problem-solving model. However they both have **Awareness** as the starting point and **Adoption** as the end point. It is therefore possible to produce a single model incorporating both approaches.

No matter how sophisticated the model, they are all variants of the original five stage model. The basis is a progression from Awareness through applications of Interest, Trial and Evaluation to Adoption. Whatever form this progression may take in practice it is firmly grounded in appropriate and effective communication. The sources of such communication vary in relation to the stage reached, from being initially quite impersonal to being eventually highly personal indeed.

REFLECTION

It would be advantageous for you to try to understand why the original investigators devised the classic adoption model in the form which they actually did. Reflect on the influences of which you have been aware (either at the time or now, retrospectively) in respect of any process of adoption involving you personally. Where did you receive your original information? What was it that aroused your interest? Did you try to

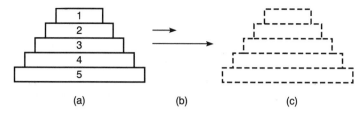

Fig. 5.6   The Hanoi game.

make any prior assessment or trial? How long or short a process did you go through before committing yourself? How realistic is the classic model (or indeed any model) in the light of your own experience? Re-read any appropriate section of this chapter in order to examine the possible relationship between theory and practice.

APPLICATIONS

Part A

Devise some alternative, but simple, model of an adoption process which allows for the fact that not all decisions may be rational, logical or even methodical. There are people who are impulsive buyers, for example, and it should be possible to represent them (together with their more rational contemporaries) on one diagram. For the purpose of the exercise assume that the representation is in respect of one particular product only, and on a limited time-scale.

There are several possible ways of doing this. There is no 'right' way. As usual, some suggestions are given in the Appendix.

Part B – The Hanoi Game

Using a systematic approach move the five counters in Fig. 5.6 from position A to position C, via B where appropriate, following the so-called **Hanoi Rules**. These are that only one counter may be moved at a time and that no counter may be placed on top of a smaller one.

When you have completed the manoeuvre try to analyse what you have learned from the experience – in addition to exercising some patience!

RECOMMENDED FURTHER READING

There are few books which will add much to those already recommended. However, the following publications might merit your attention in respect of adoption models.

Heirs, Ben and Farrell, Peter (1986) *The Professional Decision Thinker*, Sidgwick and Jackson, London. (*Chapter 3, especially the model of the decision-thinking process*)

You may well find this more complicated than first appearances would suggest.

Robertson, Thomas S. (1971) *Innovative Behaviour and Communication,* Holt Rinehart and Winston, New York. (*Parts of Chapter 3*)
    Many of the examples dealt with here concern the sale of products but there is much very useful information on the nature and importance of stages in the adoption process.
Rogers, Everett M. (1983) *Diffusion of Innovations,* Free Press, New York. (*Parts of Chapter 5*)
    Professor Rogers writes about innovation-decision processes. Pay particular attention to his approach but defer fuller study until after reading the next chapter of the present book.

The process of diffusion 6

Diffusion is the means whereby an innovation spreads.
W. R. Spence (1982)

The essence of the diffusion process is the information exchange by which one individual communicates a new idea to one or several others.
Everett Rogers (1983)

By persuading others we convince ourselves.
Letters 35, Junius (c.1769)

This chapter considers the meaning of the term 'diffusion' and examines the personal and social aspects of the process itself in relation to the spread of new ideas. Ways of promoting the diffusion of desired information are considered in relation to a range of possible social conditions.

Objectives
After reading this chapter you should be able to:

- distinguish between adoption and diffusion;
- specify essential elements in the diffusion process;
- identify some factors which could improve, and some which might retard, the spread of innovations.

HOW DIFFUSION DIFFERS FROM ADOPTION

We have seen in the previous chapter that adoption of an innovation is the result of a personal mental process which is internal to the individual concerned. Diffusion is, as distinct from this, a social activity of which interpersonal contact and influence are inescapable and essential factors. The starting point is still with individual adoption but the process itself refers to a kind of aggregate acceptance which, in some respects at least, might be considered as a form of cumulative adoption. It is spread, like a plague, from person to person. But unlike plague, it usually takes place at a much lower speed, and it cannot proceed contrary to people's wishes. However, some of the relevant mathematical formulae for calculating both, actually share some common types of components. At its most fundamental level of theory and practice the diffusion process consists of three absolutely essential and irreducible elements:

1. a new idea;
2. someone who knows about this idea; and
3. someone who does not.

Bearing in mind these three requirements it is possible to construct a **reductionist analysis** of the corresponding process of diffusion. This could be presented as having its own fundamental components consisting of the following essential elements:

- **Acts of acceptance** – in other words, some instances of personal adoption by a number of individuals.
- **Over a period of time** – since simultaneous acceptance by everyone interested is highly improbable.
- **Of some particular innovation** – only one specific new idea, practice or product can be dealt with meaningfully at any one time.
- **By an individual or a group** – the 'unit of adoption', as sociologists would call it, can be either individual or collective depending upon circumstances.
- **Using available channels of communication** – there are many options open to participants in communication pathways, networks and linkages. These may be of a social and/or technological nature.
- **In their social structure** – the most determined individualist is still located in a social context unless he/she has renounced all society and gone to live as a hermit on some remote mountain.
- **While influenced by their cultural values** – all people value some things more than others. What they cherish indicates the foundations of their culture, ie their life-style.

DIMENSIONS OF DIFFUSION

Certain dimensions of these elements are more important than others. Here follows a more detailed summary of these key elements.

Acceptance

As discussed in Chapter 4, section 4.1, the term 'adoption' has to refer to the regular use of an innovation or, at least, the intention to continue using it regularly. A single implementation, whether by purchase or otherwise, might be a genuine example of unambiguous adoption if, for example, it applied to the acquisition of something like an encyclopaedia which is usually a 'one-off' lifetime purchase. However, for most activities in life, it is necessary to remember that single, perhaps isolated, acts of acceptance can not reliably be regarded as indicators of any personal adoption propensity. Intention of continuing acceptance is the determining factor within the terms of the generally recognized definition.

Time

This element is absolutely indispensable in attaching meaning to any study of the diffusion process, especially as it is irreversible and is probably the most major factor over which we have no control. In fact the basic concept of diffusion itself would be wholly meaningless without it. Actual elapsed time as a dimension is often ignored in social science constructs such as models but, where communication is concerned, 'real time' has immediate and obvious relevance although the means of measuring and accounting for it may be subject to some methodological criticism. It is, however, undeniably both a necessary and significant factor in respect of each of the following three issues:

1. The length of time which elapses as an individual passes from first awareness to adoption or rejection. This enables an assessment to be made of individual decision-making characteristics.
2. The relative earliness or lateness with which an innovation is adopted within a social system. This can be used to construct a continuum of adopter categories, each occupying a segment of the overall distribution curve.
3. The expression of rates of adoption within a social system, ie a measurement of the number of people who adopt within a given time. This enables a community, for example, to be classified as either progressive or traditional.

Innovation

Innovations can take the form of ideas, practices or products. Some of these will be creations which have not previously existed but many will consist in modifications, major and minor, of what is already known. In some cases it will be the use which is made of whatever is seen to be new that will constitute the innovation rather than the thing itself. The concepts of both adoption and diffusion can only meaningfully be applied to one innovation at a time although it is possible to perceive cumulative patterns that may be presented subsequently as characterizing, for example, a society. In the Western World it is commonplace to classify contemporary manufacturing and technological societies as 'modern'. This, by inference, suggests that they are more progressive or innovative than rural societies in, for example, the Third World. The latter are usually regarded as being traditional or conservative and are therefore often labelled 'backward', undeveloped or underdeveloped although there is an increasing tendency to label them, somewhat less harshly, as developing countries.

Adopters

Most decisions to adopt are made by individuals but there are circumstances in which such decisions can be made by groups, for instance in forming a savings group or Neighbourhood Watch* scheme. There are other situations in which people usually act together, for example to receive cable TV in a particular residential neighbourhood. Since it is obviously uneconomic to lay a cable for just one customer it is advisable for several prospective users to band together to ensure that the costs (and consequent charges) of providing a connection to their homes from the system can be justified.

Communication channels

These are the routes along which information normally passes from sender to receiver. In many instances, as will be seen in a later chapter when communication theory and practice are examined, the flow can be two way. Indeed it is normal to consider communication as a two-way interaction since a one-way system merely indicates transmission. The most common example of interaction is in ordinary conversation. In the case of influence exerted on potential adopters, four main communication channels have been identified in practice:

1. Mass media
2. Government
3. Commercial
4. Informal.

1. **Mass media** – for the most part this refers to radio, the press and television although, as we shall see when looking later at advertising, there are other means such as posters and illuminated display signs which also serve an important purpose here.
2. **Government** – various officials and field officers, particularly in the areas of agriculture, social work, education, environmental health and the like. These officials are mainly motivated by a desire to fulfil their duty as it is laid down, and tread a path between complete objectivity and a natural tendency to promote the official perspectives of the government department or agency concerned.
3. **Commercial** – salespeople, dealers and others whose main objectives are to influence purchasing habits. They often have an additional inducement to do so in the form of a percentage commission on sales, but do not always allow that to prevent them giving other useful objective advice.
4. **Informal** – friends, neighbours, colleagues or peer group members with whom there can be an opportunity to discuss informally matters of mutual interest. Technical accuracy has not, in the vast majority of cases, been valued by potential adopters as much as the personal concern and involvement in their decision-making process of someone they felt they could trust.

*This is a local citizen surveillance system in Britain intended to safeguard residents against household crime such as burglary. It exists under other names elsewhere, for example as *Community Alert* in the Republic of Ireland.

Social structure

The term *social* should not be confused with *sociable*. Social existence begins whenever two or more people establish some form of relationship or mode of interaction, friendly or otherwise. All communication, for instance, (other than that which we hold within ourselves!) is a social activity and the physical and mental environment within which it is made possible is called a **social structure**. The commonest examples are groups, communities and societies. These constitute 'organizations', a theme which is explored more fully (including commercial undertakings) in Chapter 13. The group and community tend to give people that sense of belonging and loyalty to family and friends which assists them to acquire and accept a personal identity. The society, which is characterized by larger conglomerates such as nations and countries, is a wider frame of reference in which other qualities such as citizenship and patriotism can develop. It is from the most basic social structure of all, ie the nuclear family (parents and children), that all subsequent human groupings, at whatever level of size or complexity, derive their characteristics. These, for the individual, include being part of a hierarchy in respect of authority, being required to contribute (eg by taxes or service of some sort) to the common good, and being obliged to conform to the main-tenance of prescribed law and social order. Whether the collective set-up is a sociable context or not depends almost entirely upon the personality characteristics of the people who comprise it.

Culture

The word culture is often used in everyday terms to mean sophisticated perspectives on the arts including literature, music and the theatre. As a common social science term it refers to the system of values and beliefs which identify the way of life of people in a particular context. This owes a lot to history and can generally be recognized in, say, an educational programme by looking at the emphasis which is placed on the main-tenance of beliefs, attitudes and practices inherited from the past. It can also be sensed in relation to the degree of freedom permitting an individual to be 'different'. All societies have a range of freedom, however limited, but those who go beyond the boundaries of tolerance are regarded not only as eccentric but deviant, and in many societies deviance of any kind is at least frowned upon – and perhaps not tolerated at all.

HUMAN INTERACTION

With regard to the vast majority of situations in which we are likely to be involved with others in connection with new ideas there are certain characteristics which, in a sense, actually emphasize the importance of personal contact and human interrelationships when it comes to ensuring the spread of innovations. These include:

- social cohesiveness;
- personal identity;
- group membership;
- individual progressiveness.

Social cohesiveness

Since virtually everyone belongs to a network of social relations, often both complex and extensive, this will exert an influence of some kind on personal adopter behaviour. The more cohesive the social organization the greater will be the pressure on the individual not to step out of line in terms of the expectations or requirements of the environment. Privileges are related to responsibilities and group members are obliged to give due consideration to their social obligations, not only to the individuals who comprise the group structure but also to the group as an entity in itself.

Individual identity

In a social structure such as is found in groups, communities and societies the place of individuals in that structure will actually serve as a partial predictor of their probable rate of acceptance of appropriate innovations. With the exception of those who are isolates or hermits, people tend to cluster reasonably well around either the periphery or the centre of the structure. This assists in confirming their identity as they themselves see it, and it has to be remembered that we are only male or female, tall or short, intelligent or stupid etc insofar as there can be comparison with other human beings. Individual identity is a social creation. Furthermore, whatever picture of ourselves is developed in this way, we all have a predisposition to behave in such a manner as to reinforce the image which we possess of ourselves.

Group membership

Both the actual group membership and the reference group aspirations serve to identify individuals in a predictive way in respect of their likelihood to be progressive or innovative. The reference group is, in reality, that social set or clique to which individuals look for the images which they need. They may also aspire to eventual membership of such a group. The group is often, however, at odds with the 'real world' in which they live and work. But although it may have 'pipe-dream' overtones it does not need to be escapist or wasteful since it can, in effect, act as a stimulant to ambition and encourage progressive attitudes towards achievement. For many people it supports ambition and provides motivation.

Individual progressiveness

The rate of diffusion within a social system, providing that the grouping is large enough, tends to follow a normal distribution. The word normal is used here in a statistical sense and means that the plotting of acceptances against a timescale produces an S-shaped curve. This demonstrates a very slow rate at the beginning, followed by a period of relatively rapid diffusion, succeeded in turn by a tailing-off process in which the rate drops fairly dramatically again. Examples of such curves appear in Figs 6.1 and 6.2. When the number of acceptances over time are aggregated and plotted cumulatively against a time scale we obtain the well-known bell-shaped or **normal distribution** which is illustrated in Fig. 4.1 of Chapter 4 (the basis of categorizing individuals in respect of personal innovativeness). Since opportunities to innovate can be modified by environmental and social factors the individual's response may be better described in terms of progressiveness as outlined earlier.

Evidence in support of the impact of human interaction on innovation may be amply demonstrated as the following approach illustrates. If the assumption is made that adoption of an innovation is an entirely personal matter then this is equivalent to saying that the numbers of adopters accepting an innovation per unit of time will be a fixed percentage of those who have not already adopted it. The curve shown in Fig. 6.1 below is a representation of a diffusion curve based on this premise.

However, the normal distribution curve already referred to is shown in Fig. 6.2 and the difference in profile can only reasonably be accounted

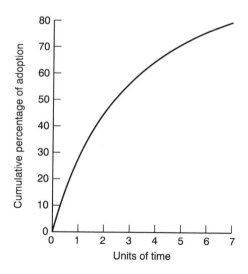

Fig. 6.1 Typical adoption curve.

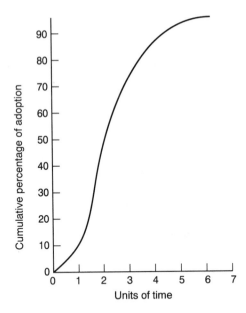

Fig. 6.2   Typical diffusion curve.

for by accepting that there is some measure of interpersonal influence between adopters. Any tendency to 'follow the leader', for example, would produce enhanced acceptance of exactly this kind. We already believe that adopters and potential adopters learn something from each other. It has become reasonably clear that, in practice, the act of adoption itself is also a probable influence on others to adopt.

DIFFUSION AND CHANGE

The very first chapter in this book was concerned with change generally and social change in particular. This was because consideration of change and communication underpins the whole process of innovation. Indeed diffusion may be regarded as one form of social change since it inevitably brings about a decided alteration in both the structure and the functioning of any social system into which it is introduced. Diffusion and dissemination are basically the same thing although **dissemination** is usually taken as being more deliberate in the sense in which, for example, a teacher attempts to spread knowledge. In actual practice diffusion is more often a gradual sort of spread, almost a kind of 'leakage', insofar as it can appear to be incidental rather than planned. The diffusion of information is not necessarily a deliberate, conscious act and there are occasions when it would not appear to have set out specifically to achieve any pre-determined objective.

DIFFUSION TIME-LAG

The time factor can vary enormously between the time of inception of an innovation and its implementation. This is true whether we are thinking of diffusion or dissemination. In practice the difference is not so much in methodology as in intention. Generally the term 'diffusion' can be taken to cover both. To quote one fairly recent example of diffusion, there was a time-lag of only a week between the discovery of the basic principle of light amplification (producing the laser and its offshoot, the *maser*) and the construction by the Bell Telephone Company in the US of the first working technological device. By contrast the introduction of penicillin was delayed for a decade. It was stumbled upon accidentally (as is so often the case with great discoveries) by Sir Alexander Fleming in 1928. It was not, however, until Rene Dubos published information in 1939 about a related antibiotic called *gramicidin* that steps were taken to ensure the recognition of penicillin as a legitimate and curative treatment for certain medical conditions. The time scale for acceptance can be even greater than this, depending on the nature of the new introduction.

The first of the innovations recounted above related to a material product and, for the most part, manufactured artefacts tend to be accepted with less difficulty than either practical techniques or abstract ideas. The second innovation, while it did relate partly to a material substance, was concerned – more importantly – with changes to established clinical practice. Whereas a modified product or new piece of equipment can be seen as an improvement without endangering the self-image of those who had owned or used the earlier model, a change of technique or practice is more threatening. It raises the possibility that the previous approach (and, by implication, those who used it) had certain serious shortcomings. This can be damaging to an individual's mental outlook, especially where standards of performance or questions of competence may arise. It is even worse with ideas because the ideas which we receive from others still belong to them. There is often a feeling of inferiority, or at least indebtedness, in becoming the receiver of such intellectual property which has originated in minds other than our own. In respect of an idea there is no way of knowing just how long the timescale could be. The precept 'Love your enemies' given by Jesus in the Sermon on the Mount is still so novel to the majority of the world's population as to be awaiting even the most limited acceptance after two thousand years! As against this, of course, there is the fairly recent concept of intellectual property just mentioned. This has been accepted unexpectedly promptly in law despite the many problems involved in analysing and legislating for any situation where something (an idea) can be given to someone else and yet remain the property of the originator. It is still being claimed that there is no copyright in ideas but that may not hold true indefinitely.

Even when there is a specific objective and the advantages of adoption can be demonstrated it still can take a long time for the process of diffusion to produce results. Technical feasibility alone is never sufficient. There must also be something else in the form of **receptivity**. In the commercial field this is called a demand. However this seems too positive a term for a condition which has more in common with lethargy, inertia or disinterested neutrality. It often is, at best, a potential or latent demand. At worst it can be active resistance such as often arises in a situation where a settled stable condition becomes threatened with at least temporary instability or uncertainty by some innovation. There is ample motivation in such circumstances for the more conservative members of the establishment to close ranks and present a unified opposition to change. This has happened in Romania in recent years where, despite the overthrow of a communist dictator and a condemnation of past non-democratic practices, virtually nothing has changed in any way for the vast majority of people in that country because the centre of power remains with those who had always exercised it in the past and obviously intend to continue to do so in the future.

RESISTANCE TO INNOVATION

Professor James R. Bright of Harvard has outlined in his book *Research, Development and Technological Innovation* (1988, Harvard University Press) a dozen reasons why antagonism may be raised to new technical innovations. These are:

1. to protect social status or prerogative;
2. to protect an existing way of life;
3. to prevent devaluation of capital invested in an existing facility or in a supporting facility or service;
4. to prevent a reduction of livelihood because the innovation would devalue the knowledge or skill presently required;
5. to prevent the elimination of a job or profession;
6. to avoid expenditures such as the cost of replacing existing equipment, and of renovating and modifying systems already in operation to accommodate or to compete with the innovation;
7. because the innovation opposes social customs, fashions and tastes and the habits of everyday life;
8. because the innovation conflicts with existing laws;
9. because of rigidity inherent in large or bureaucratic organizations;
10. because of personality, habit, fear, equilibrium between individuals or institutions, status and similar social and psychological considerations;
11. because of the tendency of organized groups to force conformity;
12. because of the reluctance of an individual or group to disturb the equilibrium of society or the business atmosphere.

Many of the items in his rationale can, with little amendment, also apply in respect of non-technical introductions since the underlying human motivation is caused by the (often irrational) fear of change itself, not necessarily the nature (much less the cause) of that change.

INNOVATION AND DEVIANCE

Everett Rogers' story of water-boiling in the Peruvian town of Las Molinos (which is included in his book under the heading of 'The innovation that failed'), helps to indicate some personal and social aspects of diffusion which cannot be ignored whatever the merits of any proposed new idea. It reminds us that those individuals who 'step out of line' can be regarded as unwelcome deviants rather than eccentrics or pioneers. I have summarized and commented on Rogers' story below as an example.

> Because of widespread water pollution the public health service in Peru introduced hygienic measures such as teaching housewives to boil contaminated water in order to make it safer to drink. In a small town of two hundred families a local hygiene worker was able to persuade only eleven housewives to adopt the new procedure: this was after repeated personal visits extending over a period of two years. The cultural beliefs held by the locals classified hot food and drink as being appropriate only for the sick – they normally ate only cold food, consequently they placed boiled water (whether it was subsequently cooled or not) in the category of being suitable only for those who were ill. It would have been interpreted as a sign of physical weakness to have drunk boiled water. As we indicated in respect of personal adoption, an innovation is not likely to succeed if it offends against inherited beliefs and values: there must be compatibility with what is held to be important. While this is of significance for the individual in respect of his or her personal belief it is sacrosanct if held by the community as a whole. Quiet conformity is the level which most of us settle for. It requires people of a very special disposition to deviate from this and we shall look at them very carefully in Chapters 8 and 9 because they have some really important roles to play in every society.

In the instance cited only those individuals who were least integrated with the culture of their community could take the risk of being non-conformist to the extent of defying the community norms on this issue. There are parallels with other more sophisticated social structures, such as manufacturing organizations, business enterprises, educational establishments and government departments today. In Chapter 3 we looked briefly at the influence of location on the individual. Now it is opportune to look again, and in a little more detail, at the consequences of the interaction which can take place.

THE INFLUENCE OF CULTURAL NORMS

Factors influencing innovativeness (Chapter 4, sections 4.3–4.5) are briefly summarized here. The very broad categories are:

1. a less innovative person in a progressive community;
2. a less innovative person in a traditional community;

3. a more innovative person in a traditional community;
4. a more innovative person in a progressive community.

It will be clear that an innovative person should ordinarily feel more at home in a progressive society than in a traditional one (point 4). Similarly a less innovative person ought to find a traditional community more congenial than a progressive one (point 2). In both cases the compatibility between individual and environment means that there is a probable absence of stress in that relationship or, at least, a lessening of the possible tensions which could be caused were the relationship less acceptable. It means also, and more importantly, the absence of any inducement or pressure for the individual to change. This ensures stability, often at the price of progress, in those sectors of society where idividuals conform to the societal norms. In extreme cases the situation can become not so much stable as almost static.

The term **norm** in a social context can have either of two different meanings:

1. actual behaviour;
2. expected behaviour.

In other words there are two distinct and separate uses of the term, namely the way in which people on the whole, actually behave, or the way in which people are expected, or even required, to behave. There is always some element of the second category contained in the first since individual and collective behaviour tends to reflect what is expected as well as what is required by law or custom. One of the ways of identifying whether or not the effects of certain innovations are good for both individuals and their society is to look at how functional they might be. In this context functional means relevant to achieving or maintaining the aims of society as a whole while furthering the objectives of the individual within it. In areas where there is difference and the likelihood of conflict of some sort the outcome would, overall, best be described as dysfunctional. This result would be likely for points 1 and 3 of the categories listed above. In such circumstances the values and aspirations (if any) of the individuals are at odds with the culture of the community because their individual reference groups lie outside that environment. The situation of each individual is very different, however, in these two cases.

In situation 3 innovators run the risk of being totally isolated in a traditional society where they will probably be able to make no headway against entrenched positions however hard they try. They may maintain their own progressive outlook since their lack of integration enables them to do so but the odds are very much against them being able to achieve any significant impact on their fellow citizens. The mass culture will normally outweigh any individual effort. Generally this is universally true of all environmental influences on the individual. Those who differ from the majority are, in effect, deviants and such people have a re-latively unhappy existence in any context. The motivation to be deviant has to be very strong indeed. This situation, therefore, is not a very pro-mising one either for the survival of the individual or for the improve-ment of the community.

However, precisely because of influences such as these, situation 1 is very much more hopeful. In fact there is every prospect of the environ-mental influences bringing about salutary change in any less progressive individuals who may find themselves located in a such a progressive society. There are frames of reference which set good examples to follow and there are acts of influence and persuasion that they will find it hard to resist. Sooner or later they will be induced, hopefully by persuasion rather than coercion, to review their attitudes as a first step towards amending them in certain operative respects. In the course of time they will change. The ways and means of bringing that situation about will be dealt with in Chapters 8 and 9.

SUMMARY

Adoption is the mental process through which an individual passes from the stage of first hearing about an innovation to the final adoption of it. **Diffusion** is the spread of a new idea from its source to the ultimate users. The first is personal; the second is social. Together they combine to form a process known as **innovation** which is directed to bringing about change. People vary in their degree of innovativeness and this is often influenced by their relationship with their community or social group. This relationship can make acceptance of new ideas easy if the individual is favourably disposed to the norms of a progressive com-munity. Otherwise an incompatible relationship would make personal innovativeness more difficult.

REFLECTION

Re-read any of the sections which you found difficult to follow on first reading. In addition, refresh your memory by looking again at the elements of adoption in the previous chapter. This should help you to respond confidently to the objectives outlined at the beginning of this chapter. Can you say that you have mastered these? If so, then you are ready to try the following exercise before having a look at the next chapter on communication theory and practice. After that you will be ready to tackle some everyday real-life issues.

APPLICATION

Some years ago, in the early days of plastic products, one manufacturer (Tupper of Florida) started to produce very good quality resealable food containers, such as sandwich boxes and other storage items. The innovative approach was in selling these items to prospective purchasers in groups rather than individually. This introduced what became extremely well-known as *Tupperware* parties. Typically, local residents would invite friends and neighbours to their homes for a coffee morning and, by suitable arrangement with the suppliers, would also mount a display, with a talk and/or demonstration of the products together with the opportunity to purchase or order some of them.

A similar approach has since been used successfully by other manufacturers in connection with cosmetics, books and clothing. If you have never attended one of these parties try to talk to some older person who has. Why do you think that, although they are not only still continuing but developing, they are less commonly heard about today? What sort of factors made this innovation possible in the first instance? What do you think supports the continuance of this approach? In what circumstances might it be difficult to maintain or develop?

On this occasion try to present your response in written form but keep it brief. Some guidelines are given in the Appendix to this book . . . but don't look just yet.

RECOMMENDED FURTHER READING

There are two books in connection with this chapter which might be worth referring to.

Bright, James R. (1988) *Research, Development and Technological Innovation*, Harvard University Press.
    Not easy reading but the sections on resistance to accepting technological changes are thought provoking. Try it if you are looking for some intellectual stimulation.
Robertson, Thomas S. (1971) *Innovative Behaviour and Communication*, Holt Rinehart and Winston, New York. (*Part of Chapter 8*).
    This is an advanced book recommended in the Editors' foreword as for 'business executives, as well as for students of innovation and communication'. Read only those snippets of Chapter 8 which appear to be of immediate relevance to your interests and needs!

Human communication 7

Great minds discuss ideas, average minds discuss events, small minds discuss people.
John Milton, 1608–74

A message must reach its target audience, be perceived as relevant and hence lead to desired action.
Colin J. Coulson-Thomas (1985)

Human communication is fraught with problems and difficulties.
Nicki Stanton (1991)

All communication involves change.
Denis McQuail (1975)

This chapter considers in detail the kind of personal and social interaction which relates to, underpins, and ultimately enables human communication to take place. The basic operation of the process is examined and those issues are explored which are of prime importance in constructing communication models, analysing techniques of operation and understanding basic individual factors.

Objectives
When you have completed this chapter you should be able to:

- identify the important parts of a simple model of human communication;
- outline ways of reinforcing a message;
- specify the main characteristics of any form of mass communication;
- recognize essential aspects of technologically-mediated communication.

WHAT IS COMMUNICATION?

The term communication is often confused with communications even by many educational institutions which offer courses in the area of communication studies. While interpretations of the terms can vary slightly the most widespread practice is to consider **communication** (in the singular) as being the social process which ordinarily operates when personal interaction takes place. **Communications** (plural) is used more specifically to indicate the channels and the technological means by which this process may be facilitated. The principal features of communication which have a bearing on innovation are presented here by considering human communication issues first (**Section A**), then those associated more with communications techniques and equipment (**Section B**).

In the preface to a recent book the editor commented 'Probably the most characteristic feature of communication is its diversity'. Much the same could be said of its definitions. Those who are interested in exploring a range of these (and there is much to be learned by doing so) will find a number of recommendations for suitable reading at the end of the chapter. It will serve our purposes at this stage, however, to think of basic communication as focusing on the exchange of meaningful messages between human beings.

Whatever may be said of systems of encoding and decoding, methods of transmission from sender to receiver, acts of persuasion and selectivity, and all the other bases for communication models there is one common foundation for understanding what is really a very sophisticated and complicated process – it is a means of trying to get an idea from one brain into another! It does not have to be in the form of oral or written language. Surely there can be few people today who are unaware of such phenomena as 'body language'? There is a story of the famous ballerina Pavlova who was asked 'What were you trying to convey in that dance?' She is reported to have replied 'If I could tell you I would not be dancing'. It is true that most communication is, however, based on the spoken or written word and this is reflected in much of the material which we will now examine. Probably the one inescapable element in any study of communication is the presupposition of a sender and a receiver, and these two elements are to be found in one form or another in every model devised to illustrate interpersonal communication. In our modern technological society it should be noted that interpersonal communication is not restricted to direct face-to-face communication. It can operate in other ways too, for example via the telephone.

SECTION A COMMUNICATION

ESSENTIALS OF HUMAN COMMUNICATION

One of the truly classic models which incorporates the basic criteria applying to human communication was constructed from the ideas put forward in 1948 by an American academic, Harold D. Lasswell. He suggested that a convenient way to describe a communication process would be to answer a few simple questions. By modifying slightly his original presentation these can be displayed in the following form.

Who?
Says what?
By which means?
To whom?
With what effect?

The essential components of communication can be shown in simple diagrammatic form:

Sender → Message → Channel → Receiver → Effect

In the format of a model this is known even more briefly as

S − M − C − R − E

The built-in assumption here, which characterizes many communication models, is that the sender has some *intention* of influencing the receiver and that therefore communication should be regarded fundamentally as a persuasive force. This has a certain attractiveness based on everyday experience as well as superficial plausibility because even the simplest statement can include an injunction – and usually does! For example, the innocuous sounding comment 'this is a house' incorporates the hidden reminder 'you will note that this is not a manor, mansion, lodge, shed, hut . . .' etc. Pressure from others, as well as influence exerted indirectly by changing fashion and habits, *do* have an important impact on the daily life of every human being. What we eat, wear, do and think are invariably affected by the persuasive influences which come from external sources. While this raises some philosophical problems it accords in practice with most observable acts of communication including that related to innovation. This is because all communication is directed towards bringing about some change of information, attitudes or actions. The elements of the model, which relate to the essential aspects of such communication, serve to direct our attention to several matters of great importance, of which a brief outline follows.

ELEMENTS OF COMMUNICATION MODELS

The S M C R E model highlights five elements, each of which involves personal, social, cultural and technical issues of considerable consequence. Some of these will be dealt with at greater length elsewhere in this book. The important dimension of feedback may be regarded as a sixth element, and also merits consideration. The six elements are therefore as follows:

1. source
2. message

3. channel
4. receiver
5. effect
6. feedback.

Source or sender

The origin of messages has a significance for the way in which the message is subsequently received and acted upon. One of the factors involved here is status. A message may be accorded more credibility, or at least regarded as of greater importance, if it originates from someone of 'high standing' rather than from an individual of lower perceived position. For instance the pronouncement of a cardinal would usually carry more weight (in ecclesiastical matters, at least) than that of a curate. Conversely, there can be an adverse reaction because of what social scientists would call a **status differential**. In other words there may be a consciousness of too much difference in levels – social, intellectual, organizational or occupational – for information to be seen as 'user-friendly'. The so-called 'generation gap' between parents and children can be viewed in such terms. Receivers of messages do not, for the most part, like to be coerced – nor do they wish to be patronized. Examples are not difficult to find, and the one which follows (taken from some 1950s child care anecdotes) will serve to illustrate the potential problems of a sender-receiver relationship.

In the early days of the National Health Service in the United Kingdom it was considered important for nursing mothers to recognize the value of proper feeding of infants but it was found that information passed on by medical staff was not readily believed in this particular respect. There was widespread reluctance on the part of patients to act on advice given by doctors in the maternity wards of hospitals. This was especially true regarding the claims made in respect of the health value of orange juice (which was provided free to supplement the growing child's normal diet). However if the same sort of advice came from women who were already mothers themselves, rather than from the white-coated doctors, it was usually accepted almost without question as being something that was useful to know. It would appear that the information and advice dispensed by doctors was regarded as 'scientific' and therefore irrelevant to 'ordinary' people. Consequently many hospitals and clinics tried to ensure that one or two volunteers with their longer experience of raising a healthy family satisfactorily, were always on hand to pass on the appropriate message to new mothers.

A further point is that there may be a sort of 'halo' effect which can colour the information given by some people whose views receive enhanced value because of some totally unrelated activities. One instance would be the opinions of a 'pop' music star concerning his belief in the harmlessness of soft drugs. His previous recognition as a person of some significance in the world of teenage music culture increases the likelihood of young people accepting his views on other topics, such as drugs. Additionally there are those who sometimes see themselves as being in a privileged position, because of their occupation, to transmit messages on issues to which they feel a commitment even if these may be somewhat marginal to their main responsibilities. For example, it is noticeable that some churchmen whose theology at times appears uncertain still manage, quite often, to demonstrate vociferous political beliefs of apparently unshakeable conviction.

The message

There is a universal attempt to make this as explicit as possible in order to aid understanding. However, it could be implicit, if adequately devised, and yet be clearly understood. For instance a current television commercial in Britain does not mention either the manufacturer or the kind of product that it is promoting but invites the viewing audience in a label of only four words to 'draw your own conclusions'. The effectiveness rests on clever construction and presentation of a few visual images totally unrelated to the product and shown without any accompanying 'voice-over'. However both the consumable item itself and its suppliers may be clearly identified from these visual clues which are very creatively employed. This is a good example of innovative communication.

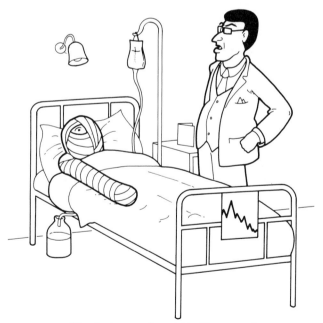

What is the meaning of this, Thompson?
Did you not receive my GET WELL card?

Fig. 7.1 Misunderstanding communication.

To be effective a message must not only be received, but must also be understood in order to produce resultant action. A simple illustration would be in respect of road traffic signals where either of the two primary colours, red and green, can act as a stimulus to the required action without any possibility of uncertainty arising. However, the basic problem with messages is that they are normally couched in language rather than visual images. Such language has to be deciphered or decoded in order to understand what is meant. The big difficulty is that no two persons may agree as to the exact meaning of a word or term. Lawyers have grown rich on such matters. So have humorists.

The cartoon (Fig. 7.1) illustrates the point. Where language is written the problems are emphasized if there is only a one-way flow of information. With spoken face-to-face language there is often, though not always, the opportunity for questions or discussion to aid clarification.

Channels of communication

It is possible, indeed necessary, to consider this feature under two different headings, ie human and technological. At this stage our attention must be on the human dimension. This underlies any other since it deals with those of the individual's personal senses which are involved in perception. The other aspect which is concerned with technology is dealt with later in this chapter in connection with mass communication.

In human terms, channels are the essential routes by which one person may succeed in getting some idea from his or her own mind into the mind of someone else. It is hardly surprising that, on occasion, one route may prove to be more effective than another. In consequence there is merit in employing all feasible and practicable routes. In this connection far too many people can operate on rule of thumb guidelines without knowing either how and why they originated or what is their justification. One well-known dictum, familiar to salespeople the world over, is 'Never write if you can phone – and never phone if you can visit'. What is the significance of this instruction? To gain insight it is necessary to recall that, while communication is frequently based on language, there are other possible dimensions too. In particular there are not only the words which are the building blocks of language itself but also the related features and subsets such as **paralanguage** and **kinesics**. The meaning of these terms may be briefly outlined as follows.

- *Language*
  Language consists essentially of words. But words in themselves actually have no objective meaning. We attach meanings based on acceptance, usage and custom which can vary from society to society, from occupation to occupation and from person to person. Written language, in particular, can leave many doubts in the mind of the reader and raise queries to which no immediate answer is forthcoming.

- *Paralanguage*

  With the employment of paralanguage we have not only words but, in addition, the sounds of those words. The term refers to inflexions, emphases, variations in volume, pitch, accent, tone of voice, hesitations and so on in the delivery of the spoken word. To many people this can convey far more clearly than ordinary print the content of a message. In respect of a radio broadcast, a tape recording or a public address system there may still be some ambiguities. If however there is a two-way connection (by telephone, for example) then it becomes possible for the receiver to ask questions, enter into debate and pursue issues further.

- *Kinesics*

  With the addition of kinesics to the other factors there is the best opportunity of all to ensure reinforcement of the message by most of the available means of human sensory perception. Kinesics, or 'body language' is the visual image of the sender in action as well as the inflexions of voice and the basic message. All the routes into the brain, except taste and touch, are being assailed at the same time; one perception reinforces another. With television or video there may still exist some unresolved areas of doubt but with face-to-face communication every opportunity is open for doubts and difficulties to be dispelled.

Body language adds a further dimension in such areas as posture and facial expression. Avoiding of eye contact, blushing, sweating, shuffling feet or twitching fingers all convey information additional to the primary message and supplements our interpretation of it. (Do you remember the television broadcast from Moscow by the uncomfortably nervous leader of the coup committee that temporarily ousted Mikhail Gorbachev?) Little wonder then, that for all their shortcomings (and they are many), interviews still form such a vital part of most personnel selection procedures.

Receiver or recipient

This term may be thought to imply a somewhat passive role for whoever is at the end of the line of communication. However, since we all have a choice as to whether or not we will receive certain messages and, if so, what we prefer to select from them and act upon, the role is as active as any other. It is for this reason that the additional component of feedback has been added to models of this kind – to indicate that observations of recipients' reactions, their own comments, changes in their purchasing habits or other activities are matters worthy of real note. They can modify subsequent message sending in the same or a similar context by influencing choice of content, timing or channel to ensure maximum effectiveness.

Effect

The effect is any outcome, predicted or not, desirable or undesirable, which can be said to result from the SMCR sequence. This can be seen in altered personal behaviour, changes in product sales figures, newspaper circulation growth and other criteria. If this element is missing there has been no communication, only transmission of information and this is not the same thing at all. All communication is essentially two way!

Feedback

It is universally expected that the effects of communication should be observable and, when they are, it constitutes what is most commonly called feedback. This does not need to be in the form of language or even human interaction as such so long as it completes what might be described as a **cybernetic loop**. This, interestingly, can apply to circuits in machines in the same way as networks linking human beings. It is the process which uses the outcome of one approach to modify those which follow. It can readily be observed in practice by watching and listening to a speaker addressing a meeting or a comedian responding with his patter to an audience. In other words it provides the means of learning from experience while that experience still continues.

One of the major failings of any theoretical model is that it has to be an artificially contrived form of presentation which, however detailed or sophisticated it may be, cannot fully reflect the wide range of issues and features to which it claims to relate. It must necessarily suffer from one or more of the following inescapable shortcomings:

- a theoretical model can be incomplete;
- it can make assumptions; or
- it can be over-simplified.

- **Being incomplete** – Considering the complexities of everyday life and the myriad of possible human interrelationships of varying directions and intensities which we all have with one another this point should not need to be laboured. Something has to be left out of even the most complex diagram or description and for some people or situations such omissions may be crucial. They will certainly be noticed and remarked upon! If the presentation is scientifically objective, however, there would be no selective deletions or rejections intended to produce a biased portrayal of any set of circumstances.
- **Making assumptions** – One of the most fundamental assumptions of any model is that things tend to proceed in an orderly fashion. Models therefore often rest on the premise that there are certain cause-effect relationships, and even contemporary chaos theory in the world of physics does not deal with isolated instances but presumes the existence of patterns of events even in the most chaotic of circumstances.

Assumptions, in other words, are not just intuition so much as informed guesses based on acute observation and previous experience. In any case no model, however refined, can be presented as though it were the whole truth. Indeed it might, while proving to be of immense value, actually contain little that could be defended as truth itself.

- **Being over-simplified** – Simplification does not consist only in a reduction of elements included in a model but often also involves a trimming down of each of those items to their most basic constituents. This is necessary in order to focus attention on the core of the process or situation under scrutiny. It *is* possible to have information overload, particularly in learning situations. This is where you encounter the problem of 'not being able to see the wood for the trees'. A good model displays the absolutely essential information and does so in such a manner as to indicate vital relationships and possible outcomes. To this extent it must be generalized and therefore simplified. The SMCRE model is a case in point.

When looking at a model in respect of any particular issue one of the first questions which we might pose could be 'How useful is this?' and we might add 'for what purpose?'. In general terms it could be said that communication models fall fairly readily into three separate but related categories, concerned with:

1. action *on* others;
2. interaction *with* others;
3. reaction *to* others.

There is no necessity to expand upon these separately here since most communication set-ups tend to involve all three. As will be seen by examining any of the material presented in this book we have considered issues which would deal adequately with any of these scenarios. For example a non-linear model provides for action by the sender, reaction by the receiver, and interaction between the two. Indeed these categories are normally specified separately more for the sake of conceptual clarity than because they relate to entirely separate and different functions. They all have the shared objective of achieving adequate transmission and reception of messages to facilitate appropriate responses. As Fig. 7.2 shows, however, not everyone is necessarily committed to achieving this objective as one of their priorities.

SELECTIVE PERCEPTION OF INFORMATION

We are all selective in our perceptions but we may not intend to be. While we sometimes make a deliberate choice (or have it determined for us by circumstances) there are other times when we are not aware that alternatives exist. For whatever reason, we see, hear, smell, taste and touch only some of the things which we might. It follows that in any communication process therefore, we are not at the receiving end of

Fig. 7.2   Message delivery.

more than a very tiny proportion of the total knowledge freely available to us. The fact that we select, consciously or unconsciously is, fortunately for us, just as well. If we were unable to exercise choice, we would be overwhelmed by the sheer volume of information in existence and be totally unable to cope with it. But often we do not realize just how rigid are the constraints which we impose upon ourselves until we pause to examine our own behaviour patterns. Naturally we only understand part of the information which we receive, and even then we only remember part of that. In the last resort we are sometimes left with very little that we can recall – a phenomenon understood only too well by students! The diagram in Fig. 7.3 below illustrates this point.

As examples of selection, we read the kind of daily newspapers which we know already support our political and social views, we buy the sort of books and magazines which cater for our acknowledged tastes and interests, we cultivate friendships with people whose lifestyles and temperaments are compatible with our own, we go on the sort of holidays which suit our habits and our pockets . . . and so on. It is only occasionally that we come face-to-face with radically differing perspectives and when we do the tendency is to ignore, reject, oppose or try to modify them. In any case we will usually identify and interpret them in the light of our preconceived value systems; indeed we can hardly do otherwise. Consequently one major objective of any innovative approach, especially in a social context, is not just to persuade people to see something as new but to get them to see anything at all.

As always, there is both a theoretical and a practical dimension to this.

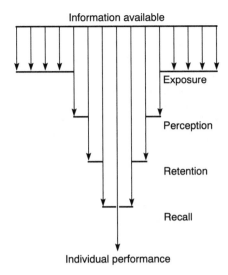

Fig. 7.3 Selective perception.

The theoretical considerations concern how reinforcement of weak or marginal perception may be assisted. These are now examined in the context of human perception and cognition. The practical approaches offered by mass media, for example, are considered later in Section B which deals with technology.

If a communication process is successful it produces an end result which marks the completion of the operation. The outcome may not, however, be what was expected or desired (by either the sender or the receiver). In spite of this the question of what constitutes effective communication need not cause us any intellectual problems at this stage because in the context of the everyday world of work, success is achieved when the sender's intentions have been fulfilled. To operate on this basis is to try to achieve an appropriate reward in return for a reasonable effort. If we accept this as a defensible aim we must pay heed to certain fundamental principles of reinforcement, which are reasonably well known to all good teachers, preachers and politicians – although possibly not by these labels.

REINFORCEMENT OF PERCEPTION

The manner in which we perceive certain stimuli such as communication signals can modify the impact which such impressions make on us. Influences can be strengthened by reinforcement, which usually operates by means of three common dimensions:

1. Frequency
2. Recency
3. Intensity.

Frequency

A self-explanatory term that says, in effect, the more often something is repeated the more likely it is to be perceived and, eventually, believed and acted upon. Advertisers, charity organizers, the clergy and social activists are among those whose endeavours depend largely upon repetition of their convictions or commitments. So, too, are trade unionists, tourist boards and marketing executives. The basic technique is not, of course, as naive as simple repetition. It consists of knowing when, how and where to return to an issue already touched upon, but avoiding unnecessary overlap or duplication (you should, I hope, be able to recognize some examples of this technique in this book). The aim may be to expand upon an earlier pronouncement, to restate a belief or principle, to revise something already adequately covered, or to paraphrase a difficult exposition. Many people use this technique in an abbreviated form for summing up a lecture or sermon to indicate the principal features which it is desired should be remembered. I have done so in this book by adding a summary to the end of each chapter.

Recency

It is something of a truism that many people (but not all) tend to remember best, and be most influenced by, what they heard last. This is why at important debates, for instance, the persons who have the duty of winding up the presentation for and against the motion are usually the most able and versatile speakers available. Also at board meetings or at conferences, it often pays to wait quietly until other speakers have had their say before delivering your own contribution. If you are both knowledgeable and competent this ensures that your viewpoint is set in the context of the previous deliveries whose authors can hardly, without loss of face, retract any firm assertions which they may have made earlier.

Intensity

It is generally believed that you will find it difficult to sell something if you, yourself, do not have faith in it. This implies that your personal conviction can come through any sales presentation which might otherwise have been thought to be sufficient in itself. It does appear to be true that there is no substitute for sincerity, especially in those face-to-face counselling sessions, tutorials and business deals where human relationships are cemented. Personal qualities like honesty and conviction colour the intensity with which any proposal or proposition can be put forward. The firmness or even fervour of the delivery can have a profound impact on the receiver. Some maturity of judgement is nonetheless required in order to ensure that confidence and assertion do not become unconscious arrogance.

While not explicitly required by any of these three concepts it is the face-to-face situations which enable them to achieve most effect. This is where the fullest possible range of sensory perception is employed by the receiver and the total integrated dimension of language, paralanguage and kinesics can be used to advantage. The objective need not be, for example, to persuade people to buy something which they do not want and cannot afford. It can quite legitimately be an effort to ensure that in the terms of the basic communication model a message has been so adequately received that it is capable of being fully understood. Whatever the skills and commitment of the sender the message which is eventually received has still been affected by selective perception on the part of the recipient as previously indicated. Many people would, of course, claim (sincerely) that they do not take this sort of action. However Fig. 7.3 indicates the probable sequence of successive filters which operate to the detriment of memory and also prompts us to reflect on the extent to which each individual's powers of comprehension are tested as a result of any stimulus.

SECTION B COMMUNICATIONS

THE ESSENTIALS OF COMMUNICATIONS

Within this section there are still human factors as well as technological ones to be considered. As indicated in an earlier chapter technology cannot be divorced from considerations of the people who develop and use it. In this section the human issues are broadly dealt with first and the technological aspects follow later.

The most basic communication models tend to look at a stimulus/response situation in its simplest terms which can be depicted as S → R. This is referred to in the textbooks as the **Hypodermic Needle** model. It is probably as close as any social science hypothesis will ever come to specifying a knee-jerk reaction. It presupposes a straight injection of information direct from originator to receiver. While this is far from unknown and is, indeed, a very important component in a situation of persuasion related to personal decision-making, it is not the most characteristic feature of mass communication. The latter comprises specialized media sources of information, such as radio, television and the press, all of whose activities are devoted to the dissemination of messages to very large and widely dispersed audiences. Despite the fact that each person in those audiences will act individually in respect of the information received it is stretching the hypodermic analogy just a little too far to suggest that it could apply in such circumstances. It is, in any case, often too simplistic a model even for those more intimate face-to-face situations which are frequently a great deal more complex than they might seem to be.

THE TWO-STEP FLOW HYPOTHESIS

The way in which most information usually travels from source to acceptance is known as the **two-step flow** in that the information goes initially to someone who is an influential or opinion leader in a social situation. It then flows from that person to a follower. (The role of opinion leader gets special attention later.) In practice nowadays this is usually regarded as a **multi-step flow** since quite a number of intermediaries may be involved. The Americans often refer to it as a trickle-down process, as shown in Fig. 7.4 below.

An everyday example could be someone who reads an item in a newspaper and then informs someone else. The latter might then tell a friend or neighbour, and so the process would continue. The important feature here is that it is not the original source of the information which actually exerts the influence, consciously or unconsciously, but the sec-

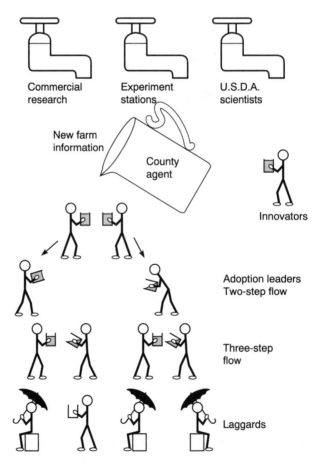

Fig. 7.4   A trickle-down process.

ondary source who relays it. The importance of those who act in this relay capacity will be seen when reflecting later on both change agents and opinion leaders. This type of sequential transmission can give rise to that word-of-mouth recommendation which is so highly sought after in the commercial marketplace where image is important and brand loyalty is at a premium. This interface between mass media and interpersonal communication serves to emphasize the overriding importance of the individual in communication relationships.

As was indicated earlier several different sources and channels may operate at various stages in the innovation/decision-making process. The mass media serves a useful purpose initially but thereafter more personalized influences become increasingly important. A little reflection will indicate one reason why this should be the case. Mechanistic models of communication place a heavy emphasis on transmission of messages. The assumption is that if messages are properly received they will be acted upon. This assumption lies behind many of the persistent campaigns which occur with rather monotonous regularity to stop people driving whilst drunk, to encourage people to stop smoking, to promote what is nowadays called safe sex, to discourage litter louts, or whatever. Always there seems to be the feeling that the message must not have got through and that people still don't know what is expected or required of them. This then can lead to even more comprehensive and expensive campaigns with equally little to show as a result.

In fact it is probably true that most of the people targeted will know well enough what message was delivered but will have decided, in the light of their own personal considerations, to pay little or no attention to it. This is one of the reasons why more individual approaches, even at mass distribution level, are being emphasized today. Radio and television programmes have phone-in sessions as well as talk-back programmes and other opportunities for audience participation. Also, in addition to the continued use of posters, television commercials and newspaper block advertisements there is an increasing tendency to personalize mass-produced letters, distribute leaflets, circulate fly sheets, send out samples and canvass door-to-door. There is also a tendency to try to use the ever-increasing availability of information technology to approach individuals more directly, say by telephone, fax or electronic mail.

In addition to the procedural problems to be overcome in respect of contemporary information transmission there is the even more important pyschological problem of role-reversal. This occurs in all situations where we become the slave of a machine instead of being the master. A computer, for example, requires you as to perform absolutely perfectly in respect of input procedures. If there is not 100% accuracy on the part of the operator it will not respond at all. No error or omission, however minor, will be tolerated. Whatever manufacturers and suppliers may claim, there is no such thing as a genuinely 'user friendly' system. What is created is a human/machine working relationship to which some people never manage to adapt. This distrust of technical aids and a failure to manage them competently is a major obstacle to the commercial expansion of information technology.

TECHNOLOGICALLY MEDIATED COMMUNICATION

Communication which involves a 'black box', ie a mechanical or electronic gadget interposed between sender and receiver, is known as **technologically mediated communication**. While the term often refers to situations where computers are used to transfer electronic mail via modems connected to the public telephone network, the black box could, in practice, be something as commonplace as the ordinary telephone or answering machine.

It is not uncommon for a caller using the telephone to find that an answering machine is operating at the receiving end. Consequently it is also quite usual for the recipient to find nothing on the machine tape when it is replayed. Some people find that being given an instruction to 'speak after the tone' leaves them bereft of any idea of how to summarize in a few words what they would have wished to talk about had the person called been available. They may have preferred to lead gradually into a topic but know that the tape allows only a matter of seconds. They may have wanted to test initial reaction to an introductory comment before being more specific. They may simply have had difficulty in composing at a moment's notice an appropriate précis of an intended longer communication. There are many reasons why there may be no message on the tape. All technological factors impinge on human perception of, and response to, the communication channels which they can employ.

Because of the range of technical communications equipment available today it is possible to collect, store and disseminate vast quantities of information at an ever-increasing rate by a variety of means. The situation is sometimes described as being one of information explosion. Inevitably two categories of citizen have arisen; those who are technically competent and feel at home with modern electronic systems and those who are, in current terminology, computer illiterate. In other words some people can not understand even the simple keyboard operation of an automated cash dispenser whereas others use a home computer daily for record keeping and correspondence. But even those who are proficient in respect of common communications technology need not necessarily feel completely at home with it.

If technology is considered as the black box previously mentioned then interposing such between sender and receiver poses a number of problems, technical and psychological. Let us look briefly at a few implications of some ordinary items of technology which are reasonably common in communication set-ups.

EVERYDAY COMMUNICATIONS TECHNOLOGY

The telephone, the answering machine, the computer with modem, and the fax machine are perhaps the technical items in most common use in Western society, not only in the business world but also nowadays increasingly at domestic level.

The telephone

This enables conversation to take place over long distances round the clock but requires caller and receiver both to be present at the same time. While interaction is high there is the absence of a visual image which prevents full utilization of all the personal senses. The idea of a video phone has not been received with any enthusiasm, however, as the audio phone can be a powerful instrument in the hands of sender or receiver. Either, for example, can control absolutely the duration of the call by appropriate means such as saying 'I'm sorry, someone has just come in. I'll ring you back' – and then putting the phone down!

The answering machine

This has its uses for brief messages. Although some of the most modern machines now employ electronic circuitry the majority still rely on magnetic tape for recording. The disadvantage of the tape is that normally it will take a message of only a few sentences, typically the name and return phone number of the caller plus a few explanatory comments. This is a real handicap as so many people find it impossible to summarize their message in a few coherent comments and the machine normally induces frustration in both parties from time to time. It is also an indication of possible absence of the resident from the location called which can be dangerous from the security point of view.

The computer/modem

This is becoming much more common in respect of communication processes such as electronic mail and access to bulletin boards. The set-up is concerned with the transference of messages from the computer via the modem which plugs into the ordinary telephone socket. Messages are transmitted from the keyboard of the sender to the screen of the receiver who does not need to be at the receiving end when a message is sent. It remains in the computer's memory until the person called is available to access it. Two-way dialogue is also possible and 'conversations' can be carried on with any number of discussants simultaneously. In addition it is possible to keep permanent records of such communications, either on computer disks or by means of paper printouts.

The fax machine

Machines for transmitting facsimiles, ie exact copies of papers and documents, are commonplace nowadays in the educational and business worlds. They too use the telephone network as does the modem, and are comparatively cheap to run. Whenever the documentation raises problems these may be dealt with by written queries or by the spoken word over the normal phone link.

All information technology can assist the accurate and speedy flow of information between sender and receiver. The method chosen will depend upon the nature and urgency of the communication and the kind of response required. The increasing deployment of such technology among enthusiasts and home-workers as well as business users has reduced the cost of equipment very dramatically in recent years and there are now courses of applied study in information technology provided by such educational bodies as the Open University and other institutions of higher education.

SUMMARY

Communication is any process whereby ideas may be transferred from one human mind to another. This action may be thought of as having certain S M C R E elements which can identify important sectors. Such communication is, in the end, personal but mass media involves the use of specialized sources to target many individual members of large populations simultaneously. Modern changes indicate moves towards more personalized technological developments of the 'black box' type. All communication is concerned with achieving and responding to change.

REFLECTION

Theory and practice go hand in hand. Models are meant to stimulate our thinking by showing how different factors relate to one another. This should enable us to see a possible relationship between cause and effect. Look back over some of the issues dealt with here and try to find everyday examples in your own experience to support or query some of the things said. In particular consider how being aware of the elements of the basic S M C R E model relates to your own particular situation. Try to identify black box examples from your own experience.

APPLICATIONS

Part A

On behalf of your employer a senior executive has let it be known that suggestions from employees for improving both working conditions and overall efficiency would be welcome. Bearing in mind the basic elements

Fig. 7.5   The chairperson's view of the committee.

of communication outlined in this chapter, what might be the best way of responding to this invitation?

Write your ideas in the form of memoranda only. There is no need to write an essay. Pay particular attention to the reasons for your proposals. Suggestions appear in the usual place at the end of the book.

Part B

Study Fig. 7.5. What message do you think that this cartoon is trying to convey? Have you any views as to how the chairperson might respond to his/her perception of the members in terms of promoting effective communication?

RECOMMENDED FURTHER READING

There is a vast library of literature in the field of general communication nowadays. An increasing amount deals with issues in human communication although technology and mass media are popular too because of continuing development in techniques and also because they constitute examination subjects for various professional bodies and training institutions. The following selection consists of a few books only but should enable you to find at least one which is appropriate to your present level of knowledge and interest. There is no advantage in wider reading at present although a glance at any library shelves or catalogues would be worthwhile, if only to see the range of titles available.

Bettinghaus, Erwin P. and Cody, Michael J. (1987) *Persuasive Communication*, Holt Rinehart and Winston, New York.

For the serious reader only. Described in the preface as for courses in 'management communication and in personal influence'.

Corner, John and Hawthorn, Jeremy (eds) (1980) *Communication Studies – an Introductory Reader*, Edward Arnold, London.
Well worth reading as it has chapters by different writers – some easy to understand, some very academic.

Forgas, Joseph P. (1986) *Interpersonal Behaviour*, Pergamon Press, Sydney.
This book is sub-titled 'The Psychology of Social Interaction' but it is not difficult to read and understand although it is quite long. At least have a look at the contents if you can find a library copy.

Jowett, Garth S. and O'Donnell, Victoria (1992) *Propaganda and Persuasion*, Sage, London.
Easy to read and contains many historical examples.

McQuail, Denis (1975) *Communication*, Longman, London.
One of the books which covers really basic topics in communication theory and practice. If you can read only one book at this stage, this is it!

Change agents 8

Almost thou persuadest me.
Agrippa to Paul, Acts 26: 28

Change Agent. A person who tries to stimulate change among people or organisations.
Van den Bàn and Hawkins (1988)

...a change agent's position is located midway between the bureaucracy to which he is responsible and the client system in which he works.
Rogers & Shoemaker (1971)

Most change agents go by rule of thumb and experience.
Loomis & Beegle (1964)

In this chapter we look particularly at the role of change agents and the influence which they may have on the adoption behaviour of other people. The operation of the change agent as a social group worker and also as an adult educator receives special attention.

Objectives
After reading this chapter you should be able to:

- identify occupations where the worker effectively operates as a change agent;
- specify several essential roles for a change agent;
- describe some personal qualities which might assist change agents to operate successfully.

THE ORIGINS OF INTERVENTION

Although the role model of the 'change agent' can be identified from biblical times and even earlier, the term first came into fairly common usage in the late 1940s and early 1950s. It refers to the involvement in a problem-solving situation of an independent person whose expertise can assist in a particular process of bringing about change. The justification for this intervention is that the change is desired by others (including the 'clients') who expect to derive benefit from the altered conditions envisaged. Such an agent would normally be a professionally qualified practitioner in some area of what is nowadays usually identified as 'the personal service industry'.

The idea of the change agent probably originated in the early days of psychoanalysis where the systematic examination of human conditions and the prospect of improvement obtainable by counselling ultimately spread to other social situations and activities. Whereas at first the approach was specifically concerned with the individual it was later extended to include small groups and eventually became applicable to operations which could involve whole communities. Today there are many occupations in which the job description incorporates a fundamental notion of the practitioner as a change agent, even although the term might be unfamiliar to many of those engaged in the occupations concerned. These include, among others, social workers, teachers, politicians, evangelists, marriage guidance counsellors and management consultants.

The essence of the work is that it is problem-oriented and that it concerns situations which can be changed, often in the context of some organizational framework or structure. There is an assumption, not always made clear, that people can organize themselves to identify desired goals and can be motivated to achieve these if they are given appropriate advice and assistance. This is where the change agents can provide the essential services which so often characterize the role of enabler, helper or facilitator in normal social circumstances.

However, there is a distinct difference between the change agent's approach and that of the more traditional professional such as the doctor, priest or welfare officer. We shall now consider this difference.

THE CONCEPT OF 'THE CHANGE AGENT'

The essential aim of the change agent is not so much to do something for people who need assistance as to help them to do whatever is necessary *for themselves*. This approach is now becoming more widespread, even in those areas which would formerly have been viewed as the province of the benefactor. For example in many African missions today, the philosophy has changed. In those districts of food shortage where formerly the concern would have been to provide meals for the people, food is still the initial response to famine and hardship but the long-term view is summed up in the cliché which has been adopted as the working motto of one relief organization: 'Give a man a fish and you have fed him for a day. Teach him how to fish and he can feed himself for life.'

It must be remembered, however, that change agents work with people of a wide range of ability and competence. Indeed they are often assisting those whose abilities are at least equal to their own. They can, perhaps, provide a sounding board for the formation of judgements and may also be able to act as a catalyst for action rather than as activists themselves. Change agents require a blend of two very different kinds of abilities. The first is that of establishing easy relationships with other people by demonstrating both empathy and sympathy where needed. The second is that of being able to pursue objectively a reasonably scientific analysis of a situation.

Such persons are often, unfortunately, regarded largely as establishment representatives by those whom they seek to serve because inevitably they are employed by some government department or a national or international agency. Such centrally funded bodies invariably seek to persuade people to follow some course of action which is intended to promote their welfare as conceived by that particular body. An authoritarian perception of change agents by the client is strengthened at times by the fact that the agents will not only work vigorously to promote some improvement but may also actively oppose any alterations which they and/or their superiors believe to be detrimental to the client's best interests. The client may have a different point of view.

Any change agent, nonetheless, will endeavour to introduce into the situation perspectives other than the purely parochial and will try to provide a communications link between different social and technological systems. Most change agents will see themselves as filling a number of roles in the community, for example as friend, teacher, expert, technician, supporter of action or contact with the outside world. The people who are clients of such agents may well see them, at times, as the agents see themselves. But they are likely also to have an even wider range of perceptions ranging from that of the representative of some vested interest to just that of an interfering outsider or even exploiter.

THE FUNDAMENTAL ROLES OF THE CHANGE AGENT

In conceptual terms the change agent has four essential and inescapable roles. These may be identified in the following generic form:

1. Observer
2. Diagnostician

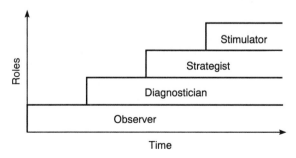

Fig. 8.1   The roles of the change agent.

3. Strategist
4. Stimulator.

The important factor in relation to these roles is that each one builds on the preceding one as indicated in Fig. 8.1.

It will be seen that the roles are successive rather than consecutive, ie they are cumulative. The previous role is never completed fully nor is it abandoned. That is why the diagram blocks are left open-ended to indicate that each extra role is not substituted for the previous one but added to it until the profile becomes more sophisticated. The essential nature of these four all-embracing roles is as follows:

- **Observer** – This is the fundamental role and is one of supreme importance. Since change agents are usually outsiders in respect of the situation in which they are operating (especially in the commercial or industrial context) they have to find out first of all what the current position actually is before proposing any changes. They should obey the old adage that 'you were given two eyes, two ears and one mouth. Use them not only in that order, but also in that proportion'. Observation consists in a great deal more than just looking. It implies seeing things in a critical way and relating them to an appropriate frame of reference such as legal requirements or publicized standards.

    To be an effective observer is the first and most fundamental task – it remains with change agents from the day they enter the agency or community until the day they leave. Consequently opportunities to practise basic observational techniques have long tended to form an essential part of appropriate training programmes for such agents as school teachers and social workers.

- **Diagnostician** – This is a rather cumbersome and pretentious label for a role which should be capable of being described more simply. It means that agents analyse the relevant information which they gather in such a way as to arrive at certain conclusions regarding what essential or possible changes are needed, and what changes (if any) would be wanted by most of the people in the target population. It calls for a great deal of skill and objective judgement to make a decision which is not unduly influenced by personal and vocational criteria or the pressures of officialdom to achieve certain organizational objectives.

    Only when a worker has gathered a relevant and sufficient body of knowledge about a locale and/or operation is he or she in any position to engage in diagnosis. Judgements made too soon after arrival are more likely to be based on prejudice or desire than on sound evidence. As with the first role this one continues *ad infinitum*, previously formed opinions being updated constantly in the light of fresh information.

- **Strategist** – This role thrusts upon agents the mantle of planner or policy maker. It is at this stage that they are in most need of the professional support of their own training and the code of ethics to which they subscribe. This is because they will be often walking a decision-making tightrope between, on the one hand, assisting people to gain what they want, and, on the other hand, persuading them to seek something else. The alternatives may be related – but different – and may be more readily approved by the establishment authority and hence more easily made available.

The action of competent strategists is not only to recognize, but to emphasize the fact that there are usually several possible ways of tackling any particular problem. Options have to be evaluated with regard to the best interests of the client subject to relevant legal and ethical considerations.

- **Stimulator**–This particular role is the most misunderstood by those who function as change agents. When properly operated it clearly distinguishes the professional from the amateur. The activity focuses on tactics rather than the strategy of the previous role from which it emerges. It is concerned with the best means of attaining a desired end. The mistake which some operators make is to become personally involved as initiators. That is not always desirable. In many cases it could be a real mistake. The wiser procedure would be to *stimulate* someone else to initiate the action.

  This serves many purposes. First of all it encourages individual initiative. Secondly it safeguards the change agent should things go wrong (seemingly a cynical view but actually very level-headed and in the interests of the community as a whole). The reasons for this do not have to be sought too hard. For example, the change agent is the employee or official representative of a body such as an organization or government whose whole image may be so tarnished by any failure that subsequent attempts to assist in other projects may well be damned by the previous lack of success. Thirdly it enables the agent to act as adviser and assessor while helping the client group as a whole to develop justifiable self-confidence. Fourthly it boosts morale and faith among those whose reservations about engaging in decision-making at all can be overcome because they know that there is a fall-back position, namely that the change agent can, if necessary, complete something which they might be unable to see through to completion themselves.

  The role of the stimulator is the most evolutionary one and it is the most difficult to acquire. It can only become operative if the previous three roles have been satisfactorily fulfilled. At this stage it is possible for several different perspectives to exist regarding the nature of the development towards which efforts are being directed. Value judgements which serve to indicate progress are bound to be subjective in many respects and, in the nature of things, there is often significant influence exerted by the agency to which the change agent belongs or owes allegiance. By relating the activities of change agents as stimu-

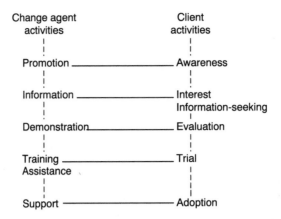

Fig. 8.2 Coordination of activities.

lators to those of potential adopters it is possible to indicate a degree of possible useful coordination between both activities as shown in Fig. 8.2.

THE CHANGE AGENT IN OPERATION

There are two major problems for every change agent. The first is that of social marginality because of being located between the employing agency and the client. This can make acceptance difficult in a particular social context. The second is an even more personal one of information overload from a wide range of sources. Because of the sheer volume of factual and procedural material which is frequently channelled to them there is often no effective way in which this can be made readily available to clients.

As a variant on the four generic roles earlier conceptualized for change agents there are at least five operational roles which are commonly thrust upon them:

1. Assisting change
2. Ensuring information exchange
3. Problem diagnosis
4. Promoting action
5. Establishing working relationships.

These roles, and variations of them, require all agents to be capable of involvement requiring them:

1. **to encourage a positive attitude towards change on the part of clients:** This requires some restraint on the part of the change agent in respect of not attempting to initiate change unless the clients become aware of a discrepancy between what is and what could be. The agent's role,

as indicated earlier, would then be to stimulate the clients to act in their own interests with the agent's encouragement, assistance and advice where necessary. It is part of the change agent's duties to alert the client to the possibilities which exist for improvement.

2. **to establish a viable information-exchange relationship:** It is necessary, in many instances, to convince clients that the nature of the working relationship is such that they themselves have something to contribute as well as receive. The qualities of the individual and the reality of the personally perceived world support the contention that the individual has knowledge and experience which are uniquely personal and that these should form part of any problem-solving exercise.

3. **to diagnose pressing problems and encourage a willingness to change on the part of the clients:** Diagnosis without intention of treatment would be a futile exercise on the part of any change agent. But treatment implies a willingness to change on the part of the client, an attitude worth encouraging and supporting as necessary.

4. **to translate this intent into action:** Change agents really come into their own here. Especially in group situations they have to ensure that the high spots of tension (as indicated, for example, in Figure 8.4 on page 114) are successfully negotiated. They have to achieve not only the full participation but also the wholehearted cooperation of all the clients.

5. **to consolidate appropriate adoption attitudes and achieve a stable working relationship:** The credibility of agents and their ability to continue exerting influence depend to a large degree on the nature and extent of their last achievement. It is therefore important to try to establish a sound basis for an ongoing relationship which will survive any of the minor trials which will undoubtedly occur from time to time.

The relative success of change agents in securing the adoption of innovations by clients tends to be a reflection of the extent to which they achieve good results in respect of, at least, the following aspects of their work:

- The amount of effort they put into contacting clients.
- The extent to which they are able to empathize with clients, ie adopt a client-orientation rather than a change-agency orientation.
- The degree to which the particular diffusion programme is compatible with the client's needs.
- Their credibility in the client's eyes.
- The extent to which they work through opinion leaders.

Change agents are, in most situations, professionally trained workers who work according to certain rules of conduct which set out a framework of ethics and appropriate accountability. It is generally accepted that their proper task involves the effective communication of information to people so as to assist them in the formation of sound opinions and good decisions. There are some questions relating to this which serve to differentiate the way in which various change agents work, for example:

1. To what extent are they concerned that clients should always try to reach *their own* conclusions and make personal decisions?
2. Do they try to build up a relevant knowledge base before attempting to identify problems?
3. Can they indicate goals and specify how best to try to achieve them?
4. Are they, on occasion, too single-minded about acceptable solutions to clients' problems?
5. Are difficulties resolved on an *ad hoc* basis or is there a genuine attempt to prepare clients for future problem-solving of a similar kind?

These questions are most relevant to situations where decisions have to be made because the present situation does not correspond to that which is desired. Problems to be overcome which prevent individuals achieving their desired goals are broadly as follows:

- Individuals may lack appropriate insight to be able to identify a problem. The first stage in problem-solving is always to recognize that a problem exists.
- They may not have sufficient knowledge or skill to be able to deal with it.
- There may be personal, social and cultural factors which are working against change.
- There may be conflicting values, eg the reluctance for a man to 'do a woman's work' in order to earn a living (a situation not uncommon in truly rural areas where manual labour is often regarded as the only real work).
- The individual may have no effective power to act or may lack the confidence to employ it.

The better the training provided for change agents the better they will be at stimulating individuals and guiding their decision-making processes. To some extent all change agents have to sell themselves to their clients before they can sell ideas or practices, therefore they must have an interventive repertoire which includes a number of role relationships. This is important in view of research evidence indicating that all change agents communicate more often, and more effectively, with higher status than with lower status individuals. This can affect adversely one of the roles thrust upon change agents–that of the adult educator.

THE CHANGE AGENT AS ADULT EDUCATOR

Traditionally the change agent has been regarded, particularly in the field of agricultural extension, as an adult educator. Today that role is much more widespread. Accordingly, the work might be identified with reference to one or more of a number of headings in respect of which the change agent:

1. assists individuals to analyse their present situation in an attempt to predict a possible future one;
2. helps them to become aware of problems which may emerge from such an analysis;
3. assists them to extend their knowledge and insight into such problems;
4. helps them to gather information for decision making;
5. develops their motivation to achieve improvement;
6. encourages objectivity.

Because the change agent so often operates as an adult educator it is useful to be able to identify appropriate educational goals for the individual or target population. These can fall into one or more of three possible categories:

1. acquiring information
2. changing attitudes
3. developing skills.

As a result effort must be directed to the undernoted objectives.

1. **Learning something so as to understand it, or at least remember it.** All learning depends on a combination of perception and cognition. Perception relates to the impact made on our senses by external stimuli. Cognition refers to how our brain interprets and understands these stimuli. For many situations mass media will be initially as effective as any other approach in transmitting the necessary information.
2. **Changing attitudes.** In this situation it is necessary to learn from the experience of being involved in appropriate situations in order to internalize any shift in value judgements or an amendment to some frame of reference.

Learning	Strategy	Methods
Cognitive (understanding)	Transfer of Information	Mass media, Lectures, Talks.
Affective (feelings)	Learning by Experience	Group discussion, Simulation.
Psychomotor (physical action)	Development of Skills	Training and Application

Fig. 8.3 Learning strategy and tactics.

3. **Acquirement or development of skills.** This necessitates methods which encourage action, especially preparatory training leading to the performance of a required task.

In order to reach desired goals different strategies and tactics will be required. In terms of the nature of the learning experience involved, these may be summarized as in Fig. 8.3.

THE CHANGE AGENT AS SOCIAL GROUP WORKER

It is in the nature of all change agents' work that they should find themselves very often involved in the organization of group meetings. In order to ensure face-to-face contact, or even to bring people together in one place, they should have a reasonable expectation of the purpose of the meeting and make this clear to participants. The relevant issues are considered in greater depth in Chapter 13.

The way in which really creative group participation tends to develop is outlined briefly in Fig. 8.4.

The following points are all of consequence although no definite order of priority is attached to them since individual circumstances determine their impact in respect of particular cases. However, they arise inevitably in the sequential order outlined in the diagram:

1. **Interest (i):** indicates the initial purpose of coming together on the basis of some perceived commonality of interest, eg in a sport, hobby, pursuit or venture.
2. **Anxiety:** relates to the early awkwardness and embarrassment often felt by people when meeting for the first time. This is a situation in which there is a great deal of 'weighing up' those whom we meet, a point mentioned earlier.
3. **Participation:** While at this stage people have begun to take part it must be understood that they are not necessarily yet collaborating. For example, some people may take part in discussion but only with the intention of killing it.

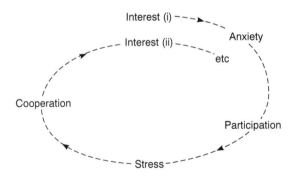

Fig. 8.4 Development of cooperation within a group.

4. **Stress:** This is more serious than the first state of tension where people were more or less searching out a suitable role for themselves. Here they are becoming more deeply involved and there are likely to be personality clashes and disputes about beliefs and values. If this stage is not resolved fairly quickly and harmoniously there is every chance of the group fragmenting or even splitting up completely.

5. **Cooperation:** When this point is reached everyone should be pulling in the same direction. This does not mean that there is unanimity of viewpoint or that reaching consensus will be easy. However it is now possible to achieve some decision-making which should lead on to action.

6. **Interest (ii):** This is the spiral effect, which perhaps is now becoming as familiar to you as the former linear presentation of relationships. The act of working together to achieve some objective, however limited in scope, nearly always leads to greater collaboration and the development of additional or extended interests for even further collaboration.

In a social context such as that which we have just examined, the activities of the change agent are different from those of the opinion leader whose role we are to examine next. Change agents, unlike opinion leaders, are seldom members of the community in which they work. They are also little known in their own right as individuals. Their own opinions are not necessarily those which they attempt to propagate since their primary obligation is to further the interests of their agency or organization. They may, in fact, experience some role conflict as they try to achieve compatibility between their clients' wishes and those of their employers. Their own self-concept often requires redefinition if only because their reference group can be far removed from that of their clients. They are required in all circumstances, whatever the difficulties, to try to achieve results whereas an opinion leader may be indifferent or even unaware of the effect, if any, which his/her influence or presence may have.

Bearing in mind these brief comments it can be accepted that group work is an essential method for change agents as they do not necessarily have any more success than anyone else when using the direct approach with individuals. This has been referred to in the previous chapter as the hypodermic needle approach. The professional change agent benefits more than most from the trickle-down process and consequently is very disposed to employ the opinion leader whenever an opportunity presents itself. How such leaders may be identified and how they may best be used is examined in the next chapter.

SUMMARY

People who exert an influence on others so as to try to bring about change in those other people and/or their circumstances are generally described as change agents. Their influence is exercised on the basis of persuasion and can be directed towards either or both of two objectives, namely to promote what is believed to be desirable and/or to discourage what is not considered worthwhile. Unlike opinion leaders change agents are professionals whose task it is to bring about change. They are usually employed as teachers, consultants, doctors, social workers, managers and in similar posts which operate on a basis of ethics and the maintenance of standards of professional conduct. While some agents deal with individuals when necessary the general nature of their work often produces the best results with groups. In order to be most effective in such social situations the agent normally would try to work in collaboration with known opinion leaders.

REFLECTION

Because the term 'change agent' is not familiar to many people, including those who actually operate in this capacity, it is necessary to look very carefully at the basic points which have been put forward here to identify the nature of the post and the post-holder. Review the definition, consider the professional dimension of the work, and reflect on the ambiguity of serving the interests of an employer and/or governing body while at the same time trying to respond honestly and objectively to individual and group needs. Examine the effectiveness of various methods of communication, the dynamics of group decision-making, the sort of qualities necessary for holders of such posts and the nature of the training which they presently receive. This is a big topic. It requires time for consideration and contemplation.

APPLICATION

Imagine that you have been asked to advise a small manufacturing firm which has just recently been formed by a few working partners. These partners are the entire workforce at present and are not making a great success of selling a common garden implement which ought to have had a reasonable market. However they have ideas for producing another product, not currently available, which they believe will prove to be more attractive. They would, however, require a bank loan to finance the production.

Consider carefully which technical and human factors would be relevant and important enough to draw to the attention of the partners.

RECOMMENDED FURTHER READING

There are several books which would be helpful here although very few of them use the term 'change agent'. It is necessary to know what kind of information each can offer towards a better understanding of a complex role relationship so be selective in reading any of these texts as there is some profound material in each. A glance through the index of any of them will indicate which pages are likely to be most useful to you.

Cummings, Julian (1989) *Sales Promotion*, Kogan Page, London.

Loomis, Charles P. and Beegle, J. Allan (1957) *Rural Sociology – the Strategy of Change*, Prentice-Hall, Englewood Cliffs, N.J.

Packard, Vance (1957) *The Hidden Persuaders*, Penguin Books, Harmondsworth.

All will prove useful in respect of reference material.

Opinion leaders 9

Opinion leaders are members . . . who influence other members.

Van den Ban and Hawkins (1985)

Opinion leadership resides to some extent in all group members.

Robertson (1971)

The question is whether there are certain leaders who can be identified.

S. H. Britt (1970)

In this chapter we examine the influence on other people's decision-making which can be exerted by opinion leaders. This may take the form of intentional assistance, guidance and example or it may be wholly unintentional to the extent that it is unknown even to the person whose influence is having an impact on others. Methods of identification of opinion leaders are explained.

Objectives
After reading this chapter you should be able to:

- outline the principal characteristics of opinion leaders;
- describe one method of identifying such individuals;
- construct a simple sociogram to show the leadership situation in a human group.

THE PROCESS OF INNOVATION

Before considering the nature of opinion leadership and the role of the typical opinion leader it is necessary to reflect on the circumstances which can give rise to opportunities for influencing others, either deliberately or unintentionally.

Previously we have examined briefly two different but very closely related processes in connection with the spread of new ideas. **Adoption**, it was said, refers to individual decision-making with regard to the acceptance of new things; **diffusion**, as a related process, concerns social interaction in 'passing on' these accepted ideas. In practice there is often advantage in dealing with issues of innovation as though adoption and diffusion together constituted a single, or at least a combined, action which could be considered as one integrated process of innovation.

One way of relating this to human problem solving, decision-making, need reduction and commitment to action of various kinds is to utilize the concept of **progressiveness** in respect of which I published (in 1969) the original methodology for computing a reliable and predictive index. Progressiveness is probably best thought of as a predisposition to be innovative. In other words it is an attitude of mind or mental 'set' which enables individuals to be open-minded with regard to new things. While not necessarily being impressed by novelty they do not reject novel things as a matter of course but examine any innovation to determine whether, for them at least, there might be merit in adoption.

The encouragement of progressiveness in individuals and the development of suitable personal attributes can often be assisted by a number of readily available means. Essentially these are all related to different communication techniques, not only in respect of mass media but also in relation to those other approaches which support and enhance personal interaction. As indicated in Chapter 7 there are many models which have attempted to demonstrate possible communication systems. The two which have implications for opinion leadership are the hypodermic needle model and the two-step flow hypothesis, both of which have already been illustrated. We should regard the latter as being of major importance since opinion leaders play a significant role in activating **diffusion networks**.

Diffusion networks comprise an interlinked series of communication channels or routes by which information is transmitted throughout any social system. They demonstrate the universality of a stepped flow of communication which can be observed in practice to operate from any source which functions via mass media channels. What happens is that information passes, in the first instance, to particular opinion leaders who, in turn, pass it on to certain of their followers. This process is actually much more understandable and acceptable than earlier theoretical assumptions about the so-called hypodermic needle model. This, you may remember, suggested that the mass media made direct impact on individuals to the extent that it could have more influence on the supposedly 'disconnected' members of mass audiences than the individuals comprising such audiences could have on each other.

It is now fairly obvious that in many everyday situations information pursues not only a two-step flow but very often follows a multi-stage journey, with quite a number of steps in some linkages between originator and eventual receiver. In nearly all instances of any process of diffusion the opinion leader appears as a vital contributor. This is especially so in respect of influencing individual decision-making concerning the adoption of innovations. Figure 9.1 demonstrates in simple terms the possible kinds of linkage which may result.

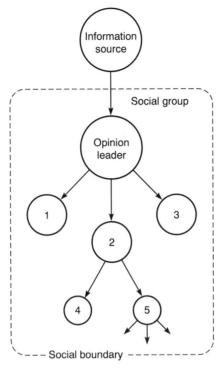

Fig. 9.1   The influence of the opinion leader.

THE CHANGE AGENT AND THE OPINION LEADER

We have already had a brief look at the work and aims of the change agent. It is worthwhile to reflect that change agents are normally **reactive**, ie they usually respond to expressed or implied wants in any given situation whilst having quietly encouraged and supported the identification of a suitable need. However there are many situations in developing countries or evolving economic circumstances when they are involved unashamedly **proactively** in openly stimulating and even (against all the rules) occasionally initiating change. For both conditions, of course, forward planning is essential if desired goals are to be achieved. Planning identifies:

- Group
- Objectives
- Message
- Methods
- Organization.

There must be information about:

1. the target group to be helped, to what extent, by whom and using what means;

2. the nature of the goal to be pursued, its desirability and feasibility;
3. the actual message to be transmitted, to whom, when, where and how;
4. the methods to be employed for adequate reception and understanding;
5. the organization of activities into a flow chart or time scale.

This involves getting appropriate details from others, and those who are potential 'influentials' or opinion leaders in the situation are in privileged positions. They can not only assist in the process of change but are often able to offer information about the factors involved. These might typically concern, for example:

- the overall goals of the community or organization;
- the target group most open to approach and persuasion;
- alternative courses of action open to the group;
- the possible consequences of each choice;
- the media which could be used to best effect in order to achieve the desired results;
- additional resources, especially those available locally.

The kind of decision made about any one of these factors must have implications for consideration of the others. In many community situations it is now widely accepted that anyone operating in the capacity of change agent can gain increased influence by working closely with opinion leaders. What is not always understood is the means of identification of such people and the emergence or creation of appropriate roles both for the change agent and for the opinion leaders themselves.

At an earlier stage we examined the fundamental roles of the change agent, identifying them as successively an observer, a strategist, a tactician and a stimulator. The value of the opinion leader tends to vary in relation to each of these roles but there is a possible input to all of them. Initially the opinion leader assists the change agent's insight into group relations by complementing those things which cannot be observed in practice. In the strategic and tactical stages he or she can participate in the necessary planning which could benefit by his/her (often unique) insight into the local machinations and politics which govern individual public behaviour. At the level of stimulation by the change agent the knowledgeable opinion leader often suggests closer examination of certain proposals about to be put before colleagues, to see precisely what benefit is likely to be derived from them.

This is especially true in a context which favours innovation and where cooperation of local people with a change agent may reasonably be expected. Opinion leaders, however, may lose their influence if they move around too quickly and change agents will find it essential to consider carefully the leadership pattern of a community before deciding how best to make use of the potential opinion leadership structure within it. One innovative method of doing so is by the construction of **sociograms**.

This term means that simple diagrams based on patterns of social inter-action are drawn. These are then examined to identify what message they may hold. The procedure is covered in more detail later in this chapter since it is relevant, not only to the identification of opinion leaders, but also to analysis of group interaction.

At this point we need to consider what meaning might be attached to the term **opinion leader** and what influence opinion leaders generally might be able to exert in an appropriate context.

THE CONCEPT OF OPINION LEADERSHIP

Leadership concerns action more than position. The opinion leader, or **influential**, is normally identified as someone from whom others seek information or advice. But the experience of many observers over the years in a wide range of countries has demonstrated that this can be too restrictive a concept. It may also, in practice, be misleading because at least two categories of influential person may be identified. The first type consists of those who know that their services are being sought and who respond to this situation. But there is a second type, the informal leaders, who exert influence without even being aware that they have been chosen by others to act in this role. In some situations they may not be trying consciously to influence others at all, and indeed, may not wish to do so. However, their position in society, community, organization or group often determines such things for them.

For such individuals a typical communication sequence (in the context of previous indications such as those in Fig. 9.1), would be of the following order:

Innovation
↓
Change agent
↓
Innovator
↓
Opinion leader
↓
Rest of the group, organization
or community.

In practice it is unlikely that one person will act as opinion leader for the whole of a large group or community. It is also unlikely that any person would have worthwhile influence over an extensive range of areas and topics, although this does happen on occasion, particularly in developing countries of the world. The most frequent situation is that each influential person acts as leader for a small cohort of followers who are themselves leaders of other groups which comprise the larger entity. This set-up was illustrated earlier in Fig. 7.4. Another variant of this situation would be that more than one opinion leader would be operating over roughly the same range of peers but each would have a particular (perhaps highly specialized) contribution to make. It is relatively uncommon for any one person to be seen as influential in respect of more than a few specialized issues or activities dependent on technical knowledge. It is in the most modern technologically dominated western countries that there appears to be the most widespread recognition and appreciation of specialist qualifications and/or experience.

CHARACTERISTICS OF OPINION LEADERS

All attributes of opinion leadership are relative. (You will no doubt remember that all attributes of the different classes of adopters were also relative.) A fairly venturesome person in a backward community might be thought of as laggard in a more progressive context. Any criteria relating to opinion leaders are not much use when specified in general terms but acquire real meaning when considered relative to the characteristics of their followers. It is this comparison which provides the basis for their identification as well as being the foundation of their influence in any particular social context. In general terms the relevant factors in defining opinion leaders is that they:

- have greater exposure to the mass media. Basically they read more, and more widely, than their contemporaries. They listen to a fairly broad range of broadcast material and watch a selective variety of television programmes including many of the educational series as well as current affairs;
- are somewhat cosmopolitan in outlook. This means that they are less parochial in many ways than most of their friends and colleagues, not only because of their attitude towards the media but also because they take the opportunity to travel further afield than many of their companions;
- have greater contact with official change agents than most of their friends, neighbours or colleagues. Their way of life often brings them into regular contact with politicians, teachers, clergy and others to a greater extent than the rest of their social set and they also tend to receive information from such sources more or less as a matter of course;
- enjoy a higher degree of social participation than would be considered normal in relation to the other facets of their lifestyle. There are few social gatherings, formal or informal, in which they do not participate and consequently they are known to virtually everyone in their particular environment, even if they do not have any more in-depth social relationships than anyone else;
- are accorded social status above the average. Invariably they are people who are highly thought of and whose identified position in society, while it might be difficult to define, is respected. This is largely because they are constantly seen to engage in socially ac-

ceptable behaviour and their perceived standards in relation to cultural beliefs and conduct meet with general approval;

- are, comparatively speaking, more innovative than average. However, this might be true only in respect of certain matters (as was the case with the innovators who were discussed earlier). Although there can be a certain blurring of identity with that of the typical innovator, the opinion leader is by no means a true innovator because he/she is never seen to be venturesome enough to be the first to try anything new. Their unique quality proceeds from a disposition to be relatively early to do so, provided that the new idea appears to have merit. It is this slight delay in responding to change which enhances the credibility of opinion leaders as people who pass considered judgement on what might or might not be acceptable and who, in this way, validate what has first found favour with them.

To briefly summarize the *personal* attributes of typical opinion leaders it could be said that generally they:

- adopt many innovations earlier than contemporaries but are very rarely first to adopt anything;
- are well educated and of sound financial position. As with the innovator this enables a certain degree of risk-taking and also supports a relative amount of independence in decision-making;
- lead active social lives and have many contacts outside their immediate surroundings. For most influentials the emphasis is on contacts rather than friends or even colleagues. Having a wide range of acquaintances appears to contribute in great measure to the favourable regard in which such persons are held;
- have a special interest in their subject area. The existence of a demonstrable interest, important though it is, does not necessarily imply any personal expertise although related specialized knowledge is often the case. What characterizes these individuals is the ability to get reliable sound comment or advice readily, and if need be quickly, from others who have the reputation of being experts.

Society by its nature can be considered as being stratified into layers determined roughly by a mixture of social and economic factors. Each particular social stratum or layer can, and usually does, have its own type of opinion leaders, not all of whom necessarily operate in face-to-face situations. They may be influential in only some particular factual matters but can also exert a much wider social influence related to the class structure. However, people who are opinion leaders about specific issues in any setting may also be opinion leaders in a wider context, particularly in traditional societies. What matters to many change agents who wish to involve opinion leaders in their endeavours to promote change in under-developed regions of the world is how to identify such people. Community activists and commercial promoters likewise often wonder whom to approach and how. While it cannot always be done with absolute certainty there are techniques for identifying opinion leaders in any context with a high probability of being right and we will now look at the methods of doing this. What to do when they are found is, of course, a matter for further consideration.

IDENTIFYING OPINION LEADERS

Leadership of any sort derives from power and this, in essence, is simply the ability to influence people. Authority is the right to exercise this power and the two terms are often confused because in practice authority is often acquired by the mere exercise of power itself. The particular characteristic of opinion leadership is that whatever power and authority it may have in any given situation is achieved and exerted *informally*. Since it rests more on subjective judgement than on strictly assessable attainment the identification process focuses on social criteria appropriate to the task in hand. To identify a good committee member, for example, would be a different matter from being sure of a good leader of a design team – but the approach to gathering information would be the same. Where it is not based entirely on intuition, there are three main methods which have been utilized in communication research to identify and measure the strength of opinion leadership:

1. sociometric methods
2. self-designating techniques
3. informants' ratings.

While the relative strength of influence is vital in some contexts the appropriate full analysis requires mathematical skills which are irrelevant to the purpose of this book. Here we need only look at this basic approach to identification. Each method has particular strengths and weaknesses – but all work! The major differences between each method are outlined below.

Sociometric methods

Using the sociometric approach respondents are questioned as to whom they have asked (or would ask) for advice or information regarding certain topics. As a general rule this approach needs a suitable environment where the nature of the matter being enquired into is not seen as threatening and respondents see no harm in answering questions even if the purpose is unclear. Naturally they are not told that it is an exercise to identify power leaders or the like.

Typically a respondent would be asked to answer a question such as 'If you had a problem with (something specified), who would you be likely to turn to for advice?' Perhaps the question would be even more factual, for example by asking 'Who *have* you recently asked for help or advice?' (in relation to a specified problem). For the most part there is no reason to distrust the responses received using this approach since there is no obligation for the respondent to nominate anyone. Indeed, there may well be some reluctance on the part of the respondent to acknowledge that it was necessary to seek assistance at all. There is, therefore, at least a superficial plausibility in this approach since it depends on the views of the followers, who are not likely to exaggerate the numbers of people they regard as more knowledgeable or capable than themselves.

In addition to finding out several nominees who are useful sources of advice and assistance it is possible to devise simple systems for allocating each a score. These scores can then be aggregated or processed so that totals may be used to designate the 'most useful' person as an opinion leader for certain purposes. In general this approach has proved to be very useful in many North American communities outside of the major conurbations.

Self-designating techniques

The self-designating technique is exactly that. People are asked to identify themselves as being approached by others for guidance or assistance in respect of some difficulty. With any self-designating technique there is, of course, a dependence on the accuracy of the reporting of any self-image. This cannot always be taken at its face value in respect of nature, frequency or range of assistance available and therefore may be open to criticism on conceptual grounds. However, as a means of verification, it is usually possible to check (tactfully and cautiously!) with those alleged to have received help and the method is, in any case, widely used in circumstances where it is particularly appropriate. Generally speaking this would include all those situations where individuals' perception of their possible influence is likely to govern their behaviour.

A person who feels able to offer an informed comment on a particular topic is usually unable to resist the temptation to do so. As was mentioned in an earlier chapter we all perceive the world uniquely and the way in which we picture ourselves will therefore cause us to try to behave in a manner which reinforces our self-image. If we think that we have leadership qualities (and who doesn't) we will make some effort to try to live up to this image by attempting to influence others at appropriate times and in those circumstances where we feel reasonably secure enough to do so. I have used this approach with advantage in a wide range of European countries. You can learn a lot about influential people by this means!

Informants' ratings

With informants' ratings we are again depending on the views of others but in this case we are asking people who might be expected to have additional information or situational insight so that their views represent more than just an opinion or a guess. Informants' ratings tend normally to be sought from a collection of judges who are in a position to be particularly knowledgeable about patterns of influence which come within their jurisdiction. They do not necessarily act as a panel on such matters and it is not even necessary that each knows who else is being consulted. Indeed there is merit in not advertising the fact that other opinions are being sought at all – although there is no necessity to maintain secrecy here, only confidentiality.

In community affairs, for example, such a group could include teachers, clergy, police, doctors, welfare workers or other suitable people. If operating as a convened panel (and in suitable circumstances this is an excellent method of ensuring cross-matching and exchange of information about potential leaders) they can compare notes and views. This ought to highlight those individuals known to them who actually have, or are most likely to hold, sway in respect of certain locations, specific affairs, or at particular times. I have found that this technique has worked extremely well in a number of African rural developmental projects.

All these methods have been tested widely and there are many instances where they have proved invaluable, particularly to extension agents in Third World countries and youth workers in the inner urban areas of some European cities. The method most likely to be used in any given circumstance is largely determined by convenience rather than by any special procedural or diagnostic merit. There are advantages to change agents (such as teachers, social workers, clergy, etc) in identifying specific peer-leadership of this kind and instead of offering resistance or attempting to compete with such leadership potential they would, instead, find it worthwhile to search for it. The opinion leader can be of particular assistance in helping those whose job it is to assist others in problem-solving. They are in a position to know, better than most, that the individual is not only seeking a solution, but an acceptable solution. The opinion leader can help to make it so!

THE OPINION LEADER IN OPERATION

Those who are able and willing to help others with their problems can often become opinion leaders in that particular location, organizational setting or group. In addition, non-verbal communication can be very important in a peer group situation and this allows a great deal of influence to be exercised, perhaps unwittingly, by the group opinion leader merely behaving in such a way as to set an example. However in vocational situations it is, for the most part, those who are reasonably well informed about relevant issues who tend to become opinion leaders. The degree to which individuals share certain characteristics such as education, income and so on tends to make them more compatible with (and acceptable to) each other and it is when this happens that communication networks can be established. The stronger the internal linkage within a particular setting the more difficult it may be to establish and maintain cross-border linkages between different settings. This is true not only of the social environment but also of commercial enterprises in the business world. The situation is little different from the creation of team spirit or community identity dealt with in an earlier chapter. The greater the creative achievement in this respect the easier it is to communicate within the system but the more difficult it becomes between systems. This is a point which merits a great deal more attention than it has ever received but this is not the place to expand upon it.

While there are many different types of opinion leader all tend to fulfil at least some of the following functions:

- they pass on information;
- they interpret communications;
- they legitimize change;
- they affect group norms.

1. **Passing on information from outside the group.** To some extent, especially in the commercial, educational and political world the opinion leader also operates as a gatekeeper, ie he or she filters out information which for personal or professional reasons he or she does not wish to be passed on. This is considered again in Chapter 13.

2. **Interpreting outside information on the basis of personal experiences and opinions.** The opinion leader may, of course, misinterpret messages from others so that a highly personal meaning may be given which results in some distortion of communication. This may not be wilful but may arise from the problems which we all experience from time to time in paraphrasing the ideas or words of others.

3. **Legitimizing or disapproving of change that others may want.** This aspect of the opinion leader's role is not always appreciated or even understood. By word of mouth and (perhaps even more importantly) by personal acceptance or rejection of certain changes the opinion leader can assist or obstruct the aspirations of others. Some opinion leaders are more influential early in an adoption process when initial interest can either be fostered or frustrated. Others will have more influence later as the time for individual decision-making draws closer.

4. **Influencing change in some of the group norms.** Any influence eventually works its way through to the modification of standards of normality in any particular social grouping. The opinion leader, in the course of time, can have quite a significant influence on the ideas of others and therefore alter their views of what is to be accepted as normal in their particular context.

Because of the dimensions of peer group communication it is commonplace for opinion leaders to be like their contemporaries in social status, size of enterprise, education, and age. They tend, however, to be sufficiently different in other respects so as to be able to provide fresh information on a basis of credibility and have its significance and relevance discussed by those whom it might concern and who are still able to concede that they might have something new to learn.

SOCIOGRAMS IN LEADERSHIP ANALYSIS

There is little that can be displayed diagrammatically that cannot also be explained in words but there are occasions when, as the old saying has it, a picture is worth a thousand words. The advantage of examining social situations in graphical form is that this often offers global overviews which might otherwise go unnoticed. Also, especially in respect of interpersonal communication, it often displays significant relationships which would not otherwise be immediately obvious. That is why the sociometric approach deserves consideration. This concerns patterns of human relationships which depend upon selection or rejection. In other words on the exercise of personal choice.

Consider a simple social group consisting of seven people. Suppose that we wish to display a situation where each individual exercises one choice in respect of another person. By 'choice' we could mean 'likes' or 'talks to' or 'moves towards' or anything else which indicates attraction, rejection or indifference. Look at the following description of a situation.

> Jack and Tom choose one another. They also choose Bob. Bob rejects Tom and is indifferent to Jack. Bob and Maude choose each other. Maude and Anne reject one another but Anne chooses Bob although this choice is not reciprocated. Alex neither chooses nor is chosen. Linda chooses Bob but gets no response.

There is no way in which this could be considered a typical group, nor could this brief account of one set of choices be other than highly artificial, improbable and comparatively meaningless. It is presented only by way of illustration of a technique. However, it will serve to illustrate the basic principle of a sociogram which gains favour when you realize just how difficult it is to recall accurately (or even at all!) information such as that which was given above. It is also impossible for most people, even if they could remember all the details, to disentangle the nature of the interrelationships from a written description of this sort. In comparison with this it is relatively simple to display clearly all the relevant features using only a few simple symbols. The sociogram in Fig. 9.2 shows how.

For example, A and B represent people and the line shows direction of choice, a solid line being positive, a dotted one negative, the absence of any line indicating neutrality or indifference. Where gender is important males are indicated by $\triangle$ and females by $\bigcirc$. The extent of the interaction or number of interactions could be shown by an increased number of lines or by additional cross-hatching on them (there is no universal convention in this connection). Readers who might wish to know more about sociometric techniques (which comprise much more than the graphical representations known as sociograms) are recommended to read Moreno's original book which also includes psychotherapy and sociodrama. Sociograms are used in the first instance for brevity and clarity of recording but subsequently they can form a powerful analytical tool for anyone involved in group work of any kind.

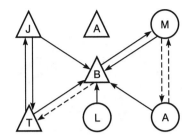

Fig. 9.2   Sociogram of a small group.

SUMMARY

The opinion leader is an influential person in any social context whether it be the office, factory, church, community or commercial undertaking. While opinion leaders influence the thoughts and actions of their acquaintances they do not all mean to do so. Many are not even aware of their influence. They may be identified by several different means, all of which are effective. They are of assistance to change agents in helping to bring about desired alterations, and elementary sociograms may serve to indicate leadership potential in those not already known to exert influence in a particular context.

REFLECTION

Reflect on the nature of the relationship between the innovator, the opinion leader and the change agent. While all three share certain characteristics and have some qualities which tend, on occasion, to blur the boundaries of their influence, all have quite specific functions and abilities to persuade others to change. List these for each and ensure that you can see the relevance and importance of the differences.

APPLICATIONS

Part A

There always have been and there always will be men and women who are much more influential than others.

S. H. Britt (1970)

In the light of your reading to date, your own experience, and your personal beliefs discuss this statement. In what kind of situations is it likely to be true? What are the social and economic consequences of accepting such a perspective?

Part B

Consider the sociogram in Fig. 9.3. It depicts a small discussion group of five people in action. They are addressing the topic which is central to the diagram.

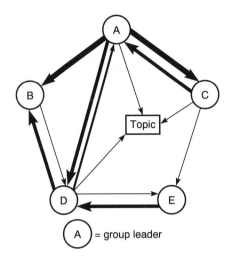

Fig. 9.3

Do you think that the discussion group leader is doing a good job? Do you think that the pattern of interaction is satisfactory, bearing in mind the purpose of the meeting?

Draw an indication of the pattern of interaction which you would have expected here and explain any differences from that shown above. (If you ever have to take charge of even a small group of people for any purpose you will – on some occasion – be glad to recall this useful technique. It can be an aid to resolving some difficulty or avoiding a problem based on interpersonal relationships.)

RECOMMENDED FURTHER READING

In respect of opinion leadership there are several useful texts available, although some of these have restricted interest, for example in the purchasing of new products. The following might be worth consulting if available on loan from a library. If you see the same title being listed for more than one chapter it is simply because some books offer material across several different topics.

Moreno, J.L. (1953) *Who Shall Survive? Foundations of Sociometry, Group Psychotherapy and Sociodrama*, Beacon House, New York.
    The original work on sociometry. There have been very few works since then and the subject does not seem to have attracted much attention, even today. This book is not light reading!
Robertson, Thomas S. (1971) *Innovative Behaviour and Communication*, Holt Rinehart and Winston, New York.
    This book offers some succint comments on several aspects of opinion leadership.

Rogers, Everett M. (1960) *Social Change in Rural Society*, Appleton-Century-Crofts, New York.

A little bit dated now and focusing largely on the American agricultural community. Not actually a great deal to say directly about opinion leadership but what it does say is useful. Don't forget the other books by Rogers!

Spence, W.R. (1984) *Sociometric Techniques*, University of Ulster, Jordanstown.

Almost certainly the only book of its kind on sociometric techniques but it is currently out of print.

Other authors and titles will be found in the general index at the back of the book but there are no requirements at this stage for further reading in connection with this chapter.

Innovative ideas 10

Ideas shape the course of history.

J. M. Keynes (1949)

One of the greatest pains to human nature is the pain of
a new idea.

Bagehot (1873)

Innovation is both conceptual and perceptual.

Drucker (1986)

There is one thing stronger than all the armies in the
world: and that is an idea whose time has come.

Victor Hugo (1875)

The line which divides ideas from practices and practices from
products is not an easy one to draw since there is often an inter-
mingling and, indeed, a fairly natural progression from one to the
other. This chapter concentrates on examining examples of what
may be classified as definite 'ideas' in the sense that each concept
itself could reasonably be regarded as being of fundamental significance apart from any resulting outcome in the form of practice
or product.

Objectives
After reading this chapter you should be able to:

- outline briefly the features of any idea which has been perceived
  as innovative;
- indicate any individual or social consequences which resulted
  from the acceptance of that idea;
- specify some criteria for assessing the 'newness' of any idea in
  respect of its content, presentation and/or consequences.

THE NATURE OF IDEAS

In any situation where we intend to examine something critically we
normally should try to ensure that our efforts are concentrated on such
aspects as:

1. what we can actually observe or in some way perceive by means of
   our normal senses;

2. what we can capture in reasonable permanent form, preferably in writing or by visual means such as video, photography or audio recording;
3. what we can subsequently analyse by applying statistical and other investigative techniques.

This approach hardly needs any defence because there is not much point in trying to examine something which cannot be perceived by ourselves and others by means of our senses. There is equally little benefit in dealing with something which, though it can be perceived personally by us, cannot be recorded in some way for others also to consider. And of course the whole object of obtaining information is that it should be relevant to the purpose for which we need it. In other words it must be appropriate (indeed essential) to the investigation and therefore be capable of being inspected, interpreted and analysed so that we may both draw justifiable conclusions from it *and be able to test it.*

But the mental process of conceptualization, ie the formation of ideas, makes it rather difficult to present innovative concepts as case studies. By their very nature ideas exist inside the heads of individuals and as such cannot be readily scrutinized by outsiders. However if we accept that all innovations start in the human mind as ideas then it might be helpful to look at them from the perspective of their practical consequences. Observations of outcome can still shed valuable light on the dimensions of innovation in the abstract sense. Having said that, the instances chosen here are not intended to be a thumbnail sketch of 'great ideas which changed the world' or anything like it. The few examples are selected principally to illustrate how the range of everyday experience which we all possess can provide suitable material to show how the establishment of a theoretical concept can lead to changes in the way in which we deal mentally with physical or 'real' situations.

Although we may not know precisely what ideas certain people have had we can still have access to what they said or wrote about them. We can also examine the possible impact which those ideas have had on others and try to explore the consequences in terms of, for instance, social change. There are plenty of ideas which have found some form of practical expression. An example might be the concept of collective bargaining as an alternative to individual negotiation of wages and working conditions which underlies the formation of the trade unions. In another example the notion of 'flexi-hours' has produced a situation where employees, particularly office workers doing fairly routine jobs, can come into their place of employment at almost whatever time best suits them provided that they actually work the full number of hours required. In a somewhat different context a curiosity on the part of many people about what the British Parliament actually did, as distinct from what it was reported as doing, has led to live broadcasting on the television of the House of Commons at Westminster, following tentative showings of the more sedate House of Lords in session. At a more bizarre level the problem of what to do with a glue which would not stick eventually led to an idea which resulted in 3M producing their commercially successful and highly popular yellow *Post-it* notes.

It could be argued, of course, that some of these outcomes are, in reality, practices. But for the most part these do not constitute practices in the sense in which the term is used in the next chapter. In Chapter 11 it largely indicates a widespread acceptance of changed, indeed improved, methods of operation. Changes in practice often refer to radical alteration in the way a community, profession or occupation operates when compared to the previous situation. The following examples, therefore, are offered as instances where ideas might reasonably be considered more innovative than the practices or products which subsequently followed from them. In some of the cases the idea which was given practical effect did not necessarily have any immediate or direct influence on the behaviour of others. A cultural time-lag occurred. At a later stage of the book we might find it worthwhile to consider why this should have been so.

The ideas selected for brief examination in this chapter relate to issues of widely differing types in various countries at different times and therefore the characteristic parameters of each are outlined in order to provide indicators for reflection.

CONCEPT: PREPAYMENT OF MAIL

Aim: Improvement of Postal Services
Location: England
Time: 1836

Those of us today who are the recipients of quantities of uninvited and largely unwanted advertising and sales literature through the post (the so-called 'junk mail') have great reason to be thankful to Sir Rowland Hill for his revolutionary view, early in the last century, as to how mail services could be improved and should be paid for. Had it not been for his concept of prepayment by the sender at a standard rate of only one penny for each item of mail we could be faced with unacceptably large bills for postal deliveries of material which, often enough, we neither expect nor want.

Hill did not invent anything. Nor did he create a postal service. In one form or another such a service has existed for at least a couple of thousand years in those parts of the world where communication was essential in respect of pursuing a war or administering a subject territory. Couriers have long carried the written instructions of kings and emperors to their subjects, or at least to the officials in charge of those subjects, on occasions when something of great moment was afoot. The epistles of Paul to the early churches are examples of such early written communications. However what Hill did was to put a great deal of written correspondence within the reach of every citizen at a very reasonable cost.

Until his idea of prepayment was formulated all mail had to be paid for by the recipient on acceptance. The problems involved in the attempted delivery, against appropriate payment, to suspicious or impecunious addressess need no description. The amount to be charged depended on the weight of the item and the distance over which it had been carried and this could be really expensive. Despite prepayment the latter two considerations still apply today in respect of certain items such as parcels sent, for instance, by airmail. In the early 1800s, however, it was a slow and costly business to engage in correspondence, with the result that only items of great importance could be dealt with economically in this way. It was necessary to go to a post office (often a great distance as there were not too many) in order to have each particular missive weighed and costed. There was no guarantee that it would, of course, eventually be accepted by the addressee who might well be reluctant or unable to pay for something which he/she might not wish to have and which he/she could not, obviously, read beforehand in order to ascertain its merit. The average postal item cost what a skilled workman would take several days to earn so this issue was of real importance. By reducing the cost to only a penny, an affordable sum (though still an hour's wages for most working people) the possibility of the mail service being used for at least some important domestic correspondence and routine business items became a more distinct possibility. Indeed it was the almost immediate increase in the postal volume (particularly from the commercial firms) which resulted from Hill's innovation that enabled the operation to survive during the initial period. Thereafter the subsequent operation of the service made great profits.

The implications went far beyond making such a facility available to those who previously could not have afforded it. It introduced a new concept for the operators of international postal services. In effect the country which originated the mail item in each instance kept the amount prepaid by the sender. The addressee country, on the other hand, which was not going to collect from the addressee on delivery often had the bulk of the delivery problem for no obvious financial return. How was this to be dealt with? As it happened, again the sheer volume of the postal items came to the rescue. Eventually the setting up of the Universal Postal Union regularized modes of financing various services that in the interim had operated on a kind of 'swings and roundabouts' principle. This was that everyone got roughly a fair enough share of the revenue by participating on the basis of prepayment for mail originating in their own country but going elsewhere, and undertaking free delivery in their own country for others in respect of the international mail which they received.

In terms of a revolutionary concept I feel that it would be hard enough today to get any government anywhere in the world to take seriously a proposal of similar kind were it to be made in respect of some other area of service where cash on the nail has, up to now, been the accepted practice. Prepayment of mail at a uniform nominal rate was one of the truly great innovative ideas.

CONCEPT: CONSUMER SEGMENTATION

Aim: Identification of a Niche Market
Location: Detroit, Michigan, USA
Time: 1957

In the course of the decade immediately following the Second World War the Ford Motor Company in the United States of America had built itself up to be a serious competitor to other car manufacturers in three of the four accepted market subdivisions. These were the low, lower-middle and upper segments. Only in the upper-middle range did they not have a vehicle which could offer competition with the models of other manufacturers. This was a vital deficiency because in the post-war years this sector was identified as being the fastest growing part of the entire car production outlet in North America. The company accordingly went to great lengths to ensure that they could produce an absolute winner for this particular corner of the market. They tried to take into account every conceivable factor which might influence potential customers and add to car sales appeal.

The result, eventually, was one of the most carefully researched and thoroughly designed cars in the world. It was to be known as the *Ford Edsel*, and was produced in 1957 after many years of tremendously intensive planning, design and production quality control. Extensive market research had influenced the product by taking account of customer preferences; the car was produced to offer a vehicle to a market segment of customers for whom there would be no comparable competitive car available from other suppliers; and the finished standard of the product reflected the outcome of the most meticulous standards of quality control. In addition it was introduced skilfully to a so-called ready market. And it was a complete flop!

What went wrong? Sometimes the unpredictable fickleness of the potential purchaser is blamed for such failures. Alternatively the sales personnel or advertising could have been held to have in some way let the side down. Something more fundamental, it seemed, had gone wrong here. What Ford management did in the circumstances was remarkable and constitutes one of the really great innovative approaches of our industrial age. They decided to find out what factors had been over-looked, misinterpreted or wrongly judged. This was not market research as it is traditionally defined. It was *pure* research in that it was fully investigative and without prior assumptions as to what reasons under-pinned the abysmal failure of what ought to have been the success story of the century. The main finding was absolutely devastating. It showed that the market was, for all practical purposes, no longer segmented – as had been categorized since the 1920s – by income groups into low, lower-middle, upper-middle and upper 'classes' but was now more oper-ationally segmented on a basis of lifestyle criteria. These criteria were judgmental and largely non-quantifiable; indeed the meaning of the term 'lifestyle' has often been queried without there being any agreement as to specificity of meaning. But using the insight gained by the investigation

Ford went on to produce, in the 1960s, the *Mustang* and, above all, the *Thunderbird* which became the greatest success story of any of their cars since Henry Ford introduced the *Model T* in 1908.

The socio-economic criteria identified by Ford, and since developed by others, are widely used today in targeting potential customers for maildrops particularly in connection with mail order promotions or direct sales. Instead of postal districts or zip codes being used to identify addresses on a distributor's area map, for example, it would be more common to see a particular road or neighbourhood categorized as 'Volvos and golf clubs' or 'Gin and tonic set'! The idea that market segmentation could change and that occasional redefinition was required constituted the innovative idea which has since underpinned all the really successful output of manufacturing production throughout the world.

CONCEPT: NON-CUSTODIAL TREATMENT OF YOUNG OFFENDERS

Aim: Rehabilitation instead of punishment
Location: Limerick, Republic of Ireland
Time: 1978

In a very large housing estate in the city of Limerick in the 1970s there was not only a shortage of recreational and other facilities for young people but also very few jobs for their elders. Unemployment was extremely high at a time when elsewhere the situation was, although poor, not quite so bad. An additional aggravation was the fact that this was the residential sector of a recently constructed industrial estate. Unfortunately for the locals this offered little work opportunity once initial involvement in the construction of the factory buildings had been completed. There was, understandably, poor morale among most of the residents and many of the parents.

In respect of the youngsters, truancy from school was high since there was little inducement to remain in attendance or to try to prepare for non-existent vocational opportunities. Idleness caused a great deal of vandalism and delinquency. Many young people were put at risk simply because there were temptations to which they could succumb in respect of criminal activities or vagrancy. In the past such young people who were in, or were likely to cause, trouble would often have been removed from their homes and lodged in a residential or custodial institution either for their own welfare or for the protection of others.

The idea was put forward in a report on Child Care Services published in 1975 that a programme might be initiated in several localities to discover the needs of deprived young people and try to respond to these. The result was the establishment of what was called a **Neighbourhood Youth Programme** in the Southill area of Limerick in the period between October 1978 and the summer of 1980. I was appointed by the Department of Health in Dublin to be consultant to this project. The aims of the programme were deliberately fairly wide and included expectations that, in a non-prescriptive way:

- individual basic skills would be enhanced or developed in respect of fundamental issues such as personal hygiene, safety and clothes sense;
- that there would be promotion of learning and personal development for each child as an individual and as a member both of a social group and of society at large.

In respect of the first category of aims the attempt was made to promote these by means of learning sessions in 'the Club' as the centre became known in the district. The custom-built centre opened in 1979 and included a multi-purpose room with kitchen alcove, a craft room, two small group rooms, an office and a store room together with toilet and washroom facilities. There was a small staff, including one temporary teacher, who operated a very flexible learning programme which functioned on a basis of rewards and punishments as no other school programme has normally ever dared to do. For example there was a small snooker table which was available for a session to those members who had learned a multiplication table, written a list of spellings, completed an exercise, or satisfied whatever other formal educational requirement had to be met.

The more difficult or complex the task the greater the leisure or recreational reward for accomplishing it. It was a system which did not meet with universal approval, especially amongst some traditionalists. However, it was condoned because there was always the comforting reflection that potential (or actual) troublemakers were at least being kept away from those who might have been adversely influenced by them. Also there was always just the faint possibility that the troublemakers themselves might conceivably eventually be changed by this approach and grow up into better, if not model, citizens!

The second category of aims followed rather logically from this approach and focused on activities which reflected more what the child wished to do than what an adult might want the child to do. But the activity was monitored by staff to ensure the eventual achievement of certain desired aims. For example, in ball games the casual observer might note nothing remarkable in the feverish activity of children pursuing a ball around a playground or sports hall. However this lowest level of involvement was only mere activity. It passed the time pleasantly enough for the participants and kept them occupied and therefore out of trouble. But it was not allowed to last too long. At a somewhat higher level games became more organized and enjoyable by encouraging the development of some skill, the gaining of expertise, learning to play in a particular position for best effect, moving away from individual gratification to becoming a team member, and accepting responsibility for performing a particular task as a member of that team.

At the highest level, for the purposes of this exercise, activity became a vehicle for improving personal interaction, social awareness and civic responsibilities. These were encouraged to emerge from team situations which ensured the acceptance of rules and decisions made by those appointed in authority such as referees – with whose opinions and judgements there was not always universal agreement. This assisted the submergence of some of the wishes of the individual in the reaching, for example, of a collective achievement by the team. The emphasis shifted from the activity in its own right to an analysis by the participants themselves of individual attitudes and behaviour. In this way they could determine the advantages of conforming to social convention and regulation without, naturally, always approving it.

The outcome of the first couple of years was that the numbers of children who were a source of concern or a cause of trouble to other people noticeably diminished and the record of attendances at school increased, while the total of young people falling foul of the law by being delinquent or criminal significantly lessened.

Since then the centre has continued to flourish and today the situation is that the personal aims expressed by the original team of youth workers for the project are still being realized far beyond the original expectations of the planners. The young people are coping more effectively than previously with the personal and social problems which they encounter, they are functioning more adequately and with both confidence and competence, and they are undoubtedly leading happier lives. So are their parents and the other residents of the housing estate! It might be noted that the centres proposed at the same time as Limerick for two other experimental areas did not last very long; indeed one barely got started before running into terminal difficulties. The idea of assisting those in trouble, and especially those who have caused problems for others, to grow up in such a way as to be able to live useful and meaningful lives rather than just being put 'behind bars' is still too novel an idea to have widespread acceptance. This is particularly true if it is likely to involve the expenditure of public funds. But the idea, whilst being innovative, is certainly not impractical and can actually produce worthwhile results when supported by community commitment as this example has demonstrated.

CONCEPT: TECHNOLOGICALLY MEDIATED COMMUNICATION

Aim: Cross-campus communication
Location: Jordanstown, Northern Ireland
Time: 1984

In 1984 the University of Ulster came into existence through the merger of existing colleges, a polytechnic and an earlier established university. In common with other academic institutions formed as a result of enforced merger of existing operations and locations there was a legacy to inherit. As with many relatively large universities throughout the world (and the University of Ulster initially had, and still has, around 13 000 students) its four campuses plus out-centres were widely dispersed throughout Northern Ireland. The problem of inter-campus communication was therefore a fundamental concern right from its inception.

The idea of distance learning was a familiar one, but could its principles be applied to the meaningful linkage of at least four physically separated sites so as not just to maintain but actually to improve educational facilities for both students and staff?

Before the new university came into being there had been a great deal of travel between campuses by planners and academics, a situation which became worse when lectures actually began and coordination of teaching provision became vital. Travel was still essential for the proper discharge of teaching or supervisory duties by many senior staff in different locations. The amount of time taken up in travel (and the financial, not to mention the opportunity, cost) became virtually insupportable. Some innovative and practical approaches were required. Because the ideas had to underpin some practical application the problems were somewhat removed from the traditional 'ivory tower' context and the procedure took the form of two phases of tactical problem solving. First was the consideration of how to reduce time lost in connection with the inevitable committee work involving staff from several campuses. Next came exploration of how to provide teaching simultaneously on more than one campus.

While indicating some differences of approach it was important that neither of these situations in their revised state should require any fundamental change in the practices related to either committee operation or teaching procedures.

1. **Committee work:** Over several years I had conducted personal experiments with both the conference telephone and the telefax machine. The experiences, which were shared with the more progressive members of staff, led to some diminution in the distrust (and lack of funds) with which technologically-mediated communication had at first been viewed. Eventually, officially approved meetings of various university committees, planning groups, working parties and departmental boards were held with definite economic benefit by way of reduced cost and, in addition, with the establishment and maintenance of satisfactory human relationships.

2. **Teaching:** While some rationalization of course provision was undertaken at the time of the merger, there was a wish to retain a basic policy of meeting student demand, in so far as was possible and practicable, wherever it might arise. Thus while some courses requiring fixed plant, particular equipment or specialized accommodation, were associated with a particular location all other educational provision had to be made available to students in such a manner that they did not have to travel between campuses in order to study any permissible combination of subject areas. If, however, students were not required to travel it was obvious that staff would have to do so unless some alternative scheme could be devised. It appeared that cross-campus communication, initially by telephone conferencing, could supply the answer subject to technological criteria being met. It could also respond appropriately in respect of situations of the following kind:

- for those courses of study where limited input is required from staff with particular expertise who are based on one campus but where there are students on another;
- where an option is offered on one campus but is desired by a small number of students on another;
- for programmes with a limited enrolment on each of several campuses where it is impractical to combine the students physically into one group. This characterizes many taught postgraduate courses;
- for the supervision of postgraduate research students where some aspects, at least, of student/supervisor consultation and monitoring of progress might be maintained at a distance;
- for the encouragement of inter-disciplinary or inter-professional studies by making arrangements for joint seminars and discussion groups;
- for the promotion of further research into both human and technological factors associated with learning at a distance.

The original audio system has since been extended even further by the creation of closed circuit television linkage which is not so economic but is a virtual necessity in the promotion and development of inter-campus programmes. There are human adjustments to be made in all cases to overcome the reluctance which some people feel about becoming involved in technologically-mediated communication, oral or visual. As the perceived threat of being seen or heard by a wider audience than usual recedes and with it the paranoia of being video- or tape-recorded there will be continuing benefit to those staff and students who can meet only occasionally face-to-face but who need to maintain constant contact in order to achieve their educational goals.

Subsequent to the initiation of experiments in Ulster, I was sponsored by the British Council to return to Canada and the United States to collaborate with colleagues there in exploring further ideas for cross-campus communication and the techniques for achieving it. At Rutgers University in New Jersey, for example, there was a set-up very similar to that of the University of Ulster, with a teaching commitment spread over four dispersed campuses each around sixty miles distant from each other. The introduction of computer-mediated communication linking Rutgers, Ulster and other universities has since added an extra dimension to the process of keeping in touch even on a transatlantic basis. The original idea of trying to overcome physical distance in a communication set-up was the starting point. In practice it was demonstrated that the concept of distance learning was not just an idea but a possibility which the experiments turned into a certainty for many staff and for thousands of students.

CONCEPT: DISTANCE LEARNING

Aim: Global communication
Location: Perth, Western Australia
Time: 1987

Some years ago I was invited to go back to Australia where I had once lectured, to present a keynote paper on distance learning to an international conference on industrial technology. Because of other commitments it was not possible for me to accept the invitation but the conference organizers still wished to have my input in respect of an issue which is taken very seriously in a country where there can be great distances between one habitation and another. The scale of travel in Australia, where a few hundred miles can be regarded as 'just down the road', means that normal attendance at educational institutions is still quite impossible for many people. This naturally includes children in outlying areas who still depend on educational radio contact to provide a reasonable substitute for attendance at day school.

After several telephone discussions it was agreed that my address could be delivered by telephone from my own study in Jordanstown. The connection 'down under' would be completed by incorporating a conferencing relay system which would broadcast the talk to the assembled delegates. Ideally there should have been printed handouts available for the audience together with visuals for overhead projection on to a screen. However time did not permit such refinements. The talk had to proceed on a basis which would not, in advance of the experiment, have raised much expectation of success.

As it turned out, however, it was extremely well received by the audience who had access to roving microphones in order to pose questions. The session lasted for over an hour and was agreed to be an outstanding example of practising what was preached. The British Government Information Service subsequently circulated details of the innovation to its outlets throughout the world and reports were published in various journals including the British Council's *Media in Education and Development*. In so far as can be judged the concept has now been accepted as feasible by several academic institutions in other parts of the world. The development of satellite communication has been of immense technical assistance in ensuring that the idea can be universally implemented.

CONCEPT: OPEN ACCESS TO HIGHER EDUCATION

Aim: Unrestricted entry to university
Location: England
Time: 1972

Perhaps the most innovative idea ever to be devised in the context of higher education was that which led to the creation, in 1972, of the Open University in the United Kingdom. It was established to provide degree studies for part-time students, particularly those who had 'missed out first time round'. It embodied the belief that access to higher education and training should be available to all, whatever their circumstances, so that each person had equal opportunity to reach his or her full potential.

Application was, and remains, open to everyone over the age of eighteen. No qualifications are required for admission to undergraduate programmes and students may follow both basic and honours programmes.

Teaching methods are based on correspondence and audio-visual material and are arranged on a regional basis. Broadcasts are normally transmitted outside normal working hours. There are packages of study materials and required assignments and some courses also have an annual one-week residential summer school. There is strong emphasis on the recognition of students as individual learners. They are supported by the provision of local study centres where a range of services and materials is available.

The Open University, needless to say, is different from all other British universities. The unique character of the 'OU', as it is universally referred to, is that:

- it is open in the fullest meaning of that word;
- it operates educationally and administratively for the most part at a distance from the student (and also from the tutorial staff who are invariably part-time);
- its students are all adults, studying part-time only;
- the teacher in such a system is in a special position, exposed, accountable, experiencing both considerable risk and, as a bonus, unusual liberation or freedom.

Openness is the dominating idea of the Open University. The name was deliberately selected to emphasize this in preference to its first working title of *The University of the Air*. The truly significant principle on which the institution was based was that adults could be trusted to select themselves for higher education, whatever their previous qualifications or lack of them. To this day students are admitted solely on the basis of their wish to study. Some left school as soon as possible; others have already gained PhDs from more orthodox universities. Furthermore the number of students with physical disabilities who study with the Open University is greater than in all the other British universities put together. The desire of most students to study is voracious and, although the initial drop-out rate is high, the number of discontinuances thereafter is minimal. Most candidates who finish the first year eventually complete at least a pass degree.

Not only are admissions open, but so are the university records. Students may inspect them at any time. The university ensures that assessment schemes are published, that assignments specify carefully what is required, that appeal procedures are well publicized and that examinations are not in any way competitive. Students are represented on all university policy-making bodies.

Open University education places the emphasis on learning rather than teaching. There are no performance measures in respect of the art of the pedagogue, only a requirement that the tutors use every effort to assist learning. For the student the tutor is the only close human element in a distance learning situation but relationships between students and tutors are of a high order of effectiveness. This fact alone means that in practice the university is neither as bureaucratic nor as impersonal as might have been feared. Its continued existence and development is a tribute to the very idea of *open access* and an indication of just how great a potential still exists for this concept in higher education.

The Open University became an integral part of the unified higher education system inaugurated in Great Britain in 1992, and at the beginning of 1993 received the highest funding of any university from the new Higher Education Funding Council for England. It is worth noting that, with the recent demise in Great Britain of CNAA (the Council for National Academic Awards) following the upgrading of vast numbers of polytechnics to university status, the Council's validating function for new courses in tertiary education lapsed. This function has now been acquired by the Open University. It has also been one of the prime movers in operating the Credit Accumulation and Transfer scheme. This system, which involves many institutions of higher education, allows students to move from one educational establishment to another within the scheme in order to complete a course of study begun elsewhere. Students are enabled by this means to be mobile in respect of employment opportunities without having to discontinue important courses of study and they may normally receive the desired award from whichever of the collaborating institutions they find most appropriate.

CONCEPT: COMPUTER LITERACY

Aim: Communication competence
Location: Western World
Time: The present

Any idea of competence necessarily introduces the mirror image of incompetence. It is one of the more regrettable sociological characteristics that in considering society there are often complementary categories for people in the sense that many social, occupational and other categories are created simply as a result of the existence of some other. For example to have some people in employment automatically labels the rest as unemployed; the existence of graduates creates, of necessity, non-graduates; winners become possible only because there are losers; skilled workers spotlight the unskilled; and so it goes on. In the days of the so-called three Rs someone who was illiterate was unable to read or write. Nowadays even honours graduates of universities are in danger of being classified as computer illiterate if they cannot handle fundamental keyboard skills and operate, at some level of competence, the ubiquitous personal computer. How has this new perception of educated (or at least knowledgeable) but technically incompetent people come about?

In the early days of computing, when a single computer tended to occupy an entire building, computer operators were, for the most part, specialists and even experts. With the technological revolution arising from the development of the personal computer and the extension of such equipment to routine tasks such as word processing the idea of basic competence has spread far beyond specialist areas. There is an expectation that many non-manual people should be familiar with the technical (or at least the basic operational) skills of keyboard operation on the assumption that this is analogous to the mechanical writing skills of former days. While it is not yet necessary to be able to demonstrate such competence in many of the traditional educational areas there is certainly an opportunity for students to acquire basic expertise and there is a preference, for example by examiners, for written work to be wordprocessed where possible rather than handwritten. Another criterion, of course, is that of potential employers who so often expect, or even require, at least some preliminary acquaintance with a computer for many occupations. In the business and commercial world of today the requirement to operate computers is definitely not restricted to specialists or experts.

Assistants in travel agencies, cashiers in building societies, storemen in factories, police in patrol cars and many others need to show that they can handle micro technology in respect of the particular requirements of their jobs. For the average citizen, too, there is advantage in being able to use the automated teller machines or ATMs provided now so liberally by banks and building societies. As distinct from the early days when these hole-in-the-wall outlets were merely cashpoints there is now the availability of a wide range of services to be called upon. It is, however, necessary to use fairly explicit icons or key in simple instructions. Those who cannot perform at this basic level would certainly be regarded as computer illiterate.

Many people would be loth to admit that they could not operate such machines. However functioning at even this elementary level is somewhat removed from any normal definition of literacy. The term *literacy* should almost certainly be replaced by some other one such as *competence*. This would – possibly – remove acquired skill from the realm of basic education and at the same time reduce the possibility of individual stigma arising from being adjudged below par when compared with the norm for a particular occupation or group. The idea of computer illiteracy is certainly innovative in respect of definition but is not particularly helpful in maintaining or restoring individual self-esteem which has been dented by feelings or actual charges of incompetence. It is one idea which is likely to prove eventually to have been more dysfunctional than useful.

CONCEPT: TIME-SHARE OWNERSHIP

Aim: Shared ownership of property
Location: Vacation sites worldwide
Time: 1980s

In a largely capitalist and materialist society there is not just a possibility but a virtual obligation to own things. This applies particularly to property, especially since most people derive some feelings of security from ownership of their own home. In days gone past the rich would have had an ancestral home or country seat and at least one town house – the town being, of course, London. The *nouveau riche* today are likely to have a residence in the 'stockbroker belt' appropriate to whatever city they commute to as well as a 'little place' in Tenerife or Marbella. Those who envy them their good fortune and are unable to afford a second dwelling, even a cottage in the country, have been introduced to a new concept in recent years – the idea of time-sharing a property which they 'own', typically, for one fixed week in the year. This means in practice that, provided they are content to travel to the same place on the same dates every year they can have, in effect, a reasonably cheap annual holiday. Furthermore they are going to their own 'little place', with all the bestowed attributes of ownership. It is not a rented property. It confers some of the benefits and all of the problems of true ownership, additionally complicated in most cases by being located in a foreign country where the legal system may not be very supportive of the rights of non-nationals.

The idea has been embraced enthusiastically by many thousands of satisfied customers who really do enjoy, as part-owners, the limited occupation of properties which would ordinarily be far beyond their financial means. The whole image of time-sharing, however, has been tarnished in recent years by the unscrupulous tactics of some operators who trap the unwary into commitments which they cannot honour or who are forced to accept hardship in order to do so.

There are many instances where property has been bought in advance of construction and when the builders have gone out of business nothing has been left but legal liabilities for the purchasers. There are other situations where planning approval has either been withheld or withdrawn, again causing legal complications. And, of course, because of the variations in different parts of the world in laws relating to contracts, ownership of property and other issues, some time-share owners have found that, as foreigners, they have very few rights indeed and are unable to defend their interests.

Even in more satisfactory situations where the property has actually been constructed, is in acceptable condition and is what the owners had expected and for which the price seemed reasonable, there can still be problems. For example there are local taxes and rates to be paid, there are inescapable charges for keeping the property in good repair, and there are payments for various services such as cleaning, security and the provision of water supply. A universal complaint concerns the escalating cost of merely maintaining what has been purchased since some charges increase enormously with the passage of time. Above all, for many people, there is the cost of insurance (when it can be obtained!) against all the things which can happen when you have a property which is one tiny unit of a large conglomerate and owned by up to 52 people, each of whom occupies it for one week per year. For some people the situation can precipitate a nervous breakdown! It appears obvious from the diminishing involvement of speculators in this type of business that time-sharing would seem to be one idea which no longer attracts really serious attention from those who were formerly most at risk – the modestly affluent.

SUMMARY

These case studies are already summaries, in some cases very brief indeed, of issues which were often both prolonged and detailed. In all cases the common feature was that someone **thought** of a new approach to dealing with a familiar situation, a recurrent issue or a predictable problem and then tested the idea in practice. The opportunity to do so characterizes the innovative approach because of the venturesomeness which is required in a situation where there is no previous experience to act as a guide or provide assurance of a satisfactory outcome.

REFLECTION

It would be useful to review carefully the possible extent to which the concept, aims and even the location and timing of each of the examples quoted above tended to be supportive of one another in producing an acceptable outcome.

APPLICATION

You will have noted that the case studies dealt with here covered a number of different situations with regard to the resources needed, the time required for development, the extent to which others had to be involved and the changes of attitude and behaviour which were necessary in order even to try the ideas in practice.

What factors do you think might have assisted those which worked well? What do you think might have hindered the achievement of those which did not do so well?

RECOMMENDED FURTHER READING

Some of the items mentioned in this chapter relate to information published in journal articles, research reports, conference papers and broadcast material not listed in the bibliography. Much relevant material will be found in any resource centre, data base or library for those who wish to pursue some matters in detail. Just a few titles are suggested for those who may wish to consider a little further the nature of ideas and their practical applications.

Bird, Drayton (1989) *Commonsense Direct Marketing*, Kogan Page, London.
  Interesting sidelights on how to sell against potential customer sales resistance.
Drucker, Peter F. (1986) *Innovation and Entrepreneurship*, Heinemann, London.
  Fairly heavily theoretical.
Jones, Trevor (ed.) (1980) *Micro-electronics and Society*, The Open University Press, Milton Keynes.
  Easy reading. Highlights ideas which have 'taken off'.
Rowe, Christopher (1986) *People and Chips*, Paradigm Publishing, London.
  Of general relevance. Not difficult to understand and apply.

Innovative practices 11

Though you think you know it – you have no certainty
until you try.

Sophocles, 400 BC

'There is no use trying,' she said: 'one CAN'T believe
impossible things.'
'I dare say you haven't had much practice.' said the
Queen.

Lewis Carroll, Alice Through the Looking Glass

If we want things to stay as they are, things will have to
change.

Lampedusa, The Leopard, Folio, London (1987)

Plus ça change, plus c'est la meme chose. (The more
things change, the more they are the same.)

Alphonse Karr, Les Guepes (1849)

In this chapter we concentrate on examining some ideas which
actually have resulted in changed practices, especially those which
are open to observation. The examples chosen illustrate new approaches related particularly to communication techniques and
employment practices.

Objectives
After reading this chapter you should be able to:

- outline the manner in which an innovative practice may arise
  from an idea;
- describe some communication practices which have caused
  changes in people's everyday lives;
- identify the personal and social consequences of adopting some
  particular practices.

THE NATURE OF INNOVATIVE ACTIVITIES

Habit assists us to perform in the workaday world almost on 'auto-pilot'.
By the sheer recurrence of actions with which we have become familiar

we lessen both the amount and the difficulty of many of those personal decisions which we have to make daily. When we are persuaded, or convince ourselves, that we should make some alteration we have to go through a phase of conscious adaptation and adjustment which most of us would normally evade if we could. The sooner we are able to familiarize ourselves with any changed activities, and develop the habits that repetition itself brings, the sooner we find ourselves able to operate the new practices and thus make life easier for ourselves.

The activities chosen to be listed briefly here are all in some way concerned with aspects of communication and information technology. They are those which have initially produced, and are still having, a profound effect on the lives of all the people involved, whether directly or indirectly. Many of the changes in practices do not necessarily require additional sophistication in terms of behaviour but their individual and social consequences can hardly be overemphasized. The effects relate to such personal factors as human attitudes towards daily work and home life. The social elements involved are relevant to the impact of new approaches to issues as diverse as marketing and teaching.

THE ELECTRONIC VILLAGE HALL, SCANDINAVIA, 1985

In the Nordic countries, ie Sweden, Norway, Finland and Denmark, a number of Information and Community Service Centres (ICSCs) have been established in recent years. These were devised as **Electronic Village Halls** or, as they are still often called, *telecottages* or *telehouses*. They were instituted to provide isolated communities with a means of using computer mediated communication and also of gaining access to useful data processing facilities. They were intended, and are at present used, as much for private as for commercial activities, for example in connection with satellite TV, teleshopping, Citizen's Advice counselling and similar services.

The concept was created, and the set-up invented, in the small village of Fjaltring in Denmark in 1984. The first working telehouse was established in Sweden in September 1985. Since then the numbers have grown and there are now a couple of hundred such facilities throughout the Nordic countries. In fact the whole set-up has become international as the scheme was copied by more than thirty other countries. The basic model employs the strategy of locating the technology at an appropriate site so that communal use may be made of all the facilities available. This is noticeably different from the approach usually adopted elsewhere, for example in networking systems, where individual provision is considered as the norm and the connecting links are then subsequently arranged to provide for any necessary collaboration.

The conditions which appear to have led to success in Scandinavia are these:

- The telehouse has to become integrated into the everyday life of the rural community. The ultimate aim is that it should be used as much, and indeed in the same way, as the village shop.

- Learning and actually doing have to support each other as complementary activities. This is catered for in the telehouse system because people have the opportunity to get any necessary instruction in information technology at the same time as they gain access to the technical facilities.
- The telehouse has to operate as a centre for social service. It should parallel some of the provision of a United Kingdom community centre but with less emphasis on leisure and recreational activities and more on counselling, supportive guidance and educational assistance.

A typical programme of services by an ICSC is what has been produced at Harjedalen in Sweden. The initial provision was for the rural community at Vemdalen, very close to the mountainous border with Norway. This village has only 800 inhabitants and is 125 kilometres from the nearest town, Ostersund. It was the first fully equipped ICSC to open in Scandinavia and plans were made at the very beginning to install satellite TV reception, two-way video access to the university at Ostersund and a micro-link access to the municipal administration in Sveg about 60 kilometres from the village. The intentions of the planners were, at first, actually thought by some people to be too ambitious.

The basic services provided included:

1. **Information:** The inhabitants can obtain much information from the offices of the local government administration, the area library, and also both national and international databases.
2. **Consultancy:** At least one full-time consultant is normally available to provide appropriate services to the small firms in the area. This person can usually develop software programs and act as tutor for courses related to community needs in information technology.
3. **Teleworking:** Because of ICSC, facilities have gradually become available for the establishment of new 'cottage industries'. These are intended to supplement the customary work-at-home clerical and other allied activities of the past by taking place at workstations in the telehouse instead of at individual residences. They are consequently beneficial in promoting local social life as well as providing new employment.
4. **Training facilities:** It is worth noting that initial interest was such that before the telehouse even opened 10% of the local population had taken a brief introductory course in computing. There is now additional opportunity for more advanced study available from the relationship built up with the local university.
5. **External communications:** Facsimile, teleprinting and other services are available to the local community. This would not have been economically viable in respect of personal access being sought by small firms or individuals but, for this neighbourhood, the overall cost

represents a modest *per capita* outlay and it provides, amongst other things, a useful type of community mailbox for the inhabitants.

The innovative approach here lies in utilizing as individual services a number of resources which are normally regarded as large scale, if only because of the inherent cost. By redefining them as public service utilities they have been made available to all those who need and/or can benefit from them.

In Western Europe alone there are over 300 000 villages which face social and cultural problems of the kind which have been effectively tackled in a few experimental areas such as the telehouses already set up in Scandinavia. What as-yet-untapped possibilities are there for collaborative, cheap, cooperatively based communication facilities to be developed in the Third World countries? Admittedly their inhabitants at the present time often have enough difficulty in surviving, without thinking about international communication and commerce! But is there any hope for their future development if some appropriate technological steps are not taken right now, even while famine relief, medical care and basic housing often constitute the first priorities? This type of innovation should stimulate some fresh approaches to enabling people to do for themselves what otherwise society will eventually have to try to do for them.

TELECOMMUTING, SCOTLAND, 1992

Ever since the modem joined the personal computer in the domestic as well as the industrial context the idea of working at home and communicating electronically with the office has been a recurring dream of commuters. No more rush-hour traffic jams, no more hurried lunches. An escape from irritable work companions. Above all, an opportunity to evade the eagle eye of the boss. As with most dreams of this kind there can be a down side to the practice since the reality can sometimes differ from the product of the imagination. It is, none the less, becoming a working reality for a growing number of people who have identified the strengths and weaknesses relating to their own circumstances and are able to establish an acceptable working environment.

In one recent example of this kind of homeworking, **teleworking**, or **telecommuting**, British Telecom has combined with Highlands and Islands Enterprise (formerly the Highlands and Islands Development Board) to set up a contemporary project. This is to determine the feasibility of telephone operators living in a wide area of the North of Scotland operating a directory enquiries service from a workstation in their own homes instead of from the Inverness Directory Assistance Centre. The operators, who are all volunteers, were chosen by questionnaire and interview and then given a two day training course. Each operator has a videophone link to the exchange which not only allows him or her to talk to his or her supervisor or colleagues but also enables him or her to see them. In this way he or she is able to maintain some reasonably acceptable social contact. In addition there is an electronic notice-board which provides him or her with any necessary service information from the Centre.

The operators are all full-time employees whose terms and conditions of service remain unchanged by the alteration of location but who are entitled to certain additional payments or recovery of costs incurred in operating from home. It is intended to include some handicapped people in the volunteer team if at all possible.

Funding for the exercise comes from joint provision by British Telecom and Highlands and Islands Enterprise. Whether the investment of several millions of pounds sterling will ever be recovered in purely financial terms is a matter for conjecture. There is obviously no short-term monetary return.

This innovative project which started in July 1992, initially for a trial period of a year, is being monitored jointly by BT and Aberdeen University to determine what technical issues require consideration; what problems (if any) remote control might pose for management; and the consequential social implications of teleworking in this particular context. It is not proposed by British Telecom, for example, to follow the operation to its ultimate conclusion of dispersing the entire directory service since this would mean that all existing directory-enquiry units would have to close down.

In addition to this service more than forty telecom exchanges have been upgraded in terms of ISDN (Integrated Services Digital Network). This can carry video as well as voice circuits and computer data and since there are internationally defined standards the potential is virtually unlimited. Already it has contributed to the extension and expansion of some Scottish business enterprises. Initially these have been in connection with such activities as hotel bookings, travel arrangements and contact with representatives working at a distance from head office. The facilities have, however, also assisted the further development of home-working in such sectors as computer software production and word processing. In addition there has been the opportunity to familiarize a much wider range of people than ever before with the advantages of electronic mail, a matter of some importance for all remote or sparsely populated regions.

The eventual aim of these initiatives is to be able to satisfy what is believed to be an increasing demand for alternative ways of working. For some people, at least, 'going to work' in the future may no longer necessarily involve travel – one of the very few genuinely innovative practices to emerge in the context of contemporary employment.

NEW HOME WORKING, ENGLAND AND WALES, 1992

The possibility of working at home is not confined to those who are computer literate or who may need constant access to a telephone and modem although the term most popularly used is 'teleworking'.

Teleworking is usually defined somewhat vaguely as 'working at a distance'. While some approaches will inevitably reinforce the image of telecottages as remote outposts for national or multinational companies, others may well characterize private enterprise in the form of purely domestic endeavour.

There is room to reflect that the first Industrial Revolution destroyed the cottage industries by taking many people out of their rural homes and moving them into the environment of the growing number of factories. Now the information technology revolution, whether recognized as being of comparable significance or not, is doing quite the reverse. Around 300 000 people in Britain are now estimated to be involved in a new home working system of some kind. It is difficult to assess how accurate this figure is, particularly since the advent of the personal computer and especially the lap-top or even smaller versions. Nowadays a surprising number of people regarded as in orthodox full time employment actually carry out a fair proportion of their work at home (or even in transit between home and office) by using such miniaturized computers. There are, accordingly, many different types of home working ranging from those who are continuously on-line to their base via a computer terminal to those who merely do some extra work at home or elsewhere outside normal working hours.

It is interesting to note an ecological remark from former President George Bush in 1990 when addressing the California Chamber of Commerce . . . 'If only 5% of the commuters in Los Angeles teleworked for one day per week they'd save 205 million miles of travel each year and keep 47 000 tons of pollutants from entering the atmosphere.' From a conservation point of view alone that might seem to be quite a persuasive argument to try the process, at least in those circumstances where it would appear to have some chance of success.

A recent survey undertaken by the National Computer Centre and others has indicated that one in eight firms in Britain now use teleworking of some sort. While there are converts who are operating purely as individuals most of the uptake generally is reported as coming from:

- firms employing more than 1000 people;
- firms in the South of England; and
- sections of the Information Technology industry itself.

The two major benefits seen by firms in respect of this type of operation are:

1. increased productivity;
2. the retention of skilled staff.

The main problems perceived by teleworkers concern lack of face-to-face contact with either senior staff or their own colleagues. The reasons for non-use of the practice seem to relate to problems with employee motivation, embracing personnel assessment and organizational difficulties.

Great diversity of opportunity in this field is now available and much of the appeal of this type of employment lies in the reasons which make it appear to offer advantages to so many different types of worker. Included are:

- opportunities for many physically handicapped people who might have difficulty coping with office or factory situations;
- relative freedom for those who seek flexibility of approach and creativity rather than control in their work;
- openings for those who wish to have only part-time employment rather than career possibilities;
- flexi-hour working for those who can undertake full-time commitment but not within the orthodox hours of attendance;
- more relaxing working conditions in familiar surroundings;
- absence of travel worries and costs, including many expenses such as fares together with hidden items such as laundry, dry-cleaning and lunches;
- few problems of holiday or leisure breaks; and
- informality of dress and general appearance.

There are other points, of course, the relative importance of the items being largely a personal matter but probably the first point mentioned above is the one which figures most prominently in arguments for establishing new enterprises.

In Dorset, for example, the Social Services run a project for disabled people. It is called *Abilities* and arose out of a sheltered placement scheme based on a day centre. Five people were employed in the first instance, two at their own homes and three others in the centre, and their work consisted mainly in tachograph analysis. This is concerned, amongst other things, with checking the automatically recorded journeys of trucks and lorries to see whether transport regulations have been obeyed regarding distances travelled, maximum speed limits, and necessary rest breaks. It is strictly a commercial project which has to pay its way, but it fortunately continues to do so.

For those who do not wish to travel to a work centre, or who are unable to do so, it is sometimes forgotten that there are disadvantages as well as advantages in working at home. In the office or factory certain things are taken care of for the employee which have to be dealt with on an individual basis at home. These include:

- the cost of heating and lighting which may offset savings on travel costs;
- the unavoidable disruption of normal home life;
- the necessity for greater self-discipline to maintain a regular average daily output or level of achievement;
- the disadvantageous rates of pay often offered to part-time workers;
- the uncertainty and discontinuity of income for freelance operators;
- the feeling of being remote from trade union or professional association contact in respect of many issues;

- general feelings of relative isolation and absence of the usual comradeship of the traditional workplace team;
- interruptions from callers, domestic chores etc which can disrupt a day's work beyond recovery (and this should *never* be discounted!);
- expenses of repairs, replacements and insurance of equipment;
- absence of incentives other than personal motivation;
- missing the opportunities for reflection, contemplation and internalization offered by the travel time formerly regarded as 'lost' working time.

A new association aimed at promoting the spread of teleworking in the United Kingdom has recently been formed to try to establish codes of conduct for both employers and employees. If teleworking is to become a universally accepted form of normal employment rather than an interesting departure from it, some rules of conduct related to professional practice or occupational custom certainly require to be devised and agreed without too much delay.

WORKING AT HOME – ANYWHERE, ANY TIME

If you are, or are likely to be, involved in home working of any kind you must heed the message given below.

> # P L A N A H EAD!

I hope that this will serve to show that much may be learned from even the briefest of messages – and why should learning not also be fun? Isn't it in the *Talmud* that it is said that a lesson with fun is a lesson remembered? However, some practical advice in greater detail follows.

Guidelines for home working

1. Have an office-type working environment. If you cannot set aside a whole room specifically for your home working at least lay claim to one for the designated work periods. If all else fails then settle for operating always in the same special corner of a room which becomes your work station. You must have somewhere that is familiar, contains your equipment, files and papers, and is likely to be, on the next occasion you need it, as you left it the last time you were working there.
2. Set your alarm clock for your usual time. Enjoy the sheer luxury of not having to rush your preparations for facing the day ahead.
3. Start the day as usual by getting washed and dressed. Take as much care of your appearance as you would if you were going to the office or other workplace. You might even, with psychological advantage, wear what you would normally have worn to travel to work!

4. Enjoy a leisurely breakfast. You are in no rush to hit the highway! Eat a proper meal so as not to be tempted to break up a working day more than usual by having unlimited snacks. You may, of course, have morning and afternoon breaks and could build the time for these into your work schedule.

5. Work office hours if your job is to be full-time. You can, of course, be somewhat indulgent in specifying these but whatever you decide on you should stick to. Practice saying *and believing*, 'I work from 9 till 5' (or 10 till 3.30 or whatever). Be available for phone calls during those hours. Switch off, if you can, outside that time. And do allow yourself an official lunch hour – you'll find that a midday break never was so good before.

6. Get started to work on time – you have no excuses. Since you can't get stuck in a traffic jam you should be up and running by opening time. A routine is vital and punctuality is the backbone of it.

7. Always try to quit on time too unless there is a very good reason not to. Make a special point of going outside into the fresh air regularly. Let the dog take you for a walk. Leave the office or workroom behind until tomorrow.

8. Don't become isolated from other people. There is no reason why your walk should not include a stop at your 'local' (ie pub, tavern, hotel, bar-room, whatever). Additionally make a point of meeting other people in leisure, recreational or social activities on a regular basis.

9. Don't forget to maintain professional, business and mutual interest contacts. It is even more essential to 'keep in touch' when you are not meeting colleagues regularly.

10. Enjoy it. Remember *you* are the boss!

TECHNOLOGICAL PIRACY, WORLD-WIDE, 1992

This is perhaps a doubtful example of a practice. It might be better identified as a definite social malpractice because of the way in which computers and other technological equipment have created for crime many opportunities which never previously existed. What we are about to consider concerns briefly, for the most part, both unethical and illegal practices related to and arising from innovative advances in technology.

Technical developments which enabled sound to be recorded on magnetic tape soon led to the do-it-yourself home recording of broadcasts off-air, followed by the unauthorized copying of commercially published audio tapes. Since the more recent creation of appropriate techniques and equipment for recording vision also in this form, the amount of unauthorized video recording, duplicating and unlawful distribution has been, by any standards, phenomenal. The importance of the problem can be gauged from the fact that pirating of audio and video tapes as well as illegal copying of computer software constitutes the major industry of south-east Asia. Hardly anyone can claim not to hold or have used at least one illegal tape or computer disk. In respect of information technology in the financial world the situation appears to be even worse but less is known about it since there is a reluctance to admit the extent of the technical piracy which is going on, or to give any estimates of its possible cost. Banking appears to constitute the major area for concern.

One reason for this would appear to be the touching faith which senior bank officials display in the apparent infallibility of the systems installed by their suppliers. Other organizations realize that there are no perfect mechanical or electronic devices. Bankers, however, appear to have unshakeable confidence in theirs. Another concern is the apparent complacency with which they regard the adequacy of 4-digit PINs (Personal Identification Numbers). These do provide for many hundreds of thousands of separate codes from 1111 to 9999, but do they offer sufficient uniqueness and security to cover the millions of individual identities of all customers, even when the PIN is combined with a distinctive bank code? Many customers have had occasion to wonder whether they were the only user of a particular code number! A legal decision in Britain in 1993 has ruled that banks generally do now have a case to answer in respect of claims concerning 'phantom' withdrawals whereas previously any complaints or claims of this kind were dismissed out of hand on the grounds that all withdrawals via automated teller machines must be valid and therefore chargeable to the cardholder. Some banks in Scotland have already installed miniature pinhole cameras to record all those who withdraw or attempt to withdraw cash from these outlets. In this way it is possible to identify genuine instances of unwitting or irregular operation.

In respect of plastic bank cards alone the losses were (in 1992) admitted by British banks to be more than £165 million per annum. While part of that is no doubt due to the possible shortcomings of the technology there is another important factor – that of the extreme carelessness of customers who lose an incredible 5500 cards per day, or over two million per year! This is in addition to the tampering with magnetic strips on cards and the other dodges which give rise to phenomena like 'ghost withdrawals' which, by the time they are discovered, make it difficult to investigate how they happened. There is even one recorded instance of a bank employee who installed his own computer inside a cashpoint in order to ensure that he had a full record of all the customer accounts and guaranteed means of access to them.

Information systems, by their very nature, have provided virtually unlimited opportunities for unauthorized access to data or money. Probably the best known term in this connection is **hacking**. Nowadays this refers to the apparently compulsive and obsessive process of accessing computer sources of information whether there is legitimate right of entry or not. Often the practice is simply the end product of a genuine and insistent curiosity but there are occasions when opportunity to benefit from chance encounters with something significant proves too much for the intruder and some sort of mayhem results. This may be caused by the alteration of accounts, actual transfers of funds, acquirement of confidential information, or just a temptation to corrupt data and cause inconvenience or even disaster. Although some of this can be brought about by people who have only a basic working knowledge of particular computer systems the worst damage arises when hackers can use fairly sophisticated techniques. These include approaches such as the so-called *Trojan Horse*. This comprises unauthorized buried instructions which are timed to operate at some date in the future. When that time arrives hackers can perform such actions as transferring cash balances from one account to another or amending other forms of data. They can then delete themselves and thus make it impossible to trace the fact that they ever existed. An even more sinister development is the virus or '*Logic Bomb*' which causes severe disruption, corruption or even complete erasure of a system.

The amount of computer fraud, while commonly believed to be of huge proportions, is difficult to assess because of the unwillingness of those involved (especially the victims!) to provide any information even to the extent of admitting that a system has been breached. However it should be remembered that virtually every organization and company which has at least one computer is almost certainly the victim of some computer fraud from time to time. Often this is nothing more than the theft of computer time by unauthorized word-processing of an individual's CV or club newsletter. To that extent it is in the same category as the office phone which is so often used for personal calls. However the word processor, unlike the typewriter, is designed to store the information which passes through it and this facility often provides the basis for activities ranging from industrial espionage to individual blackmail.

One thing about computer fraud which *is* known is that it is getting easier as world-wide communication techniques improve. It is now possible to be in Monrovia and rob a bank in, say, Rio de Janeiro if that was what you wanted to do. The chances of success are high and the possibility of being caught is minimal. Even then the probability of being prosecuted is virtually nil. It would be difficult to think of a more innovative, although antisocial, practice. Unfortunately it appears to be one which shows every indication of increasing in the future.

DIRECT MARKETING, UNITED KINGDOM, 1992

Direct marketing includes, and for the most part comprises, direct mail and indeed shopping by post is what most people think of when the term is mentioned. There are people, and perhaps you are one of them, who either dislike the thought of going into a shop or store to ask an assistant for some particular item or are, for one reason or another, unable to go shopping at all. Such people provide the foundation for the mail order or direct mail business. They choose goods from catalogues and are normally assured of fairly prompt delivery. Their purchases usually arrive under plain sealed cover, a matter of some consequence to many people who are spared possible embarrassment or discomfiture. In addition, the supplier (by cutting out the middle party in the process) is often able to supply what is needed at a lower price than a retail outlet and yet make a higher profit. Whatever the classical view of demand producing supply it is nowadays commonplace for many people not to know that they want something until they see that it has actually been produced. It is the task of direct marketeers to bring to the attention of potential customers items which they believe that person may be interested in purchasing. This is most commonly done by direct mail and although this is only part of the greater perspective of direct marketing it is by far the most important sector of the market, both in terms of scale and of financial turnover.

Direct sale from producer to consumer is, of course, as old as the hills. It is possible to see the system in operation in relation to many cottage industries in various countries where those who spin and weave sell their products to passing tourists. Similarly with pottery, woodcarving, beads, lace and other artefacts. However, direct marketing has become much more sophisticated in recent years and is now really big business. The emphasis is no longer on responding to customer demand but on creating it.

There are four major objectives which motivate the direct marketeer:

1. To persuade people to buy by post or telephone (preferably by quoting a credit card number).
2. To request catalogues or other information regarding products or services.
3. To seek a demonstration either in the home or, preferably, in some more public place.
4. To visit a shop, store or other sales outlet including exhibitions.

In order to function effectively it is necessary to construct a database of potential customer information relating to place of residence, occupation, purchasing habits, interests and hobbies as well as any other information likely to be relevant to the identification of a would-be purchaser. Circular letters, catalogues etc can then be mailed to selected individuals, having been created in a personalized form by computer. It is important to send purchase information to the right 'target market', ie those who would be most likely to want the goods or services offered for sale. Only the material which goes to people who do not want it is actually 'junk' mail and there is no profit to anyone except, possibly, the Post Office in sending it. It is essential, therefore, to target a specific audience and to do so in a manner which relates to their own level of sophistication.

There are a number of advantages built into this system, namely:

- it personalizes the approach to the potential customer;
- it offers the customer a (reasonably) speedy despatch of an order;
- it often offers a lower price than a normal retail outlet;
- it enables a continuing relationship to be built up between supplier and consumer so that future sales may more readily result;

- it is convenient for the customer who can choose at leisure and often with a guarantee of return or refund if not satisfied; and
- it is discrete, a point which is highly attractive to many purchasers.

The European Commission has recently produced a directive aimed at protecting prospective customers from unscrupulous salesmen. This is important since the largest distance selling firms in the world are European (American companies come a close second). Mail order is particularly popular in the UK where it regularly forms around 3% of the total retail trade. Don't be misled by this figure – 3% is a very significant proportion indeed in this context.

The directive has three main aims:

1. to provide legal safeguards for the consumer;
2. to establish and protect the consumer's right of choice, freedom from intrusion and right to privacy;
3. to ensure repayment to the consumer in the case of non-performance of the contract.

Distance selling operates through a suitably wide range of media including advertisements in newspapers, 'commercials' on television, announcements on teletext, spoken messages by telephone and literature delivered by postal services. Former practices such as 'inertia selling' have been made illegal in most European countries. Inertia selling means that failing to reply to unsolicited offers or actual delivery of goods does not constitute a purchase. In practice the recipient of goods which were not ordered need not return them and cannot be held to have agreed to accept and pay for them merely by retaining them. On the other hand if a prospective purchaser *does* order goods the supplier should deliver within thirty days.

This is one innovative practice which definitely appears to be here to stay.

SOCIOMETRY IN THE CLASSROOM, PORTUGAL AND CANADA, 1987

The creation of individual student profiles has always been a difficult and contentious issue in school record keeping. In an attempt to introduce a realistic as well as an innovative approach to such records an experiment in studying classroom interaction was set up in a number of schools in different cultural settings between 1987 and 1990. The principal experiments were in Canada and Portugal, for both of which locations I acted as adviser. Preliminary consultations were held with education and psychology staff at Laval University, Quebec and the University of Minho in Braga, Portugal. The nature of the exercise was to explore with teachers how best to record group situations quickly, meaningfully and efficiently so that subsequent analysis of pupil relationships might be carried out.

A sociometric approach was chosen with the sociogram being accepted as the easiest and most effective way of collecting and displaying data and consisted, as shown earlier in this book, of simple lines connecting symbols representing people, the direction indicated on each line representing the direction of a choice. Teachers were advised that such a diagram, if properly recorded, could assist in showing the nature and extent of pupil-to-pupil and pupil-to-teacher interaction and might therefore be useful in identifying children in need of either assistance with learning or individual counselling in respect of personal problems.

Sociometry relies on the exercise of choice in personal relationships. Since to be socially acceptable is a highly desirable characteristic for most people it is important for teachers to understand the factors which make children acceptable to one another. This can then provide guidance for the social training of the pupils.

Human choice may be depicted as selection, rejection or indifference. In a classroom situation these choices can be expressed in many ways. One of the most obvious, and most observable, is our choice of the person we might wish to sit beside. Some pupils might opt to sit beside the best workers, some boys might elect to sit beside the prettiest girls. Whatever the reason there is something worthwhile to be found from an examination of patterns of behaviour recorded in this way, particularly if certain patterns tend to persist. For example if one pupil always chooses the same other person instead of mingling from time to time in a wider circle of young people there may be a need to look at the nature of the relationship in case it has become too restrictive or has led to one child becoming too dependent on another.

Of course if sociometry could deal only with pairs of people there would be little point in spending much time on it. It is, however, really useful in group situations and that is where its analytical potential shows to best advantage. It is not just a mechanistic device or a form of shorthand for recording situations. It is an analytical tool which can show up phenomena which never become visible to the naked eye, however perceptive the observer. Figure 11.1 will help to explain one such situation.

In this context what had been believed to be a friendship group of long standing was demonstrated by sociogram to be actually two sub-groups held together by one pupil (no. 6) who chose a 'star' in each group but was not chosen by either in return. Why does someone become rejected or neglected in a situation like this? Children who are not well-accepted by their class-mates often have social problems which go beyond the average level and there may be factors involved which relate to issues of self-reliance, lack of social skills, feelings of inferiority or just an absence of shared interests.

Sociometry is not a cure-all for social problems nor does it help in the treatment of insecurity or other problems. But it is a very useful tool for the teacher to use in diagnosing problems of this kind. As such it is an innovation which ought to have a future in the schools of many countries if only more teachers were aware of it and its potential in practice.

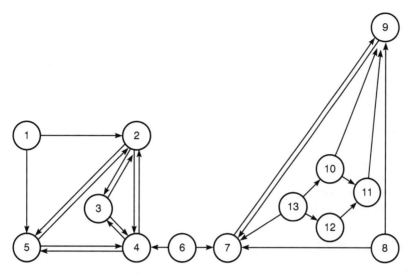

Fig. 11.1 Sociometry in the classroom.

SUMMARY

The examples given here are not intended to be in any way representative of the field as a whole. They do, however, indicate a certain range of both technical and social possibilities for future development. In looking at the locations, practices, scale of enterprise and other factors, try to identify where basic elements of innovation theory offer some assistance in understanding the way in which these practices have come about.

REFLECTION

For this chapter the term 'reflection' might include a reading again of anything that was of interest or, more importantly, not understood in its essentials or possible applications. If the examples given here have contributed to your insight into changes of practice then they have, at least, been relevant to the theme of the book. If, in addition, they have enabled you to look with sharpened perception at practices of your own which might, with advantage to yourself and others, be altered then that would be the ultimate justification for their inclusion.

APPLICATION

Imagine a local authority endeavouring to reduce refuse collection costs in a particular area. One idea being considered is that of reducing by half the number of journeys each operative has to make to individual households when a dustbin has to be emptied. Normally the workperson would go to the door or gate, collect a full bin, take it to the lorry, empty it, return the empty bin then go to the next house and repeat the process.

There is a suggestion that the lorry should carry an empty bin to start with. The operative (usually called a technician nowadays because most of the local authority cleansing departments have been renamed Technical Service Departments) could start by taking this empty bin to the first house. This would be left in place of the full one which, when it is emptied would then be taken to the house next door, to be left when that full one is collected, and so on. This approach, it is believed, could reduce door to transport journeys by half, shorten collection times, and save money whilst still offering a full service. However what do you see as primary reasons why this system would be unlikely to be viewed with much enthusiasm by householders?

RECOMMENDED FURTHER READING

Some of the items mentioned in this chapter relate to information published in journal articles, conference papers, research reports and broadcasts not included in the general bibliography. There are, however, many books well worth reading in connection with innovative practices and, if you wish, you could consult those now listed below.

Burnham, James (1945) *The Managerial Revolution*, Penguin Books, Harmondsworth.

Chesterman, John and Lipman, Andy (1988) *The Electronic Pirates*, Routledge (Comedia), London.

Forester, Tom (1987) *High-Tec Society*, Basil Blackwell, London.

Hills, Philip (ed.) (1980) *The Future of the Printed Word*, The Open University Press, Milton Keynes.

Spence, W.R. (ed.) (1989) *New Technologies and Social Intervention*, University of Ulster, Coleraine.
    Now out of print although still much in demand. Available on many college and university bookshelves.

Spence, W.R. (1989) Sociometry in the Classroom, in *Psicologia E Educacao, Investigacao E Intervencao*, Associacao dos Psicologos Portugueses, Porto.
    Despite the title this volume is available in many college and university libraries since some of the contributions are in English or French. The chapter on sociometry is in English.

Innovative products 12

To every thing there is a season.

Ecclesiastes, ch3.v1

Innovation means change.

A. W. Pearson in Henry and Walker (1991)

Whatever we are, it is but a stage on the way to somewhere else... it is only a preparation to do something else that shall be different.

Robert Louis Stevenson in Chesterman and Lipman (1988)

Some be so new-fangled that they would innovate all things.

Book of Common Prayer, Original Preface (1549)

The focus of attention in this chapter is on a small selected range of 'products', ie material artefacts, which have contributed something which was new, or was perceived as new, to most of our everyday lives. Examples include items which vary from the commonplace to the weird or spectacular.

Objectives
When you have completed this chapter you should be able to:

- identify several innovative products, eg some inventions;
- suggest some products which, while not new, can still be used in innovative ways;
- describe any recent product which has had a profound influence on the lives of ordinary people.

IDEAS, PRACTICES AND PRODUCTS

By having read the previous two chapters you will have become only too well aware that the distinction between ideas and practices can be an extremely dubious one and may be regarded as being a matter more of emphasis than of demonstrable differences of kind.

Perhaps you thought that products ought to be somewhat easier to distinguish in that they should, at least, be readily recognizable as material artefacts. But this is not always necessarily so. And, even when it may appear to be, is the distinction really so clear-cut? For example when we talk about a church or a football team are we referring to a concept, a practice or an end-product? There may be similar, or even more, ambiguity if our concern is with aspects of transport, education or government in all of which there have been dramatic changes throughout the world in recent times. Only the circumstances will make clear, if at all, whether we are considering primarily an idea, a mode of operation or a product. Usually whatever the thrust of our deliberations there is likely to be some sort of amalgam of two or more of these features within it, the context determining the more precise meaning. The complexities of specifying innovations as belonging exclusively to one category or another should be borne in mind in studying the following brief accounts of some innovative products.

THE TRANSISTOR, TOKYO, JAPAN, 1950

In 1947 Bell Laboratories in the US invented the transfer resistor or, as it became known later, the **transistor**. This was a direct replacement for the thermionic valve or vacuum tube formerly used in radios and in the early experimental television sets. It was thought that the transistor would remain a scientific curiosity for a number of years although it might be employed in some form by around the 1970s. The Japanese firm of Sony was not at that time involved in electronics at all and was actually unknown outside its own country. The president of that company had, however, heard about transistors and became interested in the possibility of exploring some way of using them commercially. He managed to buy a manufacturing license from Bell Laboratories for the rather low sum of $25 000. Two years after this Sony introduced to the world the first transistor radio. It was one-fifth the weight of a traditional set and one-third the cost. Five years later the Japanese had effectively captured a major slice of the world's radio market.

The impact of the transistor on the development of computers was even more dramatic. From the 1940s until the 1950s first generation computers needed thermionic valves and occupied whole rooms (and occasionally even entire buildings). They were primitive and unreliable since the valves had a very short life. In many ways they were a very basic forerunner of today's common pocket calculator but without either its versatility or its speed. The second generation computers of the mid-1950s were able to replace the old thermionic valves with transistors, with a consequent increase in efficiency and reduction in size. Those people who are used to the idea that millions of personal computers are in existence today might like to remember that around 1955 there were less than 100 computers in the entire world and half of these were in the US. None of the manufacturers expected anything other than a slow and modest increase in demand from the business sector over the years ahead because personal ownership was not envisaged.

The third generation computers of the following decade also had an additional advantage in being able to incorporate the recently devised silicon chip. This was able to hold masses of electrical circuits because hundreds, sometimes thousands, of tiny transistors could be built in to act as exceedingly fast automatic switches. The process of miniaturization which has led to the present fourth generation tiny laptop and notebook computers really began in earnest in the mid-1960s. The Japanese again capitalized on their ability to be both innovative and hard working and are now in the process of producing fifth generation machines of quite unbelievable performance. As Tom Forester (1990) puts it rather dramatically in his book '. . . if the automobile and airplane businesses had developed like the computer business, a Rolls Royce would cost $2.75 and run for 3 million miles on one gallon of gas'. Whatever the outcome of all the micro-electronic enhancements of the future, none of them would even have been possible without the development of the transistor.

CONDENSED BUSINESS BOOKS, UNITED KINGDOM AND THE US, 1993

It is now many years since the *Reader's Digest* first made its impact on the international publishing world by its innovative approach. Unlike most other magazines and journals it did not depend entirely, or even largely, on its own staff to provide the material for its readers. Instead the usual presentation comprised a selection of journalistic articles on a wide range of themes reproduced from publications already issued in many countries. There was also a lengthy story or condensed version of a book to complete each issue of the magazine. This latter item was very popular and at a later date the first volume of *Reader's Digest* condensed books appeared. Each volume contained several novels, biographies, travel accounts or similar. This was more controversial because every contribution was dramatically shortened in comparison with the original version. How was it possible to get the true feel for the various authors' presentations by reading abbreviations of their books? In fact the condensations were skilfully done and, since most books – especially works of fiction – often have several strands running through them (some only marginal to the main theme), the condensed version inevitably had a crispness and a directness of approach which actually found favour with an increasing number of readers.

Now there is a comparable methodology being adopted in respect of 'serious' reading taken from the field of business literature. An American organization in Vermont, which operates as *Executive Book Summaries*, offers a regular monthly subscription service of summaries of two or three current professional works on invention, marketing, management, strategy leadership . . . the list is comprehensive. It is emphasized that the publications are summaries, not reviews or digests. The typical book of around 200–500 pages is reduced to just eight. It is claimed that, as a result, fifteen minutes' reading can accomplish what otherwise could involve perhaps ten hours or more. The promotional material for this service has remarkable similarities to that for another product recently offered in the United Kingdom.

In the UK it is not a written condensation of the books but an audio presentation which characterizes the approach. Advertisements for the concept of *Booktalk*, as it is called, quote the Wall Street Journal (as do *Soundview Executive Book Summaries*) as saying 'An inventive answer to what is becoming an increasingly irksome management problem: too much to read'. The operation of the process is as follows. Leading business writers review published material, chosen from the *Business Books Best Sellers* list. They then identify the key facts, ideas and conclusions, and transform their précis on to a thirty minute audio tape. This can be listened to on the plane or train in much the same way as many people learn foreign languages nowadays by using a personal stereo machine. A number of advantages over orthodox study of the written word are put forward. It is claimed that:

- ideas are made clear for use right away instead of being buried in masses of verbiage;
- there is development of personal confidence arising from the ability to converse about the latest business publications intelligently;
- ideas in a brief review are more easily remembered than those 'buried' in a book;
- there is a reduction of perhaps hundreds of hours reading time since the reader gets to the 'meat' of a publication quickly;
- there is a money saving since the purchase of the original texts would cost much more than the annual subscription to the scheme.

There is a market to be found, especially among busy young executives, for this kind of innovative approach. The written word has more orthodoxy of presentation but perhaps the audio type of product will develop and extend into other contexts in the future if it succeeds in winning over those who still like to have traditional written material, whether books or not, which they can personalize by marking significant comments, pages or paragraphs.

TECHNOLOGICAL SHOPPING AIDS, NEW YORK, US, 1992

Throughout North America technological developments have influenced the operation of supermarkets to an impressive extent. Several examples will illustrate the impact micro-technology has had on something as basic as the weekly routine of shopping for the family groceries. In one food emporium in New York the shopping trolleys have little video screens attached to the handle. Each screen displays a list of special offers and these change as the trolley passes from one display stand or aisle to the next. In addition an overhead electronic billboard is constantly updated with special store promotions other than the bargain items of each shelf. Even when in line at the check-out the trolley offers the shopper an opportunity to use the video screen for playing games, using as a calculator, or for receiving further information likely to be of interest to a potential purchaser.

In other emporia there are 'talking aisles' with computerized voices explaining particular items to passers-by. Not everyone finds this helpful as the persistence of these 'canned' voices can cause great annoyance to those who do not wish to hear them. In fact this is one technological novelty that is very rapidly going out of fashion.

It is commonplace in most countries nowadays to expect an electronic check-out point for computing the cost of purchases. Bar codes normally ensure that products have only to be passed over a scanner for the item to be identified and priced as well as being recorded on a printout for the information of the buyer. Within the store there is usually also an electronic scale which the customer can use for weighing and pricing consumable produce such as fruit which is not pre-packed. All that has to be done is to place a chosen quantity on the scale, press an icon illustrating the product in question, and the machine indicates the nature of the item as well as its weight, the price per kilo or whatever, and the cost of the actual amount purchased. It then issues an adhesive label incorporating a bar code to be affixed to the purchase prior to the check-out. What has not yet advanced beyond the experimental stage is the operation of an automated process for packing goods neatly, compactly and securely into a suitable container for transport home, but work continues on the development of several technological prototypes. Even more ambitious, but quite feasible, schemes are in the process of being implemented whereby, for example, the headquarters of a chain of retail outlets can electronically re-price any goods on the shelves in all of its branches simultaneously, together with alteration of the relevant shelf display labels and cash till bar codes.

Interest is being displayed in the possibility of introducing checkout-free stores in the light of some experiments recently conducted in the Netherlands by the Albert Heijn company. In this situation the shopper runs a hand-held wand scanner over bar codes on the goods he/she is putting into the trolley. At the checkout the wand is slotted into a payment console which displays the total amount due. The customer then swipes a credit card through a machine located where the cash till would normally be and verifies his/her identity by means of a palm scan or fingerprint. He/she then exits through a security arch which would sound an alarm if there were any malpractice, mistake or attempt at fraud. Virtually no staff would be needed to supervise the operation and movement through the traditional bottleneck of the checkout would be considerably speeded up.

Smart Store Europe plans to open a complex of this kind at Windsor in England during 1993.

ELECTRONIC TELEPHONE DIRECTORY, SAINT MALO, FRANCE, 1980

Most people are aware that it is impossible to find a printed telephone directory anywhere that is absolutely up-to-date. Even internal lists within business organizations invariably carry manuscript alterations pending issue of the latest official version. Telephone companies accordingly have to maintain a directory enquiries service for telephone users who have the name of a person whom they wish to contact but cannot find or remember the number which they need to call. Even when a printed directory is available to the caller it is likely to be at least one year, and more likely two years, out of date simply because of the time lag in compilation, printing and distribution. On occasion the enquiries operator is unable to help because the enquirer's information is inaccurate as well as incomplete. To pursue a lengthy investigation of names with variant spellings, streets which have undergone name changes, and other factors would be both frustrating and uneconomic.

As a possible means of tackling this problem the French telephone service (PTT) started looking, in the early 1970s, at the possibilities of providing some sort of interactive videotext service. An experimental set-up was introduced in 1980 which would allow the user to obtain directory information in quite a number of different forms. For example a sought number could be looked for:

1. by name, even when there was doubt as to how to spell the name correctly;
2. by occupation, for example by searching listed numbers of all opticians or dentists;
3. by street address and district;
4. by any combination of these or other partially known facts.

Although initial trials with the first groups of volunteers produced enthusiastic responses there was a certain resistance to be overcome in respect of the average user because of public perception of micro-technology and the apparent sophistication of having to use a keyboard instead of just leafing through a book. These reservations have not entirely disappeared even today, particularly with older people, but the *Teletel* system generally got off to a very good start with PTT giving the necessary terminals free of charge to all subscribers. This encouraged people to familiarize themselves with the new type of directory, especially since they were not going to get any replacement of the traditional ones anyway! When users discovered just how easy it was to operate the minitel keyboard there was a demand for additional types of services, even if these involved some extra payment.

The Teletel soon included advertisements and access to other features. It is still constantly being extended by the inclusion of further services for which a modest charge is made. There are three broad areas of information available. These are:

1. Consultation of databases containing useful reference material.

2. Transactional services such as ordering goods from designated suppliers, paying accounts, and making travel reservations.
3. Using electronic mail and bulletin boards for interpersonal communication.

For all these services there is a composite charge which represents a compromise between the connect time payment which is retained by the PTT and the service fee charged by the providers in return for making appropriate information available. The Teletel service as a whole has expanded enormously since its beginnings and it looks as though there is still quite a future ahead for it to develop even more sophisticated services for its clients, perhaps by incorporating a videophone link. The minitel terminal has, by now, become a piece of familiar domestic furniture rather than a technological item in a vast number of French households.

THE VIDEOPHONE, US, 1992

After a delay of thirty years since it was first devised the videophone is definitely making a reappearance in the United States, aided by some really high pressure sales techniques. The American Telephone and Telegraph Company obviously disbelieves the saying that 'You don't get a second chance to make a first impression'. Top executives of the corporation appear to be convinced that at last visual communication has really come about for everyone. For those who knew that the idea was not new, and that the product itself had been tried in an experimental way several decades ago, the emergence of the revamped instrument may be something of an anticlimax.

However what gives it a distinct possibility of success this time round is that the engineers have at last mastered the technology that will enable video and audio signals to be compressed so that both may be sent simultaneously down the same telephone line. This is essentially an application of a digital system, known in the UK as **ISDN** (Integrated System Digital Network). This technological breakthrough permits one ordinary phone line to carry video signals, computer traffic and voice circuits. Furthermore the cost of using the videophone on this system will be exactly the same as making an ordinary telephone call. In the early experimental set-ups, even with slow-scan video, a number of additional telephone lines to carry the visual image were required and the cost was increased proportionately. Although, as always in such circumstances, the initial purchasers of the improved equipment will have to pay a high price for their handset it is confidently expected that sales will run into millions within a couple of years and the inevitable price reductions which will follow should put the item within the reach of everyone who wants it. The question, of course, must be 'Who wants it?'

In the United Kingdom British Telecom believes that a great many people will be looking for the equipment. So much so, in fact, that in September 1992 they offered their shareholders the opportunity to get in an early order for the *Relate 2000* videophone with a 3 inch colour screen 'as soon as it becomes available'. The cost was given as £400 per phone, or £750 for two 'so that you can see the expressions on the faces, watch emotions change, the smiles, laughter and sheer joy of talking face to face' to quote the publicity leaflet. The equipment is now on general sale and is finding a limited market.

It is, however, in the business world that the new device is likely to make most impact through an extension of video-conferencing. Most companies with an international commitment should be able to save considerable sums of money by transacting at a distance the sort of business which would otherwise require face-to-face meetings involving air fares and hotel bills. A video-conferencing system (labelled *VC7000*) was available from January 1993 from British Telecom and offers digital quality, full-colour moving pictures with appropriate sound at a reasonable rental (£1300 per quarter) and normal telephone line charges. A document reader can easily be connected to send text and drawings, and there appears to be no limit to the possible number of participants. A pan-European network is in course of development.

In communication theory we have already seen that the written word depends on language and is therefore open to certain errors of interpretation. The spoken word also depends on language but, in addition, has paralanguage, ie the inclusion of spoken attributes of emphasis, hesitation, inflexion and so on which can improve an understanding of the message. Finally the visual image adds kinesics to this pattern by introducing body language and its contribution of movements and mannerisms as well as features of gesture, expression and mimicry. The more routes which are open to the brain the more likely it is that a message will find a way there. However this may not always be a desirable thing from the point of view of a videophone caller or the recipient of such a call.

The intimacy of this kind of visual togetherness will certainly be reassuring to those who long for closer contact but may be off-putting for those who wish to maintain some distance in their relationships. It is already being perceived by some people as posing an invasion of privacy. For others the prospect is on a level with being caught on *Candid Camera*. No doubt the addition of the video on/off facility (the equivalent of the audio silent button on the normal telephone) will reassure those who are reluctant to declare themselves first. But this must pose an intriguing question to someone who calls you as to what it is that you wish to hide! And will your answering machine of the future be of the sort which captures messages on video recorder as well as the more traditional audio recording? Considering the present popularity of mobile phones, which also are not cheap, there is every chance of an appropriate model of the videophone becoming a real commercial success in the very near future.

DYESTUFFS, INTERNATIONAL AIR TERMINALS, 1991

Things have come a long way since vegetable dyes were first discovered and some colours, such as purple, were reserved (on occasion upon the pain of death) for the exclusive use of rulers and monarchs. The creation of aniline dyes at the beginning of this century gave rise to 'fast' colours, ie those which did not change colour by bleaching, wash out on being immersed in water, or grow paler on exposure to strong light. Neither did they fade as a result of ageing.

Now the innovation has been to produce dyes which do exactly that but in unusual ways. The new techniques appear to have a fairly strong novelty appeal so far as young people are concerned. As so often happens in the case of innovative developments at present the ideas originated in Japan and most of the purchases appear to be made by airline passengers with time to kill between flight connections at international airports. Dyed articles of clothing, especially the cotton T-shirts so popular with young people, can now respond to changes in temperature and pressure. This can produce some eye-catching and at times startling variations in hue. For example *Global Hypercolor* heat-sensitive dyes change colour with the heat of the human body as well as in response to changes in environmental temperature.

One rather bizarre and incongruous effect is that a pink T-shirt, if touched, displays blue hand-prints at the points of contact. Another product, *Global Hypergrafix*, enables part of a dyed design to be invisible at lower temperatures and only appear gradually as the temperature rises. Yet another product responds to ultraviolet light. The stronger the light the quicker the reaction producing subtle and not so subtle changes as the wearer moves from indoors to outdoors or vice versa. Some of these products also act on man-made fibres. So far no one has come up with any industrial or domestic application which suggests a practical use for this phenomenon but it looks as though the novelty effect is sufficient to create a market for such dyed articles of clothing for a few years at least, until something even more novel appears.

AUTOMATED TELLER MACHINES, ENGLAND, 1969

When cash dispensers were introduced in England around 1969/70 they represented the most major change in British banking service since banks first came into existence. For the first time it was possible to withdraw cash (in limited amounts) outside the traditionally restricted bank opening hours. Only those depositors who were considered credit-worthy were entrusted with the necessary machine cards which allowed them, by entering a personal code on the machine keyboard, to withdraw £10. Some affluent or needy customers had more than one card because these were retained by the machine and were subsequently posted back to the customer some time after each transaction. The dispensers were all stand-alone machines which simply provided cash (and were not wholly reliable) but by 1972 the first basic online machines were in operation. These were connected to the bank's computers and were operated by the insertion of a plastic card with a magnetic strip containing elementary coded information such as the account number. The creditworthiness of clients was no longer a major problem since the computer would not allow the machine to pay out money which the client did not have in the account.

While technicians focused their attention on the software applications necessary to operate each network system efficiently, the social scientists considered the possible implications in terms of human response. Many people, for example, are still afraid of 'big brother' type surveillance of their affairs. They worry because amongst other things the withdrawal of funds from different outlets on different days could provide, if it were wanted, an itinerary of their travels and timings of their movements. However the real innovation was that people's behaviour patterns were altered and their actions regarding basic financial transactions with a bank or building society have, in a very few years, undergone a fundamental change. Many present-day bank staff and customers have never met face-to-face whereas in days gone past every customer would normally have been known by name, even in large branches. What tends to happen today is that, instead of a queue at the bank teller's counter, there are now queues at the cash dispensing machines outside. In fact there are some banks who now charge customers a fee for the privilege of having a meeting with senior staff, such as a branch manager, whereas formerly it was taken for granted that such staff were available automatically as part of the service to ensure customer satisfaction.

Indeed after their initial reluctance to do so, because of the capital expense involved, the banks have responded to customer demands for more electronic services to a very great extent. It is widely possible, for example, to obtain not only money but also a certain amount of essential information either on screen or on printout. Such information can include latest balance, proportion actually available for use, listing of last dozen transactions, and so on. Furthermore customers can often 'log-on', as it were, at any one of a very large number of outlets around the country, and in different countries, because of a wide area network system which allows transfer of information from the data system of one bank to the outlet of another. A customer is no longer restricted to a particular bank access point nor, indeed, even to a bank as such since building societies also form a substantial part of the overall network. Additionally any information not readily available at the point of enquiry or access can be requested via the machine and will be despatched by mail to the enquirer.

One of the innovative practices arising from this situation is that there is no longer any great demand for the services of junior bank officials to be available at the front counter to handle the cashing of cheques or the processing of small change. Instead they are more often in the 'back office', removed from public gaze and engaged in more profitable ventures (from the modern banking point of view). These consist largely in selling insurance services, organizing mortgages, dealing in foreign exchange, arranging hire purchase agreements, approving loans, or other allied services. In fact, it is not unusual nowadays for employees to have to meet certain monthly quotas in order to consolidate their position with their employers.

An additional offshoot of this change has been the development of telephone banking which provides what might be described as remote personal services. There is now one bank established in the UK which has no provision for face-to-face customer interaction at all but does all its business by telephone. Other banks are examining the implications of this mode of operation in case it is likely to become increasingly popular.

Perhaps, however, it is crime that hits the headlines more often than other issues in connection with ATMs, simply because it is so visible. While theft and error can occur, as described in the previous chapter, through technical shortcomings, misuse or fraudulent presentation of stolen or tampered-with cards there is a revival of a former, more primitive practice today. The modern thief sometimes resorts to the crudities of his forebears and produces the equivalent of a brick through a shop window. He is now willing to steal the automatic machine as well as its contents where this is possible and seems more profitable. The feat is often accomplished by using a JCB, bulldozer, fork-lift truck or whatever vehicle is most appropriate for separating the dispenser from the location in question. Since institutions such as banks still operate somewhat restricted opening hours the would-be criminal has the advantage of full 24 hour access to the unattended, and often unprotected, cashpoint. This is a form of 'access' which was not originally foreseen and there is now an attempt to block it by the creation of enclosures housing the ATMs, entry to these being by possession of the appropriate coded bank card.

The ATM is a product which is now considered to be indispensable but it appears to be capable of further development to ensure improved efficiency and security.

ROBOTS, ENGLAND, 1992

Robots have been the subject of much speculation in the past and are still viewed with some trepidation by those who fear that eventually robots may be able to dispense with human beings and take over the world. There are, of course, those who do not feel that this would necessarily be a bad thing. However, the form in which robots have made most impact up until now has not been in the android creations depicted in the cinema but rather in the form of machine tools or replacement for human operatives in factories. Some jobs, such as the paint-spraying of cars by hand or spot welding, are nowadays only done in local bodywork and repair shops and never in the major car production factories where assembly line spraying and welding by machine are universal. In fact at the moment the robot excels at performing repetitive precision tasks for which it can be meticulously pre-programmed.

This has many advantages from the employer's point of view. A robot does not, for example, require to be paid, or have vacations or even tea-breaks. It does not fall ill, go on strike or refuse to work overtime. However it still cannot respond in any meaningful way to unforeseen circumstances in the work situation except in the most basic sense, for example by ceasing operation. But sensory feedback is being developed which will further enhance the performance of robots in respect of those jobs where detailed coordination of complex movement is required but where little or no human judgement or decision-making would be involved.

A robotic ear surgeon is awaiting its first human patient in Bristol (indeed by now it may have performed an operation or two) after having been developed by scientists at the Advanced Manufacturing and Automation Research Centre at Bristol University. Surgeons and robotics engineers have pooled their skills to create this device which can automatically precision-drill part of the middle ear to help restore hearing. It can also be adapted to carry out some brain operations and, no doubt, will eventually be used on further parts of the body too. In some other European countries different types of robots have already been involved in major surgery involving the brain, the prostate gland and the inner ear. In California a robotic surgeon (known as *Robodoc*) has been employed to provide hip replacements. This is a fairly routine operation nowadays and normally involves using a mallet and a chisel to provide a secure lodgement in the thigh bone for a plastic insert. The robot, although devoid of bedside or other manners, can ream a cavity with mechanical precision and in really quick time. Although robotic surgery may seem weird, improbable or even unethical it could, in fact, revolutionize many surgical procedures by bringing engineering standardization and technical precision to a process which previously has had a highly individual level of performance and a variable success rate. The personal element, of course, has still to remain to a large extent since a human surgeon must always be available to guide the robot and override it in those situations where the need may arise.

Robots working on material products have become fairly commonplace in recent years. Perhaps the extension of their functions to include working on human beings is not only inevitable but desirable in the interests of efficiency alone.

ELECTRONIC CASH REGISTER, UNITED KINGDOM, 1980s

In the 1970s there was a development of 'point of sale' technology involving attempts to centralize payroll, accounting and forecasting procedures in large retail chains. This resulted ultimately in incidental changes to some familiar pieces of shop equipment including, most dramatically, the homely cash register.

In bygone days the register, or cash till, simply held the money which the customer paid over the counter and, by way of confirmation of the sum involved, displayed the amount of the transaction in a viewing window for both counter assistant and customer. Sometimes a printed receipt could also be provided. Electronic point of sale practice introduced the recording of much more detail in respect of every transaction since it was intended to provide, among other things, a form of continual stocktaking. The latter procedure was always a tedious, labour intensive and inaccurate attempt to reconcile cash receipts with stock which had been disposed of. The physical inventory was invariably wide of the mark and out of date by the time it was able to be used. In any case it provided very little useful information as to how, when, to whom or by whom the stock had been sold. Also the problem of 'shrinkage' was there, as it still is today despite electronic aids. This innocuous sounding term refers to items which are missing without any evidence of payment having been received.

When the EPOS (Electronic Point Of Sale) register made its appearance in the early 1980s it did not differ noticeably from the more traditional machine in external appearance. What was remarkably different was what happened inside, something which has now become commonplace. In operation the typical present-day machine deals with cash registration, stock notification, time of day, nature of item, date, price, colour, design, size, style, how long in stock, whether special offer, sell-by date, quantity remaining, related items purchased etc. This information is automatically and instantaneously communicated to headquarters, if necessary, where appropriate action is routinely initiated. This may include, for example, an instruction to a central warehouse to despatch a particular quantity of certain replacement items to a designated retail branch by a specific date. It may also ensure that particular information be supplied immediately to the stores' buyers who have to negotiate contracts for the supply of future stock from manufacturers or other suppliers. Many of the cash registers today, particularly in supermarkets, are operated by infra-red or laser scanning of previously bar-coded products thus reducing input errors as well as eliminating 'sweethearting' techniques whereby lower prices could be entered for friends and relatives of the check-out operators.

Incidental data picked up from the recorded information, which may have implications for staff concerned, include periods of non-activity of any particular till, number of occasions the drawer is opened for 'No Sale' transactions, periods of slack during each day, and many other details which may or may not be used by management in appropriate decision-making. The electronic cash register is perhaps a relatively minor product to receive our attention but is an indication of what is shortly to come in the development of more fully automated and integrated systems. The amount of personal data which is available nowadays in even the most commonplace of everyday transactions surely merits reflection. Information is the ultimate innovative product!

SUMMARY

The products reviewed here all contain some food for thought. It is not always evident why and how some changes take place and why some seem to make more impact than others. The limited range of products considered in this chapter suggests that whatever the technological merits of any product the eventual widespread acceptance of it is likely to be determined more by consumer demand than by the sales efforts of the manufacturer or supplier.

REFLECTION

Look again at these examples. Can you supply some from your own knowledge or experience which maybe show even better than these the ways in which some products have come about? Reflect again on the continuum from ideas to practices and products. What ideas can you discern behind any present-day products which are trying to make market impact?

APPLICATION

Consider the development and expansion of the French Teletel system since it issued the first electronic telephone directories. Why has the minitel terminal become such an accepted household item throughout France? Why is the French PTT now expanding its service to provide even more Teletel facilities? Are there any facilities which you would like to be able to access?

RECOMMENDED FURTHER READING

As with the previous chapter some of the information given here relates to items published in journal articles, research reports, conference papers and broadcasts not listed in the bibliography.

Basically the same texts as in the previous chapter would be appropriate reading but you should look more critically at the translation of ideas into both practices and associated products. It is in this connection that incidental reading will contribute more than might be expected, the following titles being examples of this.

Coulson-Thomas, Colin J. (1985) *Marketing Communications*, Heinemann, London.

Dyer, Gillian (1982) *Advertising as Communication*, Methuen, London.

Williams, John (1983) *The Manual of Sales Promotion*, Innovation Ltd, London.

Wilmshurst, John (1986) *The Fundamentals of Advertising*, Heinemann, London.

Progressiveness in organizations 13

Every manager makes assumptions about people.

Schein (1965)

By a progressive I do not mean a man who is ready to move, but a man who knows where he is going when he moves.

Woodrow Wilson speech (1919)

'Explain all that,' said the Mock Turtle. 'No, No!...' said the Gryphon in an impatient tone: 'explanations take such a dreadful time.'

Lewis Carrol, Alice's Adventures in Wonderland

All human collectivities may be viewed as organizations of one kind or another. In this chapter the term is used in its generally understood sense to mean business, manufacturing or commercial undertakings having some form of management and command structure. Progressiveness is concerned with the organization being forward-looking in respect of responding to (or, better still, initiating) change. Because a great deal of information has been condensed into this one chapter it contains a few more formal or technical terms (mostly relating to other publications and research work) than has been the case in the previous chapters.

Objectives
When you have completed this chapter you should be able to:

- suggest what constitutes a basic organizational structure;
- differentiate between social and commercial organizations;
- give examples of communication problems in large-scale social organizations such as communities;
- identify aspects of management related to communication and innovation in a commercial undertaking.

THE INDIVIDUAL AND THE ORGANIZATION

Earlier we asked ourselves 'What is an innovation?'. By this stage you have acquired some information about it and about the circumstances in which, and by which, it comes about. Now it is time to consider another relevant question, 'What is an organization?', because whatever kind of society we find ourselves in it represents a very sophisticated type of organizational structure. It is within this structure that we live and function.

The question is an important one since we have so far thought about most aspects of innovation largely in connection with personal decision-making and individual commitment. However, nearly all new ideas, practices and products arise and come to fulfilment in a collective social setting of some kind and the outcome is influenced to a greater or lesser degree by the particular context. While we normally tend to think of organizations as artificially constructed frameworks we have to remember that any setting which depends upon a network of relationships and communication may be regarded as an organization and has therefore been contrived or designed. Any such structure does not usually arise naturally but must be created in the sense that its coming into existence is intended to serve some purpose. This includes groups, communities and societies as well as business enterprises and social clubs. It is, in other words, any human aggregate which is structured in a systematic way. Inevitably this structure has layers, classes or tiers of people stratified according to function or some other quality or qualities, many of which could be judgmental rather than objective.

A working definition proposed in somewhat academic terms by Schein (1965) states 'An organization is the rational coordination of the activities of a number of people for the achievement of some common explicit purpose or goal, through division of labour and function, and through a hierarchy of authority and responsibility'. As with most definitions relating to the affairs of people this tries to include as many relevant general features as possible. In everyday terms we might think of such examples as a camera club, a commercial firm or a corporate body of some kind. In social terms it might be thought of as a formal structure regulating human relationships and involving a hierarchy of people by imposing certain controls, for example in respect of rules of behaviour.

We have already looked at the interaction of the individual and the local community. We have considered the general impact of environmental influences on personal decision-making. Additionally there could be influence from other organizations to which an individual belongs as a member or employee. Also since there is a distinction between innovations which occur *in* an organization and those which are made *by* such a body it is necessary to look more closely at those adoption decisions which are corporate or collective as well as those which are considered to be personal. It is often the former which bring about many of the changes which happen in industrial, commercial and political situations. Since any organization is composed essentially of people there still is, of course, an intimate and intricate relationship between individual and collective interests or activities.

In order for new ideas and processes to arise and be implemented in a corporate setting there must be availability of information about the innovation and this implies a systematic structure which offers channels for communication. Such an organized group of people would then interact collectively in order to achieve some desired aims. They could differ in respect of being private (such as a manufacturing company), or public (such as a government department), as well as in size, geographical location, nature of activity and so on. But all of them would have a broadly pyramidal structure with most people at basic member or operative level at the bottom and progressively fewer leaders, supervisors, managers and directors as one goes up the scale.

There is, as might be expected, a range of approaches to examining organizational structure and process. Many publications in this area have not 'dated' to the extent that books so often do. In particular, many of those issued in the early 1960s still provide the backbone for some contemporary writings in this area. A few special perspectives selected from the last thirty years to indicate the variety of insight attempted have been included in the observations which follow. Reference is made not only to more recent publications such as Wrightsman (1992) and Rogers (1983) but also to those which have stood the test of time such as Blau and Scott (1962), Maslow (1962), Etzioni (1961) and McGregor (1960).

In business settings such as commerce or industry the principles of effective organization are usually taken to include the following:

- hierarchy
- authority
- corporate responsibility
- task specialization
- line and staff control.

Within any organization, consequently, we usually find these features:

- **A hierarchical structure:** This assumes that there are people at the top who occupy positions of oversight and control.
- **Authority:** This legitimizes the instructions which those at the top may issue. It is recognition of their right to give orders.
- **Corporate responsibility:** management decisions are expected to be shared by the managers as a whole although any particular instruction may be the action of only one member of the management board.
- **Task specialization:** Not only is there division of labour on the shop floor but also in the boardroom. Directors concentrate on those features for which they are best suited, for example production, sales, exports or finance.
- **Division of line and staff:** The so-called line responsibility carries from

the top to the bottom in that every employee is responsible to another in a higher position. A typical line is shown below.

LINE MANAGEMENT

Financial Director

↑

Finance Officer

↑

Accountant

↑

Assistant Accountant

↑

Cashier

↑

Clerical Officer

↑

Clerical Assistant

Staff–management relationships are somewhat less well defined being related, for the most part, to people at similar levels interacting mostly through intermediaries such as personal assistants who do not themselves feature in the line management diagrams.

There are other dimensions characterizing levels of decision-making and specificity of responsibilities within organizations but detailed analysis of organizational structures and management functions is beyond the scope of this book. It is, however, difficult to try to consider organizations and organizational innovation while at the same time ignoring all aspects of management. Some brief references to really essential issues will therefore be made as appropriate. For our purposes we can simply accept that even commercial organizations such as manufacturers, distributors and retailers are basically just complex social systems which must initially be studied as a whole if individual behaviour within them is ever to be understood.

Rogers (1983) lists six areas of internal characteristics of organizational structure, which may be briefly outlined as follows:

1. **Centralization:** Power is in the hands of only a few people.
2. **Complexity:** There is a range of knowledge, experience and expertise in those who comprise the organization.
3. **Formalization:** Certain rules and regulations are prescribed for the approved functioning of the organization.
4. **Interconnectedness:** There is interpersonal network linkage.
5. **Organizational slack:** Some uncommitted resources are available.
6. **Size:** An important factor in innovativeness.

It might be noted that the last item mentioned is capable of many interpretations depending on the criteria used.

THE BENEFITS OF ORGANIZATION

An organization has within it many groups which generate their own norms of what is right and proper behaviour and such norms extend to the amount and type of work to be performed.

Who, then, benefits from an organization? Obviously in order for it merely to survive there must be a benefit to someone. In Western society there are at least two major dimensions to organizations. Sometimes these features are mutually exclusive and at other times they co-exist within the same organization. They are the **service ethic** and the **profit motive**. Blau and Scott (1962) have identified beneficiaries by specifying four classes of organizations:

1. **Mutual-benefit associations:** These include such bodies as political parties, clubs, religious sects and professional societies. They benefit primarily the members, the rank and file of the organization.
2. **Business concerns:** These comprise banks, stores, insurance companies and the like. They benefit primarily the owner-managers and shareholders.
3. **Service organizations:** These include hospitals, schools, social work agencies and other similar bodies. These benefit primarily their clients.
4. **Commonwealth organizations:** These are typified by the police force, the fire service and the inland revenue. They tend to benefit the public at large.

TYPES OF ORGANIZATIONS

Etzioni's 1961 typology of organizations is very briefly indicated here. This classification is based on type of power or authority used and provides interesting comparisons of change (or lack of it) with that for present-day structures. Power is generally regarded as the ability to influence people. Authority is specified as the right to use that power. In practice since the powerful legitimize their own actions simply by being able to ignore opposition the concepts of power and authority tend to become merged.

- **Type A** – Coercive authority, eg prisons and correctional institutions.
- **Type B** – Utilitarian, rational-legal authority, use of economic rewards, eg business and industry generally, peacetime military organizations.
- **Type C** – Normative authority, use of membership, status, intrinsic value rewards.
- **Type D** – Mixed structures, eg normative-coercive in the form of combat units *or* utilitarian-normative in the form of a typical trade union.

While for many people this may appear to be little more than an academic type of classification, it does lead to some really practical consequences in terms of the possible involvement of the members. These may be viewed in broad terms as being:

1. **Alienative:** The person is not psychologically involved but is coerced to remain a member.
2. **Calculative:** The person is involved to the extent of doing a 'fair day's work for a fair day's pay'.
3. **Moral:** The person does appreciate the purpose of the organization and his/her job within it and performs his/her work basically because he/she values it.

HUMAN COMMUNICATION IN ORGANIZATIONS

Line management consists of communicating up and down (particularly down!) the inevitable hierarchy. This is called, reasonably enough, **vertical communication**. It is rather more difficult, for reasons that we shall see later, for communications to pass upward than downward. There is also a certain amount of horizontal communication in respect of management staff. So far these comments all relate solely to official communication channels.

There are, however, alternatives to the official system and it is horizontal communication which characterizes the unofficial network. It is of the 'grapevine' variety and is quicker and more interpersonal than the official communications but much more liable to distortion as it passes from person to person. The message tends to become shortened and 'sharpened' so that what was first mentioned as a possibility soon becomes a probability and then a certainty as it progresses. This unofficial structure of the organization is the recognized channel for rumour and gossip.

Assumptions are always made about human behaviour in relation to the context in which the individuals find themselves. This has special implications for examining the process of diffusion of innovations in the context of the work place. This is important because everyday employment can provide many examples which serve to demonstrate the basic features of an organizational model.

In respect of shop-floor and managerial/work force meetings there can be various types of expectation as to the nature of the gathering without anyone having actually specified, or been told, the precise basis on which it is being held. Normally meetings can be meaningfully categorized as falling into one or other of four distinct categories:

1. largely ritualistic;
2. marginally informative;
3. nominally consultative;
4. democratically participative.

In practice this means that there are recognizable constraints on most meetings although these may not always be apparent either to the participants or to the organizers. For each category the characteristics are:

- **ritual**: The meeting is being held as a matter of course or convention simply because it has been listed in the annual calendar of proceedings or because it is traditional to have a briefing or debriefing session at certain points of the process or project.

- for staff to be **informed**: There are times when something occurs which is outside the control of management. A meeting may be called merely in order to ensure that everyone gets the same message. For example in a factory it may be that an expected contract has not been secured and the labour force will accordingly have to be reduced. In this case a decision has already been made by someone in authority in the organization, or it has been imposed by some external body. (An example in 1992 was the attempt by British Coal and the UK government to impose compulsory redundancies on 30 000 coal miners by closing down 31 coalmines. When challenged in the High Court this was held to be unlawful.)
- for staff to be **consulted**: In this situation the position basically may be as indicated above but this time the work force is being asked for ideas and suggestions which will be taken into account in making any decision affecting their future. The decision will, however, still be taken by those who offer the opportunity for consultation since they see it as their responsibility to make the final judgement.
- for the staff to be **involved**: This is all too often the universal expectation of the work force who may be expected to take objection to simply being told of decisions after the event. They may, however, have unrealistic ambitions of being involved in decision-making at all levels, some of which may go far beyond their ability or experience. However, on occasion, they are undoubtedly excluded from much decision-making with which they could cope perfectly well.

The terms *problem-solving* and *decision-making* are often used interchangeably. Academics might wish to debate the precise definitions of each but in practice both terms relate to the identification of at least one possible course of action likely to provide a solution to a difficulty, or the choice of the best approach from more than one option available.

Problem-solving depends on two inescapable issues:

1. Recognizing that there actually is a problem; and
2. identifying what that problem is.

Once these have been accomplished the process of trying to find a solution can begin. This necessitates a systematic and logical approach. However, being systematic is not necessarily being logical, and being logical is not necessarily the same thing as being rational. This point has already been referred to in Chapter 5 but merits mention again as it is important to recognize the implications arising in a complex setting such as an industry or community.

In addition to considerations of decision-making there are generally at least two additional possible scenarios for contemplating human involvement in any organization. These are particularly important in respect of manufacturing or production, and are at the heart of what McGregor (1960) referred to as *Theory X* and *Theory Y*.

Assumptions of Theory X are broadly that:

1. the average human being has an inherent dislike of work and will avoid it if at all possible;
2. because of this human characteristic involving dislike of work most people must be coerced, controlled, directed or threatened with punishment to get them to make adequate effort towards the achievement of organizational objectives;
3. the average human being prefers to be directed, wishes to avoid responsibility, has relatively little ambition and wants security above all else.

Theory Y, on the other hand, relates to the integration of individual and organizational goals and the assumptions here are drastically different from those above. They are that:

1. the expenditure of physical and mental effort in work is as natural as play or rest;
2. external control and the threat of punishment are not the only means for bringing about effort toward organizational objectives, nor are they necessarily the best. People will exercise self-direction and self-control in the service of those objectives to which they are personally committed;
3. commitment to objectives is a function of the rewards associated with their achievement;
4. the average human being learns, under proper conditions, not only to accept but to seek responsibility;
5. the capacity to exercise a relatively high degree of imagination, ingenuity and creativity in the solution of organizational problems is widely, rather than narrowly, distributed in the human population as a whole;
6. under the conditions of modern industrial life, the intellectual potentialities of the average human being are only partially utilized.

With regard to these theories neither is unquestioningly accepted as fully adequate today – indeed there is no universally agreed theory of management itself. However there is some continuing justification for believing in the idea of management-worker *quid pro quo*, ie a behavioural approach which recognizes the importance of motivation and gives due reward for active participation. This takes account not only of the organizational goals but also, very importantly, of the individual's needs.

INDIVIDUAL NEEDS AND ORGANIZATIONAL AIMS

In respect of the individual A. H. Maslow (1962) has specified a hierarchy of needs which condenses the vast range of human wants and desires into five broad categories. These may be regarded briefly as:

1. **Physiological** – survival, food, sleep, sex, etc;
2. **Safety** – socially organized, threat-free environment;
3. **Love** – affection, group membership;
4. **Esteem** – achievement, confidence, respect of others, reputation, independence;
5. **Self actualization** – self fulfilment, maximum use of personal resources.

These are often depicted in the form of a pyramid, the broad base comprising the more fundamental general needs relating to survival as in the first category listed above; the apex, as in category 5, focuses more specifically on personally identified human needs or the 'higher' ones such as the spiritual. This approach in practice has often been associated with certain welfare and church organizations, particularly the Salvation Army which is noted for looking after the most basic bodily needs of the 'down and out' before approaching that person in respect of matters of the soul. The sequence of its ministrations has sometimes been lampooned, albeit sympathetically as well as humorously, as 'soup, soap and salvation'. The essence of the situation is that human needs are never completely satisfied. There is, however, a hierarchy or order of priority in respect of these. Only when the 'lower' needs are responded to do the 'higher' needs attract appropriate attention.

In an organizational context this particular theoretical approach, while being meaningful, does not in itself suffice to identify the basis for motivation. There is no single simple theory which is adequate. Consequently we must consider both individual needs and desired organizational results. Many assumptions have been made throughout recorded history concerning human beings and their motivations to work. The one which held sway for a long time, particularly in basic economic studies, was that of the rational-economic man typified by the writings of, for example, Adam Smith. This led to employees in organizations often being thought of in the following (nowadays considered sexist!) terms. However as yet this attitude of mind has by no means disappeared.

- Man is primarily motivated by economic incentives and will do whatever gets him the greatest economic gain.
- Since economic **incentives** are under the control of the organization, man is essentially a passive agent to be manipulated, motivated and controlled by the organization.
- Man's feelings are essentially irrational and must be prevented from interfering with his rational calculation of self-interest.
- Organizations must be designed in such a way as to counteract man's feelings and therefore his unpredictable traits.

In respect of innovation the psychological problem for the organization is how to develop in its personnel the kind of flexibility and adaptability that may well be needed for the organization to survive in the face of a changing environment. In this respect it is more usual for business organizations to worry about responding to change than to initiating it. It is a point worth noting that commercially successful organizations, as measured in terms of profitability, are rarely those which could be categorized as genuinely innovative. In reality, however progressively minded they may be, if they are not under any great pressure to change in order to maintain or develop markets they will not do so unless and until circumstances indicate that it might be beneficial to make a move.

LEADERSHIP AND TRAINING

It is generally accepted that leadership is not so much a human dimension as a characteristic of particular human response to unique situations at specific times. This can be seen to advantage within an organization where leadership is a function of that organization's operations to a greater extent than any individual trait. Naturally personal leadership qualities such as self-assertiveness, confidence in one's own abilities and a willingness to make decisions are extremely relevant. What *is* important is that leadership potential is distributed among the members of a group and not automatically vested in someone with formal authority. Good leadership and good membership therefore tend to complement each other. Secondly, effective leadership has an excellent opportunity to improve the relationship between a system and its environment especially in respect of identifying appropriate goals which would receive wide acceptance. This is particularly true in respect of training.

Motivation to be innovative can be stimulated by specific training which by its nature can be more readily identified and implemented than the broader and more diffuse aim of education. That is not to say that training does not imply education. It is very often a sound means of ensuring that education does, in fact, take place because of the more precise goals or training objectives to be achieved within the broader long-term educational aims. The terms are being used here in the sense in which they are commonly employed, ie that education refers more to the self-development of the individual while training relates largely to the meeting of organizational needs.

Training programmes for new members of occupational organizations, no matter in what capacity, are nowadays the rule rather than the exception. The problem may be to familiarize a nurse with the special characteristics and responsibilities of a particular hospital ward or department; an air force pilot with the intricacies of a new plane; or a teacher with the requirements of a fresh system of pupil assessment. Whatever the desired outcome there has to be a systematic and methodical approach. The rationale of training implies:

- identification of the training needs or goals;
- selection of the appropriate target group for training;
- designing the training programme; and
- evaluating the outcomes as objectively as possible.

The learning principles involved in training are referred to in numerous publications and might be summarized in the following form. Learning is facilitated if:

1. the learner is motivated to learn;
2. the training itself is meaningful, sequential and developmental;
3. the outcomes do not conflict with earlier learning or the present attitudes of the learner;
4. the outcomes are fairly generalizable to other situations and uses;
5. the new responses carry some real reinforcement by way of reward for achievement;
6. the learner is an active participant rather than a passive recipient;
7. the learning situation allows practice opportunities and provides individual assistance;
8. the learning situation recognizes individual differences rather than having a convoy speed approach to progress.

This is not intended to be the only possible representation of such principles and is, indeed, only a sample of them.

The setting of objectives of some kind is regarded nowadays as relatively commonplace although there is no longer the enthusiasm that there once was for using specified objectives as the sole, or at least major, way to determine management practices. One somewhat outmoded system was actually called *Management by Objectives* and it still survives today in various forms, explicit and implicit, in a wide range of situations.

MANAGEMENT BY OBJECTIVES

While this is not a treatise on either management theory or practice the approach mentioned above deserves a little attention because aspects of it still impinge on managerial skills in so many organizational settings. Despite the blandness of the title this approach was actually rather aggressive in respect of achieving results by the systematic setting of targets for individual employees in an organization. For manual workers engaged in production this posed relatively few problems in that there were material products capable of being counted or otherwise assessed and payment by results could follow. For those in executive and managerial roles the position would obviously be somewhat more difficult.

Some years ago this approach would have found widespread favour as a means of tackling virtually every organizational problem, particularly in respect of production or efficiency. Although no longer accorded such adulation this type of procedure, in many guises, is still being used today in areas of employment where productivity cannot be quantitatively measured as such and where employees would probably be disconcerted to know that they are being judged against a background of outdated factory set procedures. One such area is education where staff appraisal is now a regular feature (and in British universities an annual requirement if central funding from government is to continue), and linked to grading and promotion. The setting of targets can succeed only when there is consultation between each staff member and head of department or immediate superior. Ideally target objectives are not imposed but agreed by discussion for maximum achievement.

There are human problems implicit in this approach. If a lecturer, for example, sets a target for a year in respect of research funding to be sought from a grant-awarding body, the individual may be regarded as allowing ambition to outrun ability if the specified sum is not eventually obtained. It could be seen as a failure of both planning and achievement. Added to any failure to attain other specified goals it may prove to be detrimental to someone who is, in actual fact, doing a genuinely good job and earning his or her keep in very real terms.

On the other hand if the applicant identifies a more modest target, well within the possibilities of achievement, then that person may be thought of as lacking in essential ambition, in assertiveness, in research credibility, in professional contacts and in motivation to make impact in the academic world. Again the consequences for a scholastic career may be little short of disastrous.

At one time it was popular to ask employees to consider their position in an organization and their work within it in respect of three headings: **responsibilities**, **indicators** and **goals**. The responsibility might, for instance, be listed as *ensuring cost effectiveness*, the indicator being *head of finance department*, and the goal *reducing overheads by 10% within two months*. Complicated schedules were often produced in an effort to focus attention on objectives and ensure adherence to personal commitments in respect of them. For many people it was a thoroughly unpopular exercise which had thinly-veiled threatening overtones should the individual fail to perform satisfactorily. It was in many ways reminiscent of the former Soviet five-year plans – and had about the same degree of success!

At the other end of the scale there are some bureaucratic organizations, particularly government departments, where such procedures are relatively unknown. Indeed personal decision-making is often reduced to a minimum to ensure uniformity of treatment, both of individuals and issues. For many people, of course, the term 'bureaucracy' conjures up all sorts of ideas of large impersonal and inefficient organizations. In fact bureaucracies survive simply because they are actually quite efficient. What makes them appear unfeeling and unsympathetic to personal variations of rules and regulations is that most decisions within them are policy decisions, not day-to-day problem-solving, and these are consequently made by people quite remote from the ordinary worker or client.

In the civil service, for example, there is a vast volume of claim forms to be dealt with daily in respect of expenses incurred by employees in undertaking business-related journeys. Without a fairly rigid frame of reference to guide the finance officers regarding whether all such claims

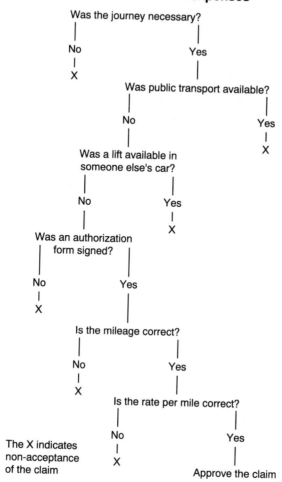

Claim for car travel expenses

Was the journey necessary?

No — X

Yes

Was public transport available?

No

Yes — X

Was a lift available in someone else's car?

No

Yes — X

Was an authorization form signed?

No — X

Yes

Is the mileage correct?

No — X

Yes

Is the rate per mile correct?

The X indicates non-acceptance of the claim

No — X

Yes

Approve the claim

Fig. 13.1   A deductive algorithm.

can be justified or not it is commonplace to produce what is known as an **algorithm** to speed approval. This is really just a checklist for the clerical assistants containing a few simple but necessary questions each capable of a 'yes' or 'no' answer. Subject to brief scrutiny a claim form can be dealt with in minutes. If there is doubt about any point it is returned to the claimant for further details. A typical, but not necessarily universal, example is given in Fig. 13.1.

Unfortunately Fig. 13.2 which now follows illustrates just how 'going by the book' can appear in practice to be so ridiculous and obstructive. It is relations with the public such as these which tend to give bureaucracy a bad name.

Fig. 13.2 Bureaucratic action.

A. INITIATION – the initiation, information gathering and planning preceding a decision.

1. Agenda setting: Consideration of organizational problems and possible innovations available.
2. Matching: Relationship between problem and innovation considered and adjusted for fit.

[The decision to adopt]

B. IMPLEMENTATION – putting the innovation into use.

3. Redefining/restructuring: Innovation is modified to fit the situation and/or organizational changes are made to accommodate the innovation.
4. Clarifying: Relationship between organization and innovation are more clearly defined in the light of experience.
5. Routinizing: The innovation loses its separate identity by becoming absorbed into the ongoing activities of the organization.

Fig. 13.3 Organizational innovativeness.

STAGES IN ORGANIZATIONAL INNOVATIVENESS

Rogers has set out a framework for displaying the stages in organizational innovativeness based on the premise that such stages commence either with an organizational problem needing solution or alternatively with an innovation which might have organizational applicability.

In modified form it could be presented as shown in Fig. 13.3.

As a result of this kind of process certain types of organizational decision-making, such as those which follow, may be specified.

TYPES OF INNOVATION-DECISIONS

1. **Optional** innovation-decisions: The choices to adopt or reject an innovation are made by an individual independent of the decisions of other members of a system.
2. **Collective** innovation-decisions: The decision to adopt or reject an innovation in this case is made by consensus among the members of a system.
3. **Authority** innovation-decisions: Choices to adopt or reject an innovation are made here by a relatively few individuals in a system who possess power, status, or technical expertise.
4. **Contingent** innovation-decisions: Choices to adopt or reject in this context can only be made after a prior innovation-decision. Any two sequential combinations from the first three shown above can constitute this fourth category.

Many characteristics of organizations are similar to those of individuals, eg larger size organizations tend to be more innovative just as are individuals with larger incomes and higher socio-economic status. But there are differences too, for instance in the nature of the structural characteristics of various organizations. In general, the openness of any system is related positively to innovativeness and the more bureaucratic formalization is usually negatively associated.

In the light of the foregoing comments it will not be surprising that one of the most basic aims of any organization remains the efficient (and effective!) utilization of human capabilities in respect of the acceptance of certain ideas and practices. Whoever is involved as the primary agent of change – usually someone in a managerial position – has to make certain judgements concerning what is likely to be 'good' or 'bad'. Although this decision-making may be complicated it still involves fundamentally the same difficulties as beset the overseers in ancient Egypt when constructing pyramids for the Pharaohs, ie how to take account of those factors which just might be important, such as how to:

- recruit a labour force;
- train the workers;
- manage them as a group;
- organize what needs to be done;

- allocate work properly;
- provide appropriate motivation;
- operate a rewards/punishment system;
- adjust to environmental changes and innovations;
- deal with competition from other groups inside the organization; and
- cope with competition from other organizations.

We have been looking just at some matters which relate to formal organizations. To examine even a few of them in more detail would require a separate book but some important points remain to be considered. It hardly needs to be said that all formal organizations breed informal ones. It is clear that only some of any individual's total activities can be relevant to the purpose of a particular organization since the individual has a life to live which comprises many facets, only one of which is concerned with, for example, employment. The organization, therefore, very quickly tends to find that there are the two communication networks previously referred to, namely the official or formal and the unofficial or informal. It is in the very complex, and absolutely essential, informal communication set-up of the organization that participants at all levels learn how to establish the working relationships which allow the organization not only to progress but actually to survive.

A brief diagram of the formal organizational structure for an organ-

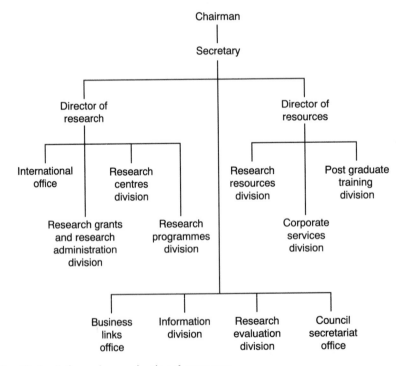

Fig. 13.4　A formal organizational structure.

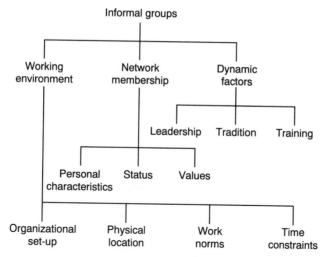

Fig. 13.5   Informal organizational relationships.

ization could look something like this one which has recently been produced for the restructured ESRC (Economic and Social Research Council) in Great Britain (Fig. 13.4).

The informal structure of any organization can not follow a specific management blueprint of this sort. It depends largely on face-to-face communication and would tend to be composed of elements something like those shown in Fig. 13.5.

The relationship between the individual and the organization is interactive, the mutual process establishing the dynamics of both. The individual's motivations and the organizational conditions and practices must be compatible if conditions for innovation are to be favourable.

HUMAN GROUPS AND ORGANIZATIONS

It is not unusual to find some inter-group problems in organizations. A little reflection will indicate that the stronger the identity of any particular group of people the greater will be the social distance between that group and any other. This is one of the reasons why, after many years of effort put into developing community groups, so little benefit seems to have arisen for society as a whole. The fact has to be faced that the process is basically divisive, not integrative. It is, for example, a helpful idea to have supporters' groups or fan clubs to encourage the sporting activities of, say, a football team. The fans can share the pleasure of a winning team in the good times and provide encouragement and a boost to sporting morale when success appears difficult to achieve. However, events in recent years in most European countries have demonstrated the ugly potential for the most extreme inter-supporter violence in connection with crucial games where there is a 'win at all costs' approach.

In organizations of whatever kind there are two problem areas which underlie all of the others which might need to be considered in respect of · groups.

1. The major problem is to ensure that the groups are effective not only in achieving organizational goals but also in meeting the needs of their members.
2. Difficulty lies in establishing as much coordination as possible between groups, initially by improving communication facilities and opportunities.

There are two basic stances which are possible in respect of group relationships. Groups may be collaborative with each other or they may be competitive. Where groups compete there are certain tendencies which can be observed:

- **within any group:**
  1. each group becomes more closely knit;
  2. each exacts greater membership loyalty;
  3. each tries to present a 'united front';
  4. members submerge (at least temporarily) internal differences;
  5. group climate becomes more achievement-oriented;
  6. each group becomes more structured and organized;
  7. groups adopt defensive postures.
- **between the groups:**
  1. each tends to see the other as an enemy;
  2. each has a distortion of perspective;
  3. each creates stereotypes based on own good points, opposition's worst;
  4. hostility disrupts communication, making it difficult to correct errors and distortions;
  5. each group listens to its own supporters and largely discounts what is said by the opposition;
  6. the clearer the identity established for each group the greater the perceived gulf between them.

Even a few moments' reflection will produce illustrative examples in abundance of any of the above points. In addition to parochial instances in our own personal experience there are the recent European Community squabbles between member states and, in more dramatic and tragic form, the extreme ethnic rivalries of Bosnia-Herzegovina highlight the dangerous potential of such situations.

In a win/lose situation the losing group will exhibit the sort of response which is commonplace among individuals. That is to say, they will never accept that they actually lost. It is usual, even at individual level, for all of us to believe that when we succeed we do so by virtue of our sterling qualities, hard work, persistence, innate ability etc. When we lose it was because of obvious external factors, the absence of a 'level playing field', someone 'moved the goal-posts', it was just the wrong time, the odds were against us, the judgement was biased and so on (listen to any football manager explaining his team's poor performance). The winners, on the other hand, may become complacent by having their self-concept confirmed. They may exhibit self-satisfaction rather like those 'how I got where I am today' individuals who sometimes talk such utter nonsense with all the arrogant confidence of those who are not accustomed to being interrupted, much less corrected.

Participant management may avert such situations by:

1. striving to avoid win/lose situations by neither promising nor threatening actions which may not have to materialize;
2. improving communication so that there is a clearer understanding of role and function for everyone in the organization;
3. instituting and developing proper objective assessment of achievement of objectives both for the organization and for the individuals who comprise it.

There is currently a positive attitude towards participative management by many people who have little idea of the implications of such an approach. It is generally believed that participative management is more advantageous than other approaches because:

1. there is a greater readiness to accept change because of information and involvement;
2. manager/worker relations are more harmonious;
3. there is generally a higher level of employee commitment to the organization;
4. there is less distrust of management;
5. there is improved decision-making;
6. communication generally is improved, but particularly upward;
7. there are better chances of building a team spirit.

Much thought and honest effort has, in the last few years, gone into devising more desirable organizational structures than have been commonplace in the past. The aim has been to satisfy the desire for personal gratification at the same time as achieving the necessary collective effort needed for commercial effectiveness. Regrettably it has to be said that no known successes have so far materialized in practice.

SUMMARY

It is virtually impossible to summarize the rather wide sweep of the contents of this chapter since the range of topics dealt with were, in themselves, all very brief summaries of really important issues. The main thrust of the material was to emphasize a point explored in a previous chapter, namely that both individual needs and organizational goals (or community norms) have to be coordinated in order to ensure reasonable success for either. When this is done properly it results in solid achievement for both.

REFLECTION

Your first impression of this chapter may have been that it was, perhaps, the most 'academic' part of this book. However, it actually relates, probably more than any other chapter, to the workaday world. Naturally the attempt to cover a wide range of fairly complicated issues in a single chapter has led to a great deal of information being presented in rather condensed form and some inevitable jargon has had to be employed in the process. It might not be a bad idea to read it again, pausing at those issues where you would like to have more details or examples, and noting the particular topics for later consultation in one of the books listed below.

APPLICATIONS

Part A
In every organizational structure there are people who act as gate-keepers in respect of the flow of information. They edit, censor or suppress information for a variety of reasons. Identify some possible gatekeepers in a typical industrial undertaking, eg a factory and comment on the influence which they could exert on communication within a commercial organization of that kind. What might their motivation be? Who is likely to benefit from their influence?

Part B
In the light of comments made about Etzioni's classification in the chapter which you have just read, what interpretation would you place on the following table and what use, if any, might it have for your own situation?

Types of power-authority versus involvement

| Involvement | Power-Authority | | |
	Coercive	Utilitarian	Normative
Alienative	*		
Calculative		*	
Moral			*

RECOMMENDED FURTHER READING

In addition to supplying supportive information about issues examined in this chapter the books listed here cover a number of points hinted at but not fully dealt with. They are all worth looking at in order to identify material about which you would like to know more.

Burnham, James (1945) *The Managerial Revolution*, Penguin Books, Harmondsworth.

Thought provoking but at a fairly philosophical level and in a very generalized way.

Etzioni, A. (1961) *A Comparative Analysis of Complex Organisations*, Free Press, New York.

If you want an analytical approach this is the book for you. For the really serious student.

Henry, Jane and Walker, David (1992) *Managing Innovation*, Sage, London.

This book focuses on management and is prescribed for the Open University course on Creative Management. However it also includes several references to innovation which is defined as 'the commercially successful use of the solution' to a problem. Don't let that put you off. You now know better and since this book has chapters on related topics by distinguished contributors you should find it interesting and useful in connection with some organizational issues raised by this present chapter.

Maslow, A.H. (1962) *Towards a Psychology of Being*, Van Nostrand, Princeton, N.J.

McGregor, Douglas (1960) *The Human Side of Enterprise*, McGraw-Hill, New York.

Penman, Robyn (1980) *Communication Processes and Relationships*, Academic Press, Melbourne.

Rogers, Everett M. (1983) *Diffusion of Innovations*, The Free Press, New York.

Schein, E.H. (1980) *Organisational Psychology*, Prentice-Hall, Englewood Cliffs, N.J.

One of the standard psychological texts related to the study of people in organizations.

Sherman, Barrie (1985) *The New Revolution*, John Wiley and Sons, London.

Wrightsman, Lawrence S. (1992) *Assumptions About Human Nature*, Sage, London.

Well worth reading – a little at a time.

The Future 14

The future influences the present just as much as the past.

Friedrich Nietzsche (1884)

There was a Door to which I found no Key: There was a Veil past which I could not see.

The Rubaiyat of Omar Khayyam,
Fitzgerald's translation (1859)

I like the dreams of the future better than the history of the past.

Sir Isaac Newton (1688)

For we know in part, and we prophesy in part . . . we see through a glass darkly.

1st Corinthians 13, 9 & 12

I said to the man who stood at the Gate of the Year, . . . 'Give me a light that I may tread safely into the unknown. . . .'

Minnie Louise Haskins, poem God Knows (1924)

At this stage we take a tentative look into the future, in so far as we can, knowing that whatever we foresee it is unlikely to turn out quite like that in the end.

Objectives
After completing this chapter you should be able to:

- suggest possible features which might characterize the home of the future;
- identify what changes might occur in respect of the office of the early twenty-first century;
- indicate developments in manufacturing procedures likely to result in different types of factories replacing those of the present day;
- recognize those factors which might have most impact on continued innovation.

PREDICTION

Prediction is a dangerous business. It is notoriously error-prone and founded on uncertainty. For the most part this is because to a large extent it is based on our awareness of, and particularly our understanding of, what has already happened. From the past we draw certain conclusions regarding, for example, cause and effect which we then proceed to project into the future. These projections rely heavily on data which, in the nature of things, are likely to be both incomplete and inaccurate. The weather forecast which was perfectly on target for the morning may be hopelessly wide of the mark by the time evening comes. The only certainty about prediction (again based on happenings in the past) is that it will, to a greater or lesser extent, always be wrong! Our attempts to foretell the future represent, for most of us, the triumph of hope over experience.

Nonetheless we all expect to see tomorrow and, to that extent at least, we tend to look ahead – some of us further than others. We also have certain expectations about the possible outcomes of developments now under consideration or even actually under way. We indulge in hopes or suffer fears. The short-range predictions which we may make are more likely to come about than those which cause us to peer further ahead. Therefore in an environment which is not only changing but doing so extremely rapidly it is necessary, whatever the possible shortcomings of any crystal gazing, to anticipate and prepare for things in the future – perhaps even in the very near future – being significantly different from their present state. Possibly the most important criterion in looking ahead is to do so on a continuous basis so that any probing of what is expected to come is constantly being fine tuned by actual observable activities supporting or retarding our predictions.

It is in the nature of human experience to internalize past experiences and previous knowledge so that even when we can no longer recall these things our expectations of the future nonetheless rest on this foundation. That being so, we usually look forward to a further development of the things about which we already have some knowledge or forewarning. This chapter is no different. Let us then consider what elements can actually make impact on human perception of what the future may bring.

THE INFORMATION EXPLOSION

The so-called **information explosion** looms large in many people's minds today. We are often said to be living in the information age (or is it now the post-information age?) and, like all processes which have exponential-like characteristics the *rate* of growth probably has not changed at all but the threshold of observability has. When developments have grown to such proportions as to attract attention the dominant features often appear to be those of a situation rapidly going out of control. Anyone who has brewed their own beer or fermented their own wines knows what this means. When you have prepared the ingredients and fed in the yeast you watch anxiously for hours and nothing seems to be happening. Unseen by you the yeast cells are dividing into two, the two into four, the four into eight and so on, yet hours pass with no visible signs of any action. Next time you look at the container the mixture is foaming over the top; really vigorous fermentation is taking place and everything seems to have happened at once. In fact nothing has changed in the sense that everything is still proceeding at the same orderly rate as before, only now it seems to be beyond control.

The following tale is an apt illustration of exponential growth.

There is an Indian legend that tells of Sissa Ben Dahir, the inventor of chess, who was rewarded by King Shirim for his invention. The king had intended to place a gold piece on each of the 64 squares of the chess board but Sissa asked instead that he put a grain of wheat on the first square, two on the second and so on, doubling the number of grains at each move. The king was astonished at the apparent modesty of the demand but sent for a bag of wheat to humour the inventor. The king's servants placed the grains of wheat as carefully as they could but by the time they came to the twelfth square they had to continue by placing the number of grains in a heap at the side of the chess board – and the bag was empty before they reached the twentieth square.

The king sent for more bags, and then for more until he had finally to give up the effort of trying to satisfy the request. Not all the wheat in India nor, for that matter, in the whole world, would have satisfied Sissa's demand.

This illustrates the kind of problem perceived by the political economist T. R. Malthus when he wrote his famous treatise on population towards the end of the 18th century. He believed that agricultural land was increasing only in arithmetical proportions, eg 100, 102, 104 etc, whereas the rate of growth of the population seemed to be proportional to population size and therefore tended to double every few years in the form 100, 200, 400 etc. It seemed inevitable, therefore, that in a relatively short space of time the world's human population would outgrow the available food supply. Changes in food production techniques and the development of family planning, amongst other factors, have ensured that the problems today are more of equitable distribution of food rather than actual shortage despite a phenomenal increase in the world's population.

Other predictions for the future have also failed to materialize. A century ago there was a prediction that personal road transport could not continue to develop indefinitely otherwise the highways would eventually be ten feet deep in horse manure. The horseless carriage put paid to that one while, in due course, producing its own kind of pollution horror. As with so much of our speculation we must make certain assumptions, the validity of which may change dramatically with the passage of time. One of the major problems in all information processing is that the human mind can carry and manipulate only a restricted quantity of knowledge, and certainly only a very limited amount at any one time. Even the storage capacity of the human brain, while remarkable, is finite and the range and complexity of technological development in particular could well be outstripping human adaptability not only to comprehend it but even to adjust to it.

CHANGING LEADERSHIP PATTERNS

It is not just a social truism but an observable fact that in every situation where there are several people there is a *de facto* leader and there are those who are led. In social science, as in physical science, nature still appears to abhor a vacuum. There is always some personal influence on individuals in a social setting and the nature and source of that influence and how it is exerted has exercised our minds in the previous chapters of this book. There are situations in which influence is brought to bear by government and the weight of authority exerted in the public interest as a matter of general policy. Other, and perhaps even more demanding, pressure comes from discovery and manufacture which seeks to promote the commercial interests of the parties involved. And there are always the inevitable forces which arise from the mere physical proximity of our fellow human beings. What things, then, are likely to change in the future – and in what way?

Change, where it occurs, will necessarily be of two kinds (or, more aptly, it will be in two very different sectors), namely human and technological. Both kinds will interact but it will, as in the past, be impossible to show them in any relationship which depicts either as necessarily being the cause of the other. In the scientific and technological field as a whole the roles of innovator and opinion leader at present tend to coincide to a greater extent than in other contexts. This may be due partly to the network systems which are created by the patterns of communication between inventors, researchers and developers in related fields. However, networks are normally composed of individuals supportive of some kind of establishment view, ie people who contribute to the construction and operation of systems or organizations. It is the fact that they actually do conform to a very large extent which enables the network to be established in the first place. Where, then, will any innovative deviants come from?

In considering this point we should accept that there are many people who use sophisticated equipment happily, without knowing anything at all about how it works. A common example would be found among car drivers. There are others with a similar approach to, say, television or personal computers. We should also bear in mind the informal networking patterns which tend to appear in society incorporating, often without their being aware of it, those who share common interests and who tend to read similar publications, engage in related activities etc. In other words there may be a black-box network of those who are not concerned with technology itself but who regularly find uses for its applications.

These are the people who are most likely to contribute to the future encouragement and adoption of innovations. The three areas in which such innovatory ideas could be most evident would almost certainly be the factory, the office and the home. Perhaps the school also should be included although, in this connection, the potential appears to be greater in the sector of adult higher education. Let us consider the three main areas first of all.

THE FACTORY OF THE FUTURE

Nothing dates quite as fast as science fiction. Today it is virtually impossible to devise fictional perspectives for applied science because developments tend to turn fantasy into reality even as we ponder the improbability of it. Bearing this in mind it is a reasonable assumption that the concept of automation will be further implemented with the passage of time. Human workers require certain standards of health, safety and even comfort in order to perform adequately in the workplace. Today there are many situations where repetitive, dangerous, noisy and dirty work is being undertaken adequately by machines which do not require human work conditions. What is likely to differ in the future is the nature of the control system for such machines.

It is possible, without too much effort, to imagine a factory where very few people are actually in attendance, and even then only for a limited time. Raw materials are automatically removed from store as needed by the manufacturing machines. The materials are loaded and moved by computer controlled robots. In a similar manner the finished products are passed through a final inspection having been carefully monitored at all stages of production, the products are packed, arranged for despatch by appropriate transport and invoices made out for the purchasers. All this and more without human intervention at all except where amendments to a programme are necessary, for example by the inclusion of the name, address and equipment requirements of a new customer.

Instead of robotic machines designed to perform specific tasks the automatons will be fully programmable for a very wide range of functions and only a keyboard alteration, the pushing of a button, or perhaps just a voice command will be needed to vary immediately the work which they are required to carry out. In addition to this, the machines will no longer merely engage in pre-set tasks without modification. Their sensory feedback, especially in respect of vision systems, will enable them to make certain amendments to processes if required, to learn from past activities, to recognize defects or irregularities and to make appropriate logical inferences in respect of alternative courses of action.

One of the inevitable consequences of such a situation will be massive redundancy in areas of employment which were formerly the preserve of human beings. This will have implications for society as a whole since the unemployment problem will hit the trades operative and manual worker harder than managerial staff although the latter category will almost disappear in the form in which it is known today. After all, management at present is essentially focused not on the oversight of resources and processes in general but of employees in particular. If they decrease almost to the point of disappearance, what is there left to manage?

THE OFFICE OF THE FUTURE

We have only to look at the typical office of today, compared to that of thirty years ago, to see just how remarkable are the changes in the nature of the work undertaken. There is hardly any writing in books or documents, very little typing and virtually no carbon copying or primitive spirit or ink duplicating. Those of us who can recall only too well the endless clacking of manual typewriters will have noted (with little regret) the closing of the Smith Corona factory in New York State in 1992. It was the last surviving mechanical typewriter factory in the whole of the USA. The ubiquitous word processor has rendered orthodox typewriters redundant, even for the addressing of envelopes which was the main reason why some were still retained in offices at all.

Gone too are the 'junior' office chores such as hand delivery of memos throughout a building or even local mail delivery to other firms in the neighbourhood. There is virtually no face to face contact with customers or even with other employees. In some instances many of the office staff rarely attend the headquarters where they are employed; they communicate regularly, perhaps daily, via their remote computer terminal or by other means. In addition there are the telex, the fax machine, electronic mail, and now the more recent voice mail systems.

When we think of the office of the future we inevitably tend to think of the electronic office. But is the office as we still know it a dying concept? Will it survive in *any* form, electronic or otherwise, in the future? The answer is probably **yes**, because with the growing complexity of society there is an increase in the volume of information to be collected, collated, analysed, stored, retrieved and transmitted. Some sort of centralized clearing house is of obvious advantage here and the concept of the office is likely to persist as the kernel of any reorganization of what has been in the past a notoriously labour intensive clerical activity. What will change most is the way in which such an office will operate.

Some of the lower levels of repetitive work and its associated bureaucracy will disappear with the removal of copy typists, filing clerks and general 'assistants'. Personal computers and associated peripherals together with a complete range of appropriate software will become easier to use, so that less secretarial help is needed and executives and managers can produce their own memos, spreadsheets, fax and other material. In fact instead of a desk the electronic workstation will be the more common piece of office equipment and will also be a node in a **LAN** (Local Area Network, eg within an organization) or even a **WAN** (Wide Area Network to external contacts, perhaps in other countries). Two developments already being worked on are going to contribute in a massive way to this change. First of all there will no longer be any need for the massive cabling with associated trunking and restructuring of internal architecture which at present is needed to upgrade a traditional office to an electronic one. Cordless networks will be not only possible but commonplace with the insertion into individual computers of a card which will enable interconnection by radio waves instead of wire cables. Also computers will finally be able to operate without any disk at all, floppy or hard, because of the further refinement of microchips which will provide all the necessary ROM (Read Only Memory) and RAM (Random Access Memory) needed to cope with the most sophisticated demands. The successful construction of voice-activated computers will also eventually minimize the present importance of keyboard skills in respect of computerized operations. And perhaps most exciting (or should it be frightening?) of all is the development of **neural networks**. These are electronic systems which simulate the activities of the human brain and accordingly consider different factors simultaneously, rather than consecutively as is the case with even the fastest computers today. Also the 'thinking' is modified by experience, ie the system is capable of 'learning'. Will machines make the really important decisions in the future?

The principal shift of focus will certainly be the long-awaited move away from paper shuffling towards faster access to information bases and consequently speedier and more universal personal decision-making at an appropriate level of staff involvement.

THE HOME OF THE FUTURE

Probably the first picture which springs to mind when we consider the home of the future is a residence which, however modest in size, is fully equipped with labour-saving devices. Lights will come on automatically when it gets dark or as people move from one room to another, heating will adjust to maintain a preset temperature and air conditioning will ensure a constant appropriate humidity. Doors will open and close as we approach them, the car can be driven into the garage virtually without slowing down as the sensitized door rises automatically to allow it entry. Meals will be ready at the desired time from cookers or microwave ovens, our favourite programmes will be automatically recorded from radio and television for us to hear and see at the times most convenient to us and our groceries ordered electronically by scanning the latest offers on the local cable network. The videophone will link us to our family and friends at home and overseas, and satellites will ensure world-wide reception of television programmes as well as extending personal communication.

So, what's new? All of these things are available at the present time for those who want them. For those with additional money to spend there are even personal helicopters and private jet planes. The technology not only exists but it is relatively no more expensive than, say, foreign holidays. Why, then, don't more people have such extra technological assistance now? What is it, really, that will be different about the future?

Well, the second picture which usually comes to mind is of almost unlimited leisure. It is generally accepted that some form of income is necessary if one is to enjoy this but there could be an absence of any necessity to go out to a place of employment in order to earn a living. Information technology links could ensure participation in the scheme of things along the lines already indicated for home working and the office of the future. For those who do have to travel, perhaps personal transport may have to be sacrificed so that road congestion is lessened and pollution decreased. High speed modified public transport could be developed out of present-day 'dial-a-bus' services which are a commercial compromise between individual transportation such as taxis and mass transport facilities. Perhaps monorail or specially adapted hovercraft could be used to free the roads by being versatile enough to offer universal transport over any terrain at minimum cost.

For those still able and desirous of undertaking personal travel it might be possible to indicate to the vehicle by pushing a button or inserting a pre-programmed card where we wish to go. The vehicle, no doubt electrically operated with the assistance of solar power, would then be guided by satellite safely to its destination, avoiding obstacles such as people and other vehicles by its in-built sensory system. Its occupants, meanwhile, would be able to get on with video-conferencing, computing or whatever task needed attention before arriving at the workplace. The wealthy individualist would, no doubt, be the possessor of one of the flying platforms which were publicly demonstrated at the Los Angeles Olympic Games in 1984. This was, of course, a primitive form of airborne locomotion (comparable with the horseless carriage forerunner to our present day motor car). Refinements yet to be developed will ensure optimum safety, speed, economy, ease of operation, and silent flight with all-weather protection for the occupant.

For those who are no longer able or willing to venture into the world outside their homes there will, of course, be the robotic servants to minister to every need. An electronic/mechanical attendant will be able to fetch and carry at a word of command, will listen to worries and complaints, offer sympathy and advice and ensure that there is variety and interest introduced into every little activity of the daily round. With its vast store of knowledge of the world and international affairs as well as more homely memories of the characteristics of the master/mistress it will ensure that for all whom it serves there will be an orderly and rewarding interaction with the environment and the tasks that relate thereto.

Should the human take ill or require medical attention there will be no problem. The robot (being able to recognize unusual symptoms calling for immediate attention) will without delay summon a fellow electronic wizard who will unhesitatingly and unfailingly diagnose the ailment and administer appropriate treatment. Should this require the replacement of ailing limbs or internal organs a suitable requisition will be made to the appropriate storage bank which maintains relevant items for spare part surgery. Transplants of basic organs will be performed as a matter of course. The fact that human hearts, lungs, kidneys and livers can be transplanted today no longer is newsworthy. Neither is the reconnection of a severed limb by micro-surgery, involving the joining together of many nerve circuits. Surely brain transplants must be the next logical step? Even if not, it is almost certain that the coming together of neuron and electrical circuitry will enable microprocessor implants to be carried out to remedy genetic defects or acquired shortcomings and perhaps to supplement brain capacity as well. Such operations would, naturally, be carried out by robotic surgeons. Should the repairs or replacements be unavailable, there may still be room for human intervention, or at least participation, by the clergy whose functions would continue to be beyond the comprehension of machines. This is one field in which technology could not compete.

LIFE AND SOCIETY IN THE FUTURE

As life becomes more sophisticated or complicated a great deal of record-keeping needs to be done to ensure that relevant information about past situations as well as solutions to former problems are retained in such a way as to be of benefit in the present and the future. One obvious example would be our personal medical records. Very often our past history of ailments and their treatment sheds light on present complaints. The problem is that human memory is limited in capacity and selective in recall, even when it is possible to remember some things at all. Written records are a help but they are, of necessity, fairly brief and subsequently open to errors of interpretation, something which every history student knows only too well. Computerized records are better because a great deal more information can be retained in a very small amount of space and it can be continuously updated with little effort. It is also possible to cross-reference issues related to any particular individual so that a sort of personal profile may be available in the form of a 'smart card' identity. This can not only identify the holder with regard to physical characteristics, age, address, sex, financial standing, educational attainment and criminal record (if any) but also any other data appropriate to the society in which that person was located. The danger is that this might (and, by many people, undoubtedly would) be considered an invasion of privacy. Much personal data is regarded by the average individual as both private and confidential and fears of a kind of electronic tagging could be well founded should a less than liberal society consider operating it.

The impact of computerization will be difficult to estimate but it must be considerable. In computer-aided diagnosis alone, medics will have available a range of information on the patient's past history, present condition, assessment of ailment and range of possible treatments and their consequences which go far beyond present computerized records and data bases. That is because much of present day computer-stored data are imprecise and lacking in both quantitative and qualitative measure because they are based, in large part, on subjective judgement which is often incomplete and therefore inaccurate. Machines, while not replacing human intervention entirely, will be able to carry out standardized diagnostic tests using advanced chromatography and ultrasonic, laser and other relevant technology. From such tests analysis of functions and conditions can be carried out, trends monitored and projections indicated. Computerized investigation of the accumulation of evidence regarding outcomes of various treatments for a wide range of patient categories will be automatic. This will lead to a presentation of the essential elements of a situation from which many of the difficulties arising from emotional, intellectual and communication influences have been removed. The information will be as complete and relevant as possible and, above all, will be immediately retrievable. When it is collected and collated then it is time for human judgement to take over. Data collection, storage and retrieval does not, of course, constitute decision-making. It is not intended to. It is only an aid to it – but what an aid!

Three-dimensional anatomic displays can be provided for detailed scrutiny and the patient can be involved in identifying from a personal perspective where that certain discomfort or malfunction appears to be located. The surgeon, if surgery is needed, can then set up a **virtual operation**. This will simulate reality, so that the entire surgical procedure may be carried out, much like car designing and testing is undertaken today. This will ensure that every reasonable eventuality is anticipated and prepared for before the actual physical operation is undertaken. Not only will procedures such as this improve diagnosis, they will also contribute to the level of subsequent treatment and, in addition, the knowledge gained will swell the store in the data banks for the benefit of others.

In respect of those with handicaps such as immobility, blindness, deafness and other disorders of normal human functions there will be a range of devices to assist such processes as speech and movement. These will be developed from the basic artefacts available today. Because the sensory signals in the human body are electrical in character it is only a matter of time, as previously mentioned, until there is a fusion of technical and neuron circuitry to remedy some of the more obvious handicaps. Perhaps replaceable cards will be inserted to bring about any necessary program changes. One of the most important developments lies in the area of electronic body implants. The idea of the pacemaker for heart patients was a real revolution when the possibility was first proposed. Nowadays there are some implants available which make it possible for certain deaf people to hear. Developments continue with similar devices to help the blind to see, if only in a limited way. In the very near future there will be other (more preventative) devices implanted to act as sensory detectors for changes of body chemistry, cholesterol accretion, coronary irregularity or general pathological disturbance. Others may be worn, wristwatch fashion, to monitor daily physical performance and indicate any significant deviations. Developments in such monitoring devices relating to human response to stress could lead to, for example, lie detectors which could simplify, for a start, many legal situations. The impact on political candidates, of course, could be devastating!

When, some years ago, I asked a physicist friend in the US what the millions of dollars spent on the space programme had accomplished for us he replied in one word, 'Accuracy'. Perhaps the key word for the future will be *miniaturization*. The trend towards making things smaller at the same time as they are being made more powerful is gaining momentum. At the present time one of the fastest growing sectors of development is in **nano-technology**. This is concerned with producing mechanical or electronic operations which can be completed in millionths of a second. In order to do this the physical construction of such machines must be of molecular dimensions. Some prototypes are already functioning under microscopes in laboratories and inevitably, in the course of time, there will be little specks of machines which could, for example, be injected into the human bloodstream to pursue and destroy malignant body cells and attack cancerous growths. Also the whole concept of implants could be revolutionized by such extremely minute constructions.

It hardly needs to be said that society itself will be different too. If we are now in a post-industrial, and moving into the post-information, society presumably sociologists might regard subsequent stages of society as post-post-industrial or (post?)post-information.

THE (POST?)POST-INFORMATION SOCIETY

At the present time there is still quite a lot of debate about the concept of intellectual property. This relates to the fact that information has become a commodity which may be exchanged, stolen or sold. It is difficult to see how it could be borrowed or lent but otherwise it behaves much in the same way as material property – with one exception. Whatever the form in which it is given to others it still remains with the originator. In many instances, for example the creation of potential customer data bases, the information on possible or actual purchasers may be sold to several different traders and manufacturers but still remain available for further use if required by the original compiler. But information need not be of this form at all. Consider advertising. It is a long time since the realization grew that we no longer sell products; we sell *images*. What woman can easily be persuaded to change from one brand of soap to another? Soap offers only cleanliness. Skin creams, on the other hand, offer the possibility of obtaining or recapturing beauty. Is any price too high for a product which holds out even a faint possibility of producing miracles? Again consider, as mentioned earlier, the stereo-type of 'the good teacher'. Could an actual role model ever effectively compete?

In a totally different context, perhaps prisons would no longer be needed except for the most violent and dangerous persons for whom physical separation from society is in their own interests as much as that of their potential victims. Convicted criminals who are not locked up in prisons may be restricted in their movements by more sophisticated electronic tagging than the primitive efforts of the present time. Not only will their whereabouts be known precisely by means of satellite surveillance techniques but they will be continuously monitored on a display screen at a control centre. Devices of a somewhat similar kind will ensure that the elderly and the infirm will have access to instant attention should it become necessary. In the political field there need no longer be the tedious delays in obtaining opinions from the populace by way of elections, plebiscites or referenda. Instead it will be possible, perhaps normal, to put the issue on telecast; hold a tele-conference with politicians of other parties; seek responses from enquirers and critics; and then invite viewers to vote yea or nay by pressing a button. That will be the matter decided in a more democratic manner than applies at present. Electronic mail will be commonplace rather than the medium of communication for the technocrat. Convergence of technologies will ensure that there will be standardization of interconnections and access codes so that the bewildering area of alternative systems at present operating becomes a coordinated network world-wide. The Open University type of higher educational system, as well as radio, television and correspondence will, by the same means, become universally available.

Practices such as visits of observation by social workers or teaching practice by student teachers in training will be unnecessary because of the development of virtual systems of the kind already mentioned. These will be able to simulate a range of conditions far beyond what are available in reality and without the consequences which inevitably arise in real life from errors of judgement or accidents. In respect of leisure too it will be customary for many people to be able to don a headpiece with the desired programme installed. It would then become possible actually to live in another situation complete with all the usual sensory perceptions of the normal physical world. In this way Walter Mitty type fantasy could become, for the individual, reality in every meaningful sense of the word. The problem of distinguishing between reality and this dream world may, of course, cause psychological problems, since for many people the artificially created and desired environment may prove to be much more attractive than their familiar, mundane daily existence. This situation could well be more acute in the future because of the extended – and enforced – leisure time which many people would have. Leisure would no longer be seen as a benefit of the privileged few who enjoy secure positions of employment; it could be the curse of the unfortunate masses who might no longer find suitable, or any, employment because of human replacement by technology. One extension of this in the artistic world might be that further refinements to the production of holograms could finally sound the death knell of two-dimensional representations of anything, except where this is done for effect, as is the case at present with black-and-white photography.

Simultaneous translation will enable all language speakers to converse with each other without difficulty. Micro translators will be worn in the same manner as present day hearing aids and similarly remote controlled by a small infra-red handset. The appropriate button is pressed, not for speech, but to receive someone else's spoken word which is then translated (as in international conferences) into the hearer's native language. Similarly in accessing data bases in other countries it will be necessary simply to indicate the language in which the information is required for it to be delivered accordingly. In respect of telephone inter-connections the caller's phone number will be indicated on the receiving phone even where it is not one of the video system types. Allowance will be made for this facility to be disabled for confidential communications, eg to the police.

Video screens which hang on the wall like pictures have been forecast for a generation now. In the near future they should become a reality with a TV receiver being capable, because of improvements in miniaturization, of being moved and hung anywhere in a convenient viewing position. Of course the wall itself may be a giant screen giving access to hundreds of broadcast channels around the world with full stereophonic sound for each individual hearer, irrespective of the seating of the listener. The picture could be three dimensional, perhaps with additional sensory dimensions in addition to sound and vision. Again the fantasy of the earlier cinema may come to life. Following the early still lantern slides came the 'movies', then the sound movies, followed by the colour movies, then the primitive 3-D, and finally variations of the extra wide wraparound screen and the dispersal of occasional odours to add an extra dimension of awareness. Why not now the feelies and the smellies too? After all, even the present 'state of the art' in virtual systems can demonstrate the comparative ease with which such provision can be made today. What, then, might *not* be possible in the future?

Is it likely that these or similar changes will actually come about? It is certainly not an unrealistic assumption since many of them are operative today, if only on a limited scale and others are already in the course of development. For example the automated teller machine has recently been developed by Olivetti. Its capabilities are far beyond the familiar hole-in-the-wall cash dispenser level. There is now an experimental interactive video setup in Rome, Milan and Turin whereby a customer can actually dial up an appropriate official who appears on screen to discuss whatever financial matter needs attention. Any necessary documentation can then be printed out on the spot and signatures can be exchanged. Further developments are in hand.

But to say that things are technically possible does not, of course, necessarily indicate that in operation they will find universal acceptance. Technology will continue to be developed and improved but human beings show every sign of maintaining the kind of attributes which they possess at present. Individual attitudes will have to change, group consensus may be needed, perhaps at societal level, for some of the more embracing measures, and communication will need to improve beyond the provision of more opportunities to exercise it in different ways. Opportunity can be seized only to the extent that people are *prepared* for it. If the secret of eternal life were contained in a manuscript written in Urdu you could not benefit from it unless you understood that particular Hindustani language. What does this tell you? I hope that you have already worked out the implications, which many people have yet to learn, that we *create* more opportunities than we *find*. The future welfare of everyone on this planet depends on many people being willing not just to respond to change but to try to bring it about – beginning with themselves.

Technological development will almost certainly continue, if only as a response to human curiosity and our normal desires for improvement in manufactured products. But in order to initiate social change there must be a degree of venturesomeness on the part of everyone involved. This requires some identification of our ultimate aims in respect of any particular society and also an ability on our part to specify more immediate objectives for individuals like ourselves to try to achieve. Everyone is involved in the exercise. As with life itself all are participants; there are no spectators.

I wish you every success in your endeavours.

SUMMARY

The so-called information explosion has already produced significant differences in the ways in which we access information and the use we can make of it. The ready availability of many kinds of data and the electronic means of manipulating it have produced important modifications of daily practice which suggest that there will be even more sweeping changes in the future. Significant alterations are likely in respect of such traditional institutions as the factory, the office and the home as well as in transport and personal communication systems. The type of society which follows on from the post-information society will be one which has unusual problems to solve, such as how to enable people to cope with extended leisure time.

REFLECTION

In the light of the comments and conjectures expressed above your reflections might take account of observations such as the following.

Whatever predictions we might make for the future depend heavily upon our interpretation of what we have previously experienced and especially those which we have cause to remember. They also are coloured by the projection of our fears, hopes and ambitions in respect of what might eventually come to pass. Our forecasts are not likely to turn out exactly as we imagined; indeed many of them will never come true at all. But the future can hardly avoid having some inheritance from the past and therefore we may speculate that:

- technological artefacts will change a great deal and the rate at which they do so will continue to accelerate. One major aspect of future technical advances must be in respect of continuing miniaturization as well as the inevitable replacement of human labour by electro-mechanical machines programmable to be able to respond to personal control at a distance;
- human nature, on the other hand, is unlikely to undergo any dramatic alteration. There is no reason to suppose that the heirarchy of personal needs will not continue to be as realistic and as insistent in the future as in the past. The prospect of fundamental changes in inter-personal relationships, therefore, seems also improbable and the interplay of forces of influence between environment and individual will continue much as before.

Society may well remain reasonably stable, at least in its structure, in many Western countries but the forces for change will continue to ensure that the situation never becomes static.

The process of innovation will continue indefinitely.

APPLICATION

It has been said in this chapter that nothing dates quicker than science fiction. What is your opinion? What items of current science fiction are you aware of? Are they largely a sort of fantasy unrelated to the real world or could they give a glimpse of the world as it might be in the future – and perhaps sooner than we think?

Illustrate your answer with suitable examples. Identify the personal, social and technical features relating to innovation and communication which would probably be instrumental in either promoting or retarding the developments which you have identified as possible or probable.

As this is the last opportunity in this book to apply theory to practice the questions posed here incorporate all aspects of the topics covered throughout this book as well as offering an opportunity for you to reflect fairly deeply on your own experience and your feelings about relevant issues. It is worthwhile spending more time than usual on probing the full implications of these questions. A few brief, but relevant, comments are provided in the Appendix.

RECOMMENDED FURTHER READING

Chesterman, John and Lipman, Andy (1988) *Electronic Pirates*, Routledge, London.

Yes, again! It not only gives insight into a great many areas of technological crime but it examines many aspects of security which will be of even more importance to all users of electronic gadgetry in the future. A fascinating account of skullduggery which should stimulate serious thought about what the future might bring!

Forester, Tom (1989) *High-Tec Society*, Blackwell, London.

The author gives his own graphic accounts of many issues of lasting significance in technological development and related social issues. Thought provoking in respect of the future.

Forester, Tom (ed.) (1990) *The Information Technology Revolution*, Blackwell, London.

A wealth of information about many issues in this book. Absolutely fascinating reading – and an opportunity for the reader to reflect just how much things have changed even in the few years since it was written – and where we might go from here.

LaPiere, Richard T. (1965) *Social Change*, McGraw-Hill, New York.

Now is the time to re-read this book and devote some time to considering the implications of the changes due to come about in people and in society as a result of both technological development and commercial advancement.

Taylor, Gordon Rattray (1972) *Rethink*, The Chaucer Press, Bungay.

A serious but fascinating book by a distinguished academic and author who tries to explain contemporary events in society such as the general disillusionment with our way of living. Well worth reading if you are looking for some mental stimulation.

Appendix

NOTES ON EXERCISES IN THE TEXT

Here is a larger selection of quotations than usual in the hope that there will be found among them at least one to encourage or cheer you at this stage of your journey through a complex but, I hope, interesting field of study.

> A little learning is a dangerous thing.
> *Alexander Pope, Essay on Criticism (1688–1744)*

> You will not learn much that counts if you do not have the urge to learn.
> *(Anon)*

> Labor omnia vincit. (Work conquers all)
> *Virgil, 70–19 BC*

> Nothing that is worth knowing can be taught.
> *Oscar Wilde (1888)*

> Learning without thought is labour lost: thought without learning is perilous.
> *Analects of Confucius, c.550–478 BC*

> I keep six honest serving men (they taught me all I knew). Their names are What and Why and When and How and Where and Who!
> *Rudyard Kipling (1865–1936)*

> Pilate said 'What is truth?'
> *John 18: 38*

THE PURPOSE OF THE 'APPLICATIONS'

The exercises posed under the heading of 'Application' at the end of the different chapters are not so much to test your knowledge as to persuade you to direct your thoughts towards the nature of those issues which most needed consideration in the context of innovation. There are therefore no 'model answers' to the questions in the sense of prescribing what you ought to have said in respect of each. Instead there are guidelines which comprise a brief review of some relevant factors already dealt with in the text, together with observations on other related issues (not necessarily mentioned previously) which also merit scrutiny or reflection. There is no suggestion that these are the 'right' comments, much less that they are the only ones which fit the circumstances. If, however, you did not take into account all the points which are mentioned here, then you will almost certainly have missed some vital matters which could be of real importance to you in dealing with adoption/diffusion issues yourself. In respect of those instances where you were asked to personalize particular views or situations I obviously cannot comment since the appropriate response must be entirely your own. The essentials of the topics are outlined below to save you having to refer back constantly to the appropriate chapters in order to read the questions again.

CHAPTER 2: CHARACTERISTICS OF SOCIAL CHANGE

At the end of this chapter you were presented with an old saying, namely *'Change is what you should prepare for in prosperity and pray for in adversity.'* You were invited to comment on the possible intentions of the message, suggest to whom it might be directed and why, and state what (if anything) it meant to you. With the exception of the last part of the exercise, which only you can supply, let us look at the factors likely to be involved here.

The emphasis in both situations is on actually doing something. When things are going satisfactorily there is every temptation to leave well alone. But change is an ongoing process, as you will have realized by now, and things are going to be different in some way with the mere passage of time. If, therefore, things are prosperous now you would be well advised to plan for the future in order to try to keep them so. You have to anticipate what might need to be done, how, by whom, in what manner and with what resources – and then try to do it.

If, on the other hand, times are adverse then you would certainly wish for change since any kind might well be better than the present condition. Obviously you must take steps to try to improve the situation since it is more positive to bring about change than merely to adapt to it when it happens. In both sets of circumstances, naturally, you will be looking for something which is not just an alteration, but which maintains at least your present position and, if possible, improves on it.

To effect change you must set yourself attainable objectives and have both the will and the means to pursue them. You should also be willing to accept the possibility of not achieving them first time. It may be necessary to try again, perhaps more than once. Persistence is a valuable quality and outweighs many others which might appear, at a first glance, to be more important. The message itself is of universal application and applies to most people in a very wide range of situations. Remember that even a stable situation is never really static.

CHAPTER 3: CONSUMER INERTIA

In this chapter you were given an extract from a publication of one of the world's leading advertising agencies. It read:

> A powerful determinant of consumer choice is habit or inertia. It suits the consumer to treat much of her activity as a matter of routine. To indulge in a process of conscious deliberation at every purchase would take an enormous amount of time and mental effort which, not unnaturally, there is a strong drive to avoid. Any satisfactory model of consumer choice is bound to give a large weight to the brand previously purchased.

You were asked to indicate what steps might be taken to overcome customer inertia towards:

1. a particular type of product; and
2. a specific brand of that product.

Who is to take the required steps here in order to influence the customer's actions? No doubt there will be different opinions on this point, especially from those whose living depends on providing part of any action! However, no matter who else is involved, this kind of situation must always include a marketing or sales promotion effort such as advertising of some kind. It may not necessarily be in the press or on television but the essential features will be there.

For instance, in respect of category 1 it is important that the potential customer becomes aware that the product in question not only exists but is readily available, preferably at a nearby location. It is also encouraging to know that it is in widespread use and is highly thought of by regular purchasers as the solution to particular personal or household problems. You will recall that the first stage of awareness is always vital in the individual adoption process.

With regard to category 2, the essential message is that all brands of the product are not the same. It is not necessary to denigrate any in order to show that some have a specific superiority. (It is often said, for example, that in respect of Scotch whisky there is no such thing as a bad one – but some are better than others!) The advantage of any particular brand may be claimed in respect of economy, speed, ease of use, environmental conservation or whatever feature can, with advantage, be emphasized. The appeal to the customer will depend on accurately identifying an appropriate consumer market with the characteristics of the target population clearly specified. For instance, while economy may be a strong selling point in one residential neighbourhood or shopping precinct there may be people in another location who respond favourably to sales promotion which claims that a successful perfume is 'the most expensive perfume in the world'. While we are all consumers some people engage more than others in **conspicuous consumption**, a topic dealt with at some length in Thorstein Veblen's (1899) classic book, *The Theory of the Leisure Class*.

CHAPTER 4: a) CAUTIOUS VENTURESOMENESS
b) INDIVIDUAL AND COMMUNITY

In this chapter you were faced with two different but related questions:

Part A In 1711 Alexander Pope, in his *Essay of Criticism*, said

'Be not the first by whom the new are tried,
Nor the last to lay the old aside.'

You were invited to state your views as to whether this was a middle-of-the-road philosophy, what kind of individual might adopt it and why, and an indication of your own attitude to it. As with the previous case the response to the last part of the question is uniquely your own. In respect of the other parts, let us look at what might be involved.

The advice relates to the avoidance of novelty for its own sake, but it also cautions against being too laggard. It would seem to fit very well the concept of the Early Majority in the classic categorization. Perhaps you might like to check again the personal characteristics of individuals in this category. If they were to have a motto it might well be *festina lente* (hasten slowly) since they manage to combine a moderate degree of venturesomeness with a reasonable degree of caution. It is a philosophy which would have an appeal for those conformists who wish to benefit from a feeling of belonging to a particular progressive type of society so long as any necessary change is not too much, too quick or too often.

Remember, however, that innovativeness categories relate only to particular innovations at particular times. They must not be interpreted as indicating the overall progressiveness profiles of any individuals.

Part B The second question focused on the relationship between the individual and the community. The question was:

In each of the following two situations what is likely to determine whether the individual specified will be able to make any real impact on the community? To what extent will community influence over the person be the dominant one?

1. a moderately innovative person who moves to live and work in a very traditional or conservative environment;
2. a very innovative individual who transfers to work in a highly progressive environment.

Notice the slight, but very significant, difference in the wording of the two situations! In the first environment a determined approach is necessary for the individual merely to survive as a 'progressive' human being. A moderately inclined person would be likely to go under in such circumstances and end up by conforming to community norms in order to live in peace. In the second situation the individual will also conform but this time it should be more happily in respect of a supportive environment within which he or she should be able to find all the necessary reference groups. It is hard, however, to maintain high standards continuously if the context is too demanding. Admittedly there is the possibility for a small number of people who have ability and stamina to become leaders and thus reap the rewards of their personal potential.

However, others may find the pace too much and look for another environment which, particularly as they get older, expects less from them. As John Donne (c.1571–1631) said in *Devotions*, 'No man is an Island, entire of itself'. He was referring to the fact that none of us can live meaningfully in isolation from others, and being in contact with our fellow human beings means that we are influenced by them and in turn exercise an influence over them. Accordingly, in the social situation all terms are relative and categories such as 'innovator' or 'progressive' serve only to indicate those who, *by comparison with their neighbours*, are inclined to operate more quickly, willingly or efficiently in respect of causing change.

CHAPTER 5: a) INDIVIDUAL ADOPTION MODEL
b) THE HANOI PROBLEM

Part A You had to devise a simple model in this case and, naturally, every response may be different while still being quite reasonable and wholly acceptable. Nonetheless in this situation let us look at the essential elements which any such model might reasonably be expected to contain. The exercise requires that it be a model of individual adoption and that it should allow for some decisions not necessarily being rational ones. For simplification only one product is considered here and the process is not portrayed against any particular timescale.

The first stage or starting point must be that of awareness. This is where every process of learning and adaptation begins. The final stage or behaviour characteristic can be thought of as decision or action of some kind. This could be typically either adoption or rejection. A kind of hypodermic needle approach (or knee-jerk reaction, if you prefer this analogy) could be depicted as:

$$\text{Awareness} \rightarrow \text{Adoption/Rejection}$$

A more likely sequence could be:

$$\text{Awareness} \rightarrow \text{Information} \rightarrow \text{Decision} \rightarrow \text{Action}$$

where the action is to adopt, reject, reconsider, seek further information or whatever. However this is a systematic layout which suggests a logical and rational approach to the decision-making. An allowance for the impulsive type of action indicated earlier would required the model to be modified, for example as follows:

Adoption Model incorporating Non-rational Element

```
                         ⌐  Impulse  Adoption
                   .          .         .
             .                .         .
                              .         .
Awareness → Impulse Rejection           .
                              .         .
             .                .         .
                   .          .         .
                        ⌐→ Information → Decision → Action
```

There is much to be explored in relation to human behaviour in the construction of models so long as you do not allow yourself to believe that they will always reveal hidden truths which would otherwise go undiscovered. Sometimes they do, but their major usefulness is in condensing into a relatively simple diagram some fundamental aspects of complex situations. This is done so as to emphasize those possible relationships which might just be of most importance for a particular purpose. In this case the purpose is decision-making in respect of something perceived as new.

Part B   The solution to the Hanoi problem may be reached by:

1. redefining the objective; and
2. accepting that many of the moves must be backwards and not forwards.

Redefining the objective means that your primary aim must be identified in its most direct terms. Inspection shows that this must be to get the largest counter (no.5) from A to C. Once the largest counter is on the required base the others will fall into place without too much difficulty. Make the appropriate moves as follows: 1 to C, 2 to B. Then 1 to B, 3 to C, followed by 1 to A, 2 to C, 1 to C, 4 to B, 1 to B, 2 to A, 1 to A, 3 to B, 1 to C, 2 to B, 1 to B, and 5 to C. Now the rest is easy! One of the lessons to be learned from this problem is that we must all redefine problems until they appear in a form where we have a clear objective. Another important point is that having identified a methodical approach we must apply it rigorously, even when it appears to be going counter to our expectations.

CHAPTER 6: THE TUPPERWARE PARTY SYNDROME

For this exercise you were provided with a reasonable amount of background information since it could not be assumed that people, younger ones in particular, would necessarily be familiar with the product or procedures referred to. Since the issues can be rather complex the question is repeated in full here.

Some years ago, in the early days of plastics products, one manufacturer (Tupper of Florida) started producing very good quality resealable food containers, such as sandwich boxes and other storage items. The innovative approach was in selling these items to prospective purchasers in groups rather than individually. This introduced what became extremely well-known as *Tupperware* parties. In a typical situation a local resident would invite friends and neighbours to her home for a coffee morning and, by suitable arrangement with the suppliers, would also mount a display, with a talk and/or demonstration of the products together with the opportunity to purchase or order some of them.

A similar approach has since been used successfully by other manufacturers in connection with cosmetics and clothing. If you do not have any personal experience of being present at one of these parties try to talk to someone who has. Why do you think that, although they are not only still continuing but developing, less is commonly heard about them today? What sort of factors made this innovation possible in the first instance? What do you think supports the continuance of this approach? In what circumstances might it be difficult to maintain or develop?

You will note that there is plenty to reflect on here! By now you will also be aware of the importance of group pressure and the extent of social influence on individual behaviour. It is part of the formative process of becoming a human being that in the act of learning anything we initially imitate others. As a result many of us carry into adult life the tendency to copy what we admire, respect or envy in other people. A small group situation is a very powerful setting for persuasion to produce results of conformity in respect of issues such as purchases of this kind.

All the relevant factors, both material and human, are there to assist the process of adoption. The products are indeed visible and can be seen to be something new. They are divisible in the sense that only a single sandwich box or a salt cellar need be purchased first, in order to see if the product lives up to expectations. The goods are not expensive but are of good quality, serviceable, durable and attractive. Having gone to the invited gathering it is difficult to refuse to purchase. The major decision is made on acceptance of the invitation. If there is any hesitation or uncertainty the conditions are ideal for the face-to-face personal influence which can assist the final decision-making in accordance with the socio-psychological model of personal adoption previously examined. There is also very strong reinforcement of the decision to purchase arising from the sense of togetherness and group action which minimizes individual accountability and strengthens the legitimacy of group actions.

One of the essential criteria for this approach to produce results is, of course, for the domestic socializing to continue to operate. It still does in many parts of the UK, but with so many women following careers at the present time as well as looking after a home the coffee morning approach is no longer possible in many of the 'white collar' districts where in the past it would have been at its strongest. Also, many people today already have most of the commonplace things that they want, including basic Tupperware, which (unfortunately for the manufacturers) appears to last forever! In addition, residential neighbourhoods are less homogeneous than they once were and there may well be less house-to-house visiting taking place than was once the case in localities which had a greater sense of community and less identity merely as a suburban dormitory area. Reflecting on alterations to socio-economic categories, changes in the social class structure, particularly of Western European countries, and the opportunities for direct mail order and other methods of purchasing should enable you to reflect on different aspects of this question, some of which will no doubt have changed anyway by the time that this book goes to print.

CHAPTER 7: a) CHANGING OFFICE WORKING CONDITIONS
b) COMMITTEE STEREOTYPES

Part A   In the first exercise you were invited to consider how best to offer an opinion on a rather sensitive issue, ie possible changes in staff working conditions. A senior executive, on behalf of your employer, had requested suggestions aimed at improving both working conditions and overall efficiency. What kind of response would be likely to benefit the work force and, at the same time, lead to better efficiency in the firm?

There is always the cynical view that these two aims are not only incompatible but are likely to be mutually exclusive. However a brief reflection will probably indicate that in all situations where a combined effort is called for a happy team achieves good results. This is true in sport, in military matters and (though still not widely accepted by either management or workers) also in the everyday workplace. It has been shown to increase efficiency in manufacturing situations, one example being that of the SAAB car company in Sweden. The breakdown of rigid job descriptions and the creation by the workers themselves of small flexible work teams who can interchange tasks from time to time (with the approval of the trade unions) has produced greater output in this situation while improving the working conditions and meriting increased rates of pay in the factory.

In this exercise it is important to check first of all what the terms of reference are. Are you being consulted as a kind of courtesy; will your ideas really be taken into account by those who will make the ultimate decision; or will you, and your colleagues, actually be involved in the decision-making? Is there any specific meaning to the terms used; for example does 'conditions' relate only to the physical environment or does it also apply to interpersonal relationships and ease of two-way communication? What is the meaning of 'efficiency'? Is this to be measured only by increased production; does it imply a reduction in numbers of those at present employed; how is it to be judged? What are the criteria? Can they be changed? Does everyone know?

You may try to give answers to questions such as these but it is important to accept that at times there is no harm – indeed there is often a great deal of benefit – in responding to a question by posing another one. It is always more important to ask relevant questions than to feel that you have at last got an answer. The essence of any solution here lies in the nature and extent of the communication network that can be established officially in the organization by building on the existing unofficial links which enable the employees themselves to relate to one another.

Part B   In respect of the second exercise you may have thought that the cartoon was rather irrelevant, or of only minor significance in relationship to the aspects of communication which you had been reading about. In fact it highlights an exceedingly important issue, and that is that we all tend to create stereotypes of those people with whom we come into contact – especially in formal relationships. Using very broad brush strokes indeed the various types of committee member may be identified, in the chairperson's eyes, in terms such as the following:

1. **Quarrelsome.** Better not to get involved with him/her. Try tactfully not to let him/her monopolize the meeting.
2. **The worthwhile type.** Very positive. Not many of them about. Use him/her whenever and wherever possible. Could be a very useful member if given some specific tasks.
3. **The 'know-all'.** We all suffer! Listen but be non-committal.
4. **Loquacious type.** Can talk – and talk. Has to be dealt with diplomatically and thanked effusively for contributions, however worthless.
5. **The shy type.** Try to avoid direct questions. Ask only those which are not too demanding. Give encouragement and support wherever possible, as well as praise for even minor contributions.
6. **Prickly and uncooperative.** Massage his/her ego. Ask for comments based on personal knowledge or experience, emphasizing unique nature of the contribution.
7. **Uninterested and fairly thick-skinned.** Encourage personal anecdotes of work and achievement, however irrelevant.
8. **Highbrow.** Don't criticize! Be wary and respectful but not subservient.
9. **Persistent questioner.** Won't be happy until chairperson concedes defeat on some issue, however minor. Try to encourage others to get involved in giving a group response to the more awkward questions posed.

What would your personal reaction be to the temptation to indulge in such stereotyping as that just outlined? Remember that the creation of stereotypes tends to obstruct meaningful and productive communication because, among other shortcomings

1. the chairperson will tend to favour those who are most likely to be agreeably disposed to his/her views;
2. there will be a tendency for him/her to give a more receptive ear to those same people when they address the chair;
3. a disproportionate amount of committee time may be spent endeavouring to get everyone to act and even think similarly while the people concerned will continue to maintain their individuality as a means of preserving and confirming their own identities.

CHAPTER 8: CHANGE AGENTS

This is a rather complicated exercise involving both human and material factors. The question is restated here in full.

Imagine that you have been asked to advise a small manufacturing firm which has just recently been formed by a few working partners.

These partners are the entire work force at present and are not making a great success of selling a common garden implement which ought to have had a reasonable market. However, they have ideas for producing another product, not currently available, which they believe will prove to be more attractive. They would, however, require a bank loan to finance the production. Consider carefully which technical and human factors would be relevant and important enough to draw to the attention of the partners.

Of the range of questions which might be asked here the following ought to find a place. First of all what is *new* about the fresh product? Is it a replacement for the item which is not doing so well at present? Why isn't the current product being taken up? Why would people want the new one? Could they afford it? Does it constitute a one-off sale or are repeat purchases likely? Is it of only limited appeal or could it be really popular if its existence became known? What kind of advertising would be necessary? Has any market research been done to indicate a target population? How many items would need to be sold to cover initial production costs?

In a sense the producers are putting themselves in the position of having to be change agents if their new implement has no existing counterpart. As such they will be dependent on performing the basic role functions of such an agent leading to the necessary stage of stimulation of a desire to purchase. If they are unable to take on any of the relevant roles themselves then they will be committed to employing someone else to do this for them. It may not work and it will, in any case, be expensive. Unless they are reasonably sure of their facts concerning possible acceptance of their innovation and of the consequences of any failure to secure a good market they ought to be very cautious about entering into loan agreements with any lender. Remember that, as with all advisory situations, the problem is theirs, not yours. You can only indicate issues which merit attention. The decision-making still rests with those who are seeking your advice. However, you would almost certainly, in these circumstances, counsel them to think again! Their chances of success are surely problematic.

CHAPTER 9: a) GROUP LEADERSHIP
b) RELATIVE PERSONAL INFLUENCE

Two issues were listed here for action and comment.

Part A Here your views were sought on whether or not the group leader was doing a good job and whether the pattern of interaction was satisfactory. You were also asked to explain any differences between the pattern of interaction and that which you would have expected. Your response will depend on how you interpret the given sociogram.

A is designated the official discussion group leader. Such an office does *not* require a change agent in that the incumbent is not (or should not be) committed to bringing about any particular outcome. He/she is

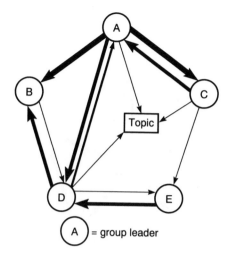

more like an opinion leader in the sense of guiding the path of the discussion without unduly trying to influence its outcome.

In this particular instance the topic itself is not being as well developed as it might and the group leader appears to have far too much to say to the individual group members instead of addressing the issues on the table and ensuring that others do likewise. As a result the group has degenerated into more of a social gathering than a work group and no alternative leadership is apparent. Such a situation will not last long before either someone with more charisma than the 'leader' attempts to control the members and focus their attention on the topic – or the group forsakes a pointless existence (or at least one of very limited value) by breaking up.

A more orthodox work-oriented situation would have appeared in something like the following form. This indicates a somewhat better balanced participation by all present, including the chairperson, and has due regard to the importance of the topic under discussion by evidently allowing and encouraging fuller participation of the members.

Part B   It has been said that 'There always have been and there always will be men and women who are much more influential than others'. You were asked to comment on the circumstances in which this was most likely to be true and to consider the social and economic consequences of accepting such a point of view.

It should not take you too long to reflect that in human society, as in the physical world, the old dictum that 'nature abhors a vacuum' may often be seen to hold true. Those who have the ability to exert influence actually do often become situational leaders provided that their peers are willing to accept the reciprocal roles of followers. When conditions are such that 'influentials' of this kind can operate they tend to show up very well on sociograms in the role of, for example, *de facto* discussion leader. This, like the position of opinion leader, does *not* necessarily

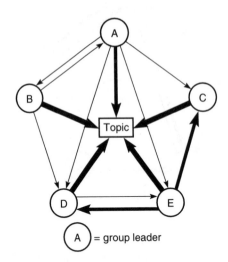

coincide with official leadership of the group. It has become routine to expect that economically and socially there will be those who will 'set the pace' whether it be as innovators, entrepreneurs, opinion leaders or change agents. There is fairly universal acceptance of this situation without everyone necessarily agreeing that it is right. The consequences of according others leadership roles of any kind are that, in a hierarchical society, the followers often suffer from some personal feelings of inferiority or injustice.

CHAPTER 10: INNOVATIVE FACTORS

The case studies in this chapter dealt with different situations with regard to resources, development time, involvement of others, and changes in attitudes and practice.

In respect of these case studies you were asked to express an opinion as to what factors might have assisted those which worked well and what might have hindered others.

Do you recall the various attributes of innovations? Factors related to visibility, divisibility, cost and so on are not just theoretical niceties. They are the sort of considerations which carry a lot of weight in the 'real' world. Chapters 5 and 6 cover the essentials in respect of availability, suitability, satisfaction of needs, compatibility with personal values, community traditions and social norms. In essence, lack of approval would inhibit adoption and there might even be open antagonism to something new, however beneficial it might claim to be. Whatever other factors might be relevant to ensuring legitimation of new and hitherto untried ideas the support of appropriate opinion leaders by the early majority would be decisive in ensuring a reasonably ready acceptance.

CHAPTER 11: A TECHNICAL SERVICES PROBLEM

Perhaps this seems to you to be an unusual type of question but, in the context of acceptance of new ideas, it is as relevant as any other to indicate the extreme range of situations to which adoption/diffusion theory and practice may be applied.

The circumstances of the situation, restated, are:

Imagine a local authority endeavouring to reduce refuse collection costs in a particular area. One idea being considered is that of reducing by half the number of journeys each operative has to make to individual households when a dustbin has to be emptied. Normally the workperson would go to the door or gate, collect a full bin, take it to the lorry, empty it, return the empty bin, then go to the next house and repeat the process.

There is a suggestion that the lorry should carry an empty bin to start with. The operative (usually called a technician nowadays because most of the local authority cleansing departments have been renamed Technical Services Departments) could start by taking this empty bin to the first house. It is then left in place of the full one which, when it is emptied, would then be taken to the house next door, where it is left when the full one there is collected, and so on. This approach, it is believed, could reduce door to transport journeys by half, shorten collection times, and save money whilst still offering a full service.

However, what do you see as primary reasons why this system would be unlikely to be viewed with much enthusiasm by householders?

Again we have to bear in mind the norms of our Western society and the personal values which are supported by the nature of capitalist systems which place a premium upon possessions. While many residents do not own their dustbins (although thousands do) virtually all of them lay claim to the particular one with which they were issued and often identify it by painting the house number on it. Many of them meticulously clean and disinfect the bins regularly and maintain a high order of cleanliness. The same thing cannot always be said about all their neighbours. There is bound to be a feeling that, in a situation such as this, any alteration could be a change for the worse. Even if the property rates or council tax had to be increased to maintain the old way of doing things it is nearly certain that this would have majority support except in those areas where there is little interest in maintaining any standards which smack of 'keeping up with the Joneses'. There can be a complex mixture of personal values and societal norms involved in decision-making of this kind and it would be well worthwhile for you to consider the personal and social implications of such situations at greater length.

CHAPTER 12: THE FRENCH TELETEL SYSTEM

The question requires you to:

> Consider the development and expansion of the French Teletel system since it issued the first electronic telephone directories. Why has the minitel terminal become such an accepted household item throughout France? Why is the French PTT now expanding its service to provide even more Teletel facilities?

This particular case study is covered in some detail in the chapter. In essence, the total acceptance of the minitel terminal in French homes owes much to the fact that telephone users really didn't have much choice in the beginning. The printed telephone directory was being discontinued throughout the country and that was that! When the decision with which you are faced is whether to do things the hard way by opposing the system or follow the easier way of doing what you are told it does not take too long for common sense to assert itself. Once the people had decided to find out how to use the new system virtually imposed on them they discovered, as often happens, that it did actually have something worthwhile to offer. Indeed familiarity and increasing competence brought requests for more features to be provided, even at additional cost, so that access could be had to personal services which had previously been unobtainable. Shopping, buying shares, arranging holidays, having fortunes told, hearing the latest 'top of the pops' and many more facilities have all become welcome additions with something for everyone in the average home. The initial impetus came from the push of technological development but the ultimate success, as always, rested on market demand from human beings who saw a ready means of satisfying some personal needs in a socially acceptable and economically affordable manner.

You were asked whether there were any facilities which you would like to be able to access. Your response to this part of the question must depend on your own interests and on your knowledge of what relevant services would currently be available.

CHAPTER 13: a) ORGANIZATIONAL GATEKEEPERS
b) POWER/AUTHORITY INVOLVEMENT

Part A Here you were asked to identify some gatekeepers in a typical industrial factory and comment on the influence which they could exert on communication within that commercial organization.

In every communication situation involving more than two persons there are certain to be gatekeepers in some sense of that word. These are people who act in much the same way as newspaper editors who receive reports from many sources and decide which ones are newsworthy. A gatekeeper also receives snippets of information from a wide range of contacts and decides which ones to let through by 'opening the gate' and which ones to suppress or delay by 'closing the gate'. The analogy is a fairly appropriate one and in respect of organizations it applies particularly to vertical communication. A moment's reflection will indicate why this should be so.

All organizations by their nature have different levels in their construction. In any such hierarchy it is noticeable that people in gatekeeping positions do not often venture to delay or modify communication downward because it is dangerous to interfere with messages from 'the top'. However, they will, almost as a matter of course, scrutinize, hold back, modify or 'lose' messages from those below them which they consider it better not to convey upward, at least in the original form. This often applies to their own personal communications also. For example a school teacher will be reluctant to confess to having disciplinary problems with a troublesome class in case the school principal might consider him/her incompetent. A junior officer may not put troublemakers on a charge since his/her promotion prospects might be somewhat dented by admitting that there are some 'other ranks' nominally under his command whom he cannot control.

In the factory the occupants of gatekeeping positions could include shop stewards, foremen, managers and personnel or welfare officers. All will have their own reasons for wishing to vet or sanitize any communication which refers to their areas of responsibility or might be thought to have their assistance in its onward transmission. In former times hapless messengers bearing bad tidings tended to suffer the wrath of the recipient. While the consequences are not so dire nowadays there is still a natural reluctance to be associated with any communication which is unlikely to be popular. It is not too difficult to identify everyday gatekeepers in virtually any area of employment where more than a few people are engaged. At times they perform a useful function in maintaining harmony where conflict might otherwise result. They also act as legitimizers in situations where information to be passed on benefits from their handling of it by gaining a credence that might otherwise be lacking. They tend to operate almost exclusively in official communication systems since the unofficial networks are so flexible and ill-defined as not to permit many opportunities for action of this kind.

Part B   This posed a different type of question, ie an interpretation of a table indicating power-authority versus involvement. On the face of it this is a more 'academic' sort of exercise but it has definite relevance for many situations where the attitude of individuals involved in collective activity is concerned.

Whatever your interpretation of the table there should be little hesitation in identifying an individual who may be characterized as falling into the 'moral' category as being preferred to one in the 'calculative' sector and definitely desirable as compared to someone with the 'alienative' label. The working relationship between employer and employee improves as one goes along the scale from individual compulsion to personal commitment in respect of both! As with many diagrams or models the presentation is simply a summary or condensation of what is already known or believed about particular situations which have been labelled in a particular way to highlight certain characteristics.

CHAPTER 14: SCIENCE FICTION

This last exercise is a wide-ranging one.

> It has been said in this chapter that 'nothing dates quicker than science fiction.' What is your opinion? What items of current science fiction are you aware of? Are they largely a sort of fantasy un-related to the real world or could they give a glimpse of the world as it might be in the future – and perhaps sooner than we think?

You were asked to illustrate your answer with suitable examples and to identify the personal, social and technical features relating to innovation and communication which would probably be instrumental in either promoting or retarding the developments which you chose. Since this is the last exercise in the book it therefore involves aspects of all the topics previously dealt with. Naturally it also rests on your own judgements, experiences and beliefs in respect of the issues which you consider to be relevant. These must surely centre around the concept of change and how it is viewed by different types of people in a wide range of domestic, social, geographical and occupational settings. All of the most relevant factors have been referred to throughout the book.

You will probably look at revisions, perhaps even major modifications, of existing things. You may be inventive enough to propose some things which are beyond our ken at present. Whatever your response you will not, I hope, feel let down by having no 'model' answer indicated here. What the future holds for anyone must be a matter for conjecture. Only time will tell whether you saw more clearly into that future than the rest of us.

RECOMMENDED FURTHER READING

Don't forget that the books in the Bibliography have bibliographies of their own, many of which are much more extensive than this one.

Rather than adding any titles to the list of those already selected I would refer you to such books and their associated works of reference if you wish to delve more deeply into any of the subject areas introduced here.

POSTSCRIPT

Samuel Johnson (1709–1784) once said 'Knowledge is of two kinds. We know a subject ourselves, or we know where we can find information upon it.' In respect of the first kind of knowledge postulated by Johnson our own experience and learning constitute our 'primary' sources of knowledge. It might be noted in passing, however, that experience is a bad teacher: it gives the test before the instruction!

In respect of the second kind of knowledge an encyclopaedia, a text-book, a railway timetable or a telephone directory are examples of 'secondary sources' which we all have used at some time. I trust that you now have a bit more of both kinds of knowledge than when you started to read this book. I hope also that you will be able to put it to good use.

What next? Perhaps another quotation from Lewis Carroll might not be inappropriate.

'Would you tell me, please, which way I ought to walk from here?' 'That depends a good deal on where you want to get to,' said the Cat.

Wherever it is, I wish you every success.
Bon voyage.

Bibliography

The list given here comprises only those titles or authors mentioned in the different chapters together with a few additional publications, other than research reports and conference papers, which could be of interest to those who wish to find out other opinions about human perceptions and personal decision-making.

There are very few books relating to innovation included, simply because only a handful of publications on this topic can be found anywhere in the world. Conversely, only a few titles on communication have been covered because currently there are hundreds to choose from, many of which will be on the shelves in your local library. The most likely catalogue sections in which to look for relevant titles will be **Human Communication**, **Mass Communication**, **Media**, **Rural Sociology** and **Social Psychology**. This bibliography refers only to those volumes from my own bookshelves to which I have referred in the preparation of the present book.

Ackoff, Russel L. (1978) *The Art of Problem Solving*, John Wiley, Chichester.

Argyle, M. (1975) *Bodily Communication*, Methuen, London.

Bagehot, W. (1873) *Physics and Politics*, Appleton-Century, New York.

Bettinghaus, Erwin P. and Cody, Michael J. (1987) *Persuasive Communication*, Holt Rinehart and Winston, New York.

Bird, Drayton (1989) *Commonsense Direct Marketing*, Kogan Page, London.

Blau, Peter M. and Scott, W. Richard (1962) *Formal Organisations*, Chandler, San Francisco.

Bright, James R. (1970) *Research, Development and Technological Innovation*, Richard D. Irwin Inc., Homewood, Illinois.

Bryman, Alan (1986) *Leadership and Organisations*, Routledge and Kegan Paul, London.

Burnham, James (1945) *The Managerial Revolution*, Penguin Books, Harmondsworth.

Calouste Gulbenkian Foundation (1974) *Community Work and Social Change*, Longman, London.

Carlson, Richard O. (1965) *Adoption of Educational Innovations*, University of Oregon, Eugene.

Carty, Francis X. (1992) *Farewell to Hype – the Emergence of Real Public Relations*, Able Press, Dublin.

Chesterman, John and Lipman, Andy (1988) *The Electronic Pirates*, Routledge (Comedia), London.

Corner, John and Hawthorn, Jeremy (eds) (1980) *Communication Studies – an Introductory Reader*, Edward Arnold, London.

Coulson-Thomas, Colin J. (1985) *Marketing Communications*, Heinemann, London.

Cummings, Julian (1989) *Sales Promotion*, Kogan Page, London.

Curran, J., Gurevitch, M. and Woollacott, Janet (eds) (1977) *Mass Communication and Society*, Edward Arnold, London.

Das Gupta, S. (1962) *Sociology of Innovation*, Cultural Research Institution, Calcutta.

Davis, Martin P. (1990) *The Effective Use of Advertising Media*, Hutchinson Business, London.

Drucker, Peter F. (1986) *Innovation and Entrepreneurship*, Heinemann, London.

Dyer, Gillian (1982) *Advertising as Communication*, Methuen, London.

Ehrenberg, A.S.C. and Pyatt, F.G. (eds) (1972) *Consumer Behaviour*, Penguin Books, Harmondsworth.

Emery, F.E. and Oeser, O.A. assisted by J. Tully (1958) *Information, Decision and Action*, Melbourne University Press, Carleton.

Etzioni, A. (1961) *A Comparative Analysis of Complex Organisations*, Free Press, New York.

Evans, K.M. (1966) *Sociometry and Education*, Routledge and Kegan Paul, London.

Festinger, L. (1957) *A Theory of Cognitive Dissonance*, Stanford University Press, Stanford.

Finnegan, Ruth, Salaman, Graeme and Thompson, Kenneth (1990) *Information Technology: Social Issues*, Hodder and Stoughton, Sevenoaks.

Fiske, John (1982) *Introduction to Communication Studies*, Methuen, London.

Forester, Tom (1987) *High-Tec Society*, Basil Blackwell, Oxford.

Forester, Tom (ed.) (1990) *The Information Technology Revolution*, Basil Blackwell, Oxford.

Forgas, Joseph P. (1986) *Interpersonal Behaviour – the Psychology of Social Interaction*, Pergamon, Sydney.

Hart, Norman A. and O'Connor, James (eds) (1985) *The Practice of Advertising*, Heinemann, London.

Heirs, Ben and Farrell, Peter (1986) *The Professional Decision-Thinker*, Sidgwick and Jackson, London.

Henry, Jane and Walker, David (eds) (1992) *Managing Innovation*, Sage, London.

Hicks, Michael J. (1991) *Problem Solving in Business and Management*, Chapman & Hall, London.

Hills, Philip (ed.) (1980) *The Future of the Printed Word*, The Open University Press, Milton Keynes.

Jefkins, Frank (1988) *Public Relations*, Pitman Publishing, London.

Jefkins, Frank (1988) *Public Relations Techniques*, Heinemann, London.

Johnson, Elizabeth S. and Williamson, John B. (1980) *Growing Old*, Holt Rinehart and Winston, New York.

Jones, Trevor (ed.) (1980) *Micro-electronics and Society*, The Open University Press, Milton Keynes.

Klein, Josephine (1963) *Working with Groups*, Hutchinson, London.

Krech, D., Crutchfield, R.S. and Ballachey, E.L. (1962) *Individuals in Society*, Kogakusha, Tokyo.

LaPiere, Richard T. (1965) *Social Change*, McGraw-Hill, New York.

Laver, Murray (1980) *Computers and Social Change*, Cambridge University Press, Cambridge.

Lawton, Denis (1973) *Social Change, Educational Theory and Curriculum Planning*, The University of London Press, London.

Leigh, Andrew (ed.) (1973) *Better Social Services*, The National Council of Social Service, London.

Leiss, William, Kline, Stephen and Jhally, Sut (1988) *Social Communication in Advertising*, Nelson Canada, Ontario.

Loomis, Charles P. and Beegle, J. Allan (1957) *Rural Sociology – the Strategy of Change*, Prentice-Hall, Englewood Cliffs, N.J.

McGregor, Douglas (1960) *The Human Side of Enterprise*, McGraw-Hill, New York.

MacIver, R.M. and Page, Charles H. (1967) *Society – an Introductory Analysis*, Macmillan, London.

McQuail, Denis (1975) *Communication*, Longman, London.

McQuail, Denis and Windahl, Sven (1986) *Communication Models*, Longman, London.

Malthus, T.R. (1798) *Essay on the Principle of Population* (various reprints), London.

Maslow, A.H. (1962) *Towards a Psychology of Being*, Van Nostrand, Princeton, N.J.

Merrill, John C. and Lowenstein, Ralph L. (1979) *Media, Messages and Men*, Longman, New York.

Miles, M.B. (1964) *Innovation in Education*, Teachers College Press, New York.

Moreno, J.L. (1953) *Who Shall Survive? Foundations of Sociometry, Group Psychotherapy and Sociodrama*, Beacon House, New York.

Mulkay, M.J. (1972) *The Social Process of Innovation*, Macmillan, London.

Myers, Kathy (1986) *Understains*, Comedia Publishing Group, London.

Nielson, James (1967) *The Change Agent and the Process of Change*, Research Bulletin 17, Michigan State University, East Lansing.

O'Sullivan, T., Hartley, J., Saunders, D. and Fiske, J. (1983) *Key Concepts in Communication*, Methuen, London.

Ottaway, A.K.C. (1962) *Education and Society*, Routledge and Kegan Paul, London.

Packard, Vance (1957) *The Hidden Persuaders*, Penguin Books, Harmondsworth.

Parsons, Talcott (1967) *Structure and Process in Modern Societies*, Frank Cass & Co., London.

Penman, Robyn (1980) *Communication Processes and Relationships*, Academic Press, Melbourne.

Reed, Stephen K. (1988) *Cognition – Theory and Applications*, Brooks/Cole Publishing Co., Pacific Grove, California.

Robertson, Thomas S. (1971) *Innovative Behaviour and Communication*, Holt Rinehart and Winston, New York.

Rogers, Everett M. (1960) *Social Change in Rural Society*, Appleton-Century-Crofts, New York.

Rogers, Everett M. (1962) *Diffusion of Innovations*, Free Press of Glencoe, New York.

Rogers, Everett M. (1983) *Diffusion of Innovations*, The Free Press, New York.

Rogers, Everett M. with Shoemaker, Floyd F. (1971) *Communication of Innovations: A Cross-Cultural Approach*, The Free Press, New York.

Rokeach, M. (1968) *Beliefs, Attitudes and Values*, Jossey-Bass, San Francisco.

Rowe, Christopher (1986) *People and Chips*, Paradigm Publishing, London.

Schein, E.H. (1980) *Organisational Psychology*, Prentice-Hall, Englewood Cliffs, N.J.

Sherman, Barrie (1985) *The New Revolution*, John Wiley and Sons, London.

Smith, Adam (1776) *An Inquiry into the Nature and Causes of The Wealth of Nations* (various reprints), London.

Spence, W.R. (1976) *Basic Descriptive Statistics*, Dundee College of Education Press, Dundee.

Spence, W.R. (1980) *Limerick Neighbourhood Youth Programme*, PIRC, Newtownabbey.

Spence, W.R. (1982) (ed.) *Innovation in Education*, Ulster Polytechnic, Jordanstown.

Spence, W.R. (1984) *Sociometric Techniques for Social Group Work*, University of Ulster, Jordanstown.

Spence, W.R. (1989) Sociometry in the Classroom, in *Psicologia E Educacao*, Associacao dos Psicologos Portugueses, Oporto, Portugal.

Spence, W.R. (1989) *New Technologies and Social Intervention*, University of Ulster, Coleraine.

Statt, David (1981) *A Dictionary of Human Behaviour*, Harper and Row, London.

Tarde, Gabriel (1903) *The Laws of Imitation*, Holt Rinehart and Winston, New York.

Taylor, Gordon Rattray (1972) *Rethink*, The Chaucer Press, Bungay.

Toop, Alan (1978) *Choosing the Right Sales Promotion*, The Sales Machine, London.

UDACE (1986) *The Challenge of Change*, The Unit for the Development of Adult Continuing Education, London.

Van den Ban, A.W. and Hawkins, H.S. (1988) *Agricultural Extension*, Longman, London.

Veblen, Thorstein (1899) *The Theory of the Leisure Class*, Scribner, New York.

Watson, James and Hill, Anne (1984) *A Dictionary of Communication and Media Studies*, Edward Arnold, London.

Wheeler, Ladd *et al.* (1955) *Interpersonal Influence*, Allyn and Bacon, Boston.

Williams, John (1983) *The Manual of Sales Promotion*, Innovation Ltd., London.

Wilmshurst, John (1986) *The Fundamentals of Advertising*, Heinemann, London.

Wrightsman, Lawrence S. (1992) *Assumptions About Human Nature*, Sage, London.

Index

Some important terms – such as *communication, change, adoption* and *innovation* – have whole chapters devoted specifically to them and there are also many instances in the book of aspects of decision making and human behaviour. References to such material are therefore included in this index only where this is likely to be of most assistance to the reader.

Page numbers in **bold** indicate illustrations or figures in the text.